P9-ELH-281

DISCARDED

26
SMIGA, GEORGE M., 1948-
PAIN AND POLEMIC

Pain and Polemic

**DO NOT REMOVE
CARDS FROM POCKET**

ALLEN COUNTY PUBLIC LIBRARY

FORT WAYNE, INDIANA 46802

You may return this book to any agency, branch,
or bookmobile of the Allen County Public Library.

DEMCO

 A STIMULUS BOOK

Editor in Chief for
Stimulus Books
Helga Croner

Editors
Lawrence Boadt, C.S.P.
Helga Croner
David Dalin
Leon Klenicki
John Koenig
Kevin A. Lynch, C.S.P.
Richard C. Sparks, C.S.P.

STIMULUS BOOKS are developed by Stimulus Foundation, a not-for-profit organization, and are published by Paulist Press. The Foundation wishes to further the publication of scholarly books on Jewish and Christian topics that are of importance to Judaism and Christianity.

Stimulus Foundation was established by an erstwhile refugee from Nazi Germany who intends to contribute with these publications to the improvement of communication between Jews and Christians.

Books for publication in this Series will be selected by a committee of the Foundation, and offers of manuscripts and works in progress should be addressed to:

Stimulus Foundation
785 West End Ave.
New York, N.Y. 10025

George M. Smiga

PAIN AND POLEMIC
Anti-Judaism in the Gospels

A STIMULUS BOOK
Paulist Press
New York/Mahwah, New Jersey

Allen County Public Library
900 Webster Street
PO Box 2270
Fort Wayne, IN 46801-2270

*For My Parents
With Love*

Copyright © 1992 by Stimulus Foundation

All rights reserved. No part of this book may be reproduced or transmitted in any form or by any means, electronic or mechanical, including photocopying, recording or by any information storage and retrieval system without permission in writing from the Publisher.

Library of Congress Cataloging-in-Publication Data

Smiga, George M., 1948–
    Pain and polemic : anti-Judaism in the Gospels / by George M. Smiga.
        p.   cm. — (A Stimulus book)
    Includes bibliographical references and index.
    ISBN 0-809i-3355-5 (pbk.)
        1. Bible. N.T. Gospels—Criticism, interpretation, etc.
2. Christianity and antisemitism.   3. Judaism (Christian theology)—
History of doctrines—Early church, ca. 30-600.   I. Title.   II. Series.
BS2555.6.J44S65   1992
261.2'6'09015—dc20

                                                        92-28044
                                                        CIP

Published by Paulist Press
997 Macarthur Boulevard
Mahwah, New Jersey 07430

Printed and bound in the United States of America

Contents

v

LIST OF PERIODICALS CITED

PREFACE

The motivation to write this book emerged as a result of the 1988 Jewish-Catholic Colloquium which was held at St. Mary Seminary in Cleveland. After that event, I became convinced of the importance of making the contemporary research into the anti-Jewish polemic of the New Testament more readily available. With that conviction, a two-year effort was launched. The book began to take shape in the discussions afforded by two graduate seminars. The first was held at St. Mary Seminary in the fall of 1988, and the second was held at John Carroll University in the summer of 1989. I would like to thank the participants in those seminars for the enthusiasm and insights which they so freely offered.

The assistance of Alan Rome, the librarian of St. Mary Seminary, must be recognized for the genial manner in which he was able to locate the most remote sources. My sincere thanks are extended to Steven Brunovsky, Kathleen Flannery, and Stephen Moran for their careful reading of the final text when I could not look at it one more time.

Abbreviations follow the suggestions of "Instructions For Contributors" which are found in the *Catholic Biblical Quarterly* (46 [1984] 397–408). The scriptural translation is that of the New Revised Standard Version Bible, copyrighted in 1989 by the Division of Christian Education of the National Council of the Churches of Christ in the United States of America.

George M. Smiga

Cleveland
January 6, 1991
Feast of the Epiphany

INTRODUCTION

This book attempts to be honest. It may not be pleasant. For those of us who treasure the New Testament as a privileged source of divine revelation, it may prove profoundly disturbing. The following pages will examine the polemic of the canonical gospels as it applies to Christian evaluations of Jews and Judaism. Overall, the evaluations are not good. Polemic is understood as an aggressive attack on the beliefs of another party. We Christians who cherish a gospel of peace, reconciliation, and love may be shocked to realize how frequently the four gospels seem to attack Jews and Judaism in sentiments filled with violence, depreciation, and even hatred. This is not to say that every polemical statement of the gospels should be understood as offensively as it may sound to modern ears. Nuances and circumstances must be appreciated in assessing such statements, and no small part of this book will be devoted to just such contextualizations. Nevertheless, to the modern Christian living in the United States, with his or her high valuation of religious freedom, the polemical stance of the canonical gospels is likely to emerge as narrow and offensive.

Futhermore, the extent and depth of this negativism regarding Jews and Judaism may strike the average Christian as something new and surprising. Christians who have read and prayed the canonical gospels for their entire lives are often taken aback when this negative strain is pointed out to them. This is understandable because Christian believers approach the New Testament primarily seeking "good news" for their own lives. In the light of this positive orientation, aspects of the scriptures which assert "bad news" tend to become invisible. It often requires a perspective from outside the Christian community to emphasize the seriousness of the problem.

3

This perspective was provided for me in a dramatic way in 1988 at a Jewish-Catholic Colloquium held at St. Mary Seminary in Cleveland. Toward the end of a session that was characterized by warm and respectful dialogue among a number of Jews and Christians, Dr. Michael J. Cook, a Jewish scholar from Hebrew Union College in Cincinnati, was asked to frame the question of the role of the New Testament in Jewish-Christian relations. Taking up a copy of the New Testament, he read the following passage from the gospel of John (8:31, 37, 44, 47).

> Jesus then said to the Jews who had believed in him, . . . "I know that you are descendants of Abraham; yet you look for an opportunity to kill me, because there is no place in you for my word. . . . You are from your father the devil, and you choose to do your father's desires. He was a murderer from the beginning, and does not stand in the truth, because there is no truth in him. When he lies he speaks according to his own nature, for he is a liar and the father of lies. . . . Whoever is from God hears the words of God. The reason you do not hear them is that you are not from God."

Dr. Cook looked up from the text of the gospel and asked simply, "What am I to make of this?"

The unanswered question hung in the silence of the room. To have that question posed by a learned man and respected colleague was both vexing and embarrassing. It was not a question that a Jew could answer, for it was the Christian scriptures that Dr. Cook was holding in his hands. His question is a question for the Christian church—a moral mandate to explain this disturbing, polemical dimension of our own scriptures. It is the aim of this book to examine the recent efforts of scholars to understand this polemical strain in the canonical gospels—to respond to the question, "What are we to make of this?"

THE RELATIONSHIP OF EARLY CHRISTIAN GROUPS TO JUDAISM

On one level, the explanation of the polemic against Jews and Judaism in the canonical gospels is not difficult. As a religion, Christianity has clearly emerged from Judaism. In their beginnings, the early Christian communities both saw themselves and were seen by others as sects within Judaism. Although it would surprise many Christians today, those who first spread the good news of the resurrection—including all the first apostles—saw themselves as a certain kind of Jew. In the first half of the first century, Judaism was a vital and diverse religion. There were many kinds of Jews who differed from each other in significant ways and yet continued to accept each other's status as members of Israel. Christian Jews, therefore, could take their place rather easily among Pharisees, Sadducees, Essenes, Zealots, and perhaps other Jewish groups whose names have not come down to us.

It took some time for the early Christians to see themselves as a group distinct from Judaism. In other words, it took time for Christian Jews to become Jewish Christians. A variety of theological and sociological factors eventually brought this about, but it was a process of development. A part of this process was an increasing need for Christians to establish their own identity apart from their parent community. Just as an adolescent's need to assert her or his own identity frequently involves the scorn and rejection of certain values in the parent, so it is often the case that an emerging religion will strike out polemically against the parent community. This phenomenon is not unique to Christianity's emergence from Judaism. Anti-Jewish and anti-Christian polemic can be found in the Koran and in the Book of Mormon. The polemics in these writings are a sign of the need of Islam and Mormonism to establish their individual identities apart from their parent communities.[1]

Thus the common pattern of a new religion emerging from its parent can provide a context in which to understand the devaluations of Judaism found within the New Testament. Well-established Jewish groups possessed a security in their own status. Christian groups, however, proclaiming the new message of Jesus' resurrection, were inclined to justify their own less-established identity. This often resulted in the evaluative claim that other Jewish groups were inferior to those of the Christian community.

JEWISH-CHRISTIAN RELATIONS
AFTER THE NEW TESTAMENT:
THE EFFECT UPON PRESENT SCHOLARSHIP

In the general sense just described, polemic against a religion's parent is understandable within its foundational literature. However, when—as in the case of Judaism and Christianity—the parent religion continues to exist alongside the new community and that younger community rises to the position of social and political dominance, a disturbing new dynamic can occur. In such a case, the scriptural polemic originally used to establish the new religion's identity can be turned against the parent community not only in verbal abuse but also with political force. Frequent examples of this kind of persecution can be documented in the treatment of Jews by Christians since the fourth century of the common era. This odious behavior against Jews sank to new and profound depths in the atrocities leveled against the Jewish people during the Second World War. Then, as in earlier times, the polemic of the New Testament was employed as a supportive rationale and warrant for such injustices.

Johann-Baptist Metz has declared that it is no longer possible to engage in Christian theology with our backs toward Auschwitz. In this book I am persuaded that it is no longer possible to engage in scriptural interpretation with our backs to Auschwitz. Although it is wrong to equate the polemic of the New Testament with the polemic of Nazism, the horrendous injustices of Christian persecutions of Jews culminating in the Holocaust are the unavoidable contexts in which the issue of anti-Jewish polemic in the scriptures must be faced and ultimately resolved.

THE PURPOSE AND SCOPE OF THIS BOOK

The purpose of this book is to provide the interested reader with a summary of the recent efforts to grapple with the polemic of the canonical gospels toward Judaism. As the reader who perseveres will soon discover, the debate which surrounds this issue is at once complex, painful, and elusive. I do not presume to resolve the debate in these pages nor even to offer some radically new perspective from which to view it. My goal is more modest. I only strive to bring together in one place both the range and intricacy of the discussion.

The year 1974 will serve as a beginning point for this survey. In that year Rosemary Radford Ruether's *Faith and Fratricide* was first published. This book marks a watershed in the post-Holocaust discussion. Few scholars would accept Ruether's methods or conclusions without qualification. Nevertheless, her thesis that anti-Judaism is the "left-hand" of classical christology has raised the stakes in the debate by insisting that the New Testament's depreciatory stance toward Judaism is not a marginal matter but a fundamental aspect of Christianity itself.[2] Biblical scholars writing since 1974 have not been unaware of Ruether's claims, and much of the writing concerning anti-Judaism in the last fifteen years has attempted to deal with the implications of her thesis. This book, therefore, will attempt to provide an overview of what biblical scholars have been saying about anti-Judaism since the publication of *Faith and Fratricide*. Of course it will prove impossible to treat every point of view or to submit each position which is mentioned to extensive critique. Yet an effort will be made to introduce the reader to the debates which surround the major writings of the canonical gospels on this topic, as well as to divide modern scholars according to the positions they assume within those debates.

HISTORICAL-CRITICAL PRESUPPOSITIONS

It is best to state at the outset two presuppositions upon which the following analysis will build. Neither of these will surprise the reader who is familiar with modern biblical criticism. It is of utmost importance, however, that these presuppositions be understood if the chapters which follow are to make any sense.

The New Testament writings as documents of faith

The first historical-critical presumption is that the New Testament writings are documents of faith. They are testimonies written by believers, for believers. This means that they are not "objective" documents in the same way that modern historical writing strives to be objective. It cannot be denied that the New Testament contains historical information. However, the literary forms which the authors of the New Testament employ have been chosen primarily to serve the function of faith proclamation. Therefore, in many areas of scriptural interpretation, the level of historical accuracy within the text will

remain a matter of dispute even among experts. This is not because
the authors of scripture strive to deceive nor because the modern
interpreters of the scripture are unqualified, but simply because it is
not the function of the text to provide the kind of unbiased reporting
which would make the attainment of historical accuracy secure.

The New Testament writings as the result of a complex process of
formation

The second historical-critical presupposition of this book asserts
that the New Testament writings as we now possess them are the
result of a complex process of development. It is not likely that any
work of the New Testament was written in its final form by an author
who personally knew Jesus of Nazareth. It is common to speak of
three dimensions of the final text which can be related to three historical stages of composition: (1) some material in the text may be
traceable to the historical Jesus; (2) the majority of material in the text
has been formed and reshaped by the postresurrectional church for
use in proclamation; (3) the final text has been reshaped by authors
who have adapted earlier material and created some of their own
according to a particular historical context and theological viewpoint.

It is crucial for the reader to appreciate this developmental dimension of the canonical gospels. Frequently in the discussions which
follow it will be asserted that very clear descriptions of Jesus in the
biblical text may not be accurate presentations of the historical Jesus.
It is only by understanding the complex process of biblical composition that the reader will be able to understand how those claims can
be made. It will be presumed that the picture of the person and times
of Jesus which the biblical text presents may have been significantly
altered by the subsequent creative reshaping of the postresurrectional
church and the biblical authors.

THREE POSSIBLE QUESTIONS BY WHICH TO APPROACH
A TEXT

There are a variety of dimensions to every text. It is therefore
possible to ask different questions of the same text, knowing that each
question will lead in a different direction of inquiry and seek to uncover a different aspect of truth. Since no inquiry can begin to deal
adequately with all the dimensions of a text, it is important for me to

identify what will be the focus of this inquiry into the polemical evaluations of Jews and Judaism within the canonical gospels.

In examining gospel texts which seem to carry a negative attitude toward Judaism, it is possible to specify at least three different questions that engage biblical interpreters.

The question of historical accuracy

The first question is that of historical accuracy. Based upon the presuppositions discussed above, interpreters will often question whether the picture of Jesus or Judaism that the text presents accurately reflects historical reality. Consciously or unconsciously, have the biblical authors drawn a picture which is closer to the characteristics and issues of the postresurrectional church than to those of Jesus' life and ministry? This question is often posed by interpreters seeking to evaluate Jesus' relationship to the Judaism of his day or the alleged circumstances which led to his death. Frequently the judgment is made that historical inaccuracies are present in the New Testament and that these inaccuracies conspire to present a negative description of Judaism. Taking the quotation from John 8 which was given earlier in this introduction as an example, the question of historical accuracy would ask: Did Jesus actually say these or similar words to the Jews of his day? Did Jesus really call "the Jews" the offspring of the devil, or is this polemic present in the text as a result of later reshaping by the church or the evangelist?

The question of evaluative claim

A second question which can be posed to a biblical text is the question of evaluative claim, which seeks to determine what is the evaluative stance that a particular text makes regarding Judaism. This question does not focus directly on the issue of historical accuracy, but rather reads the text as it stands and simply asks what attitudes toward Judaism are proposed within it. Such an approach draws less on outside historical sources and seeks rather to interpret specific passages within the themes and patterns of the work as a whole. Turning again to John 8, questions of evaluative claim would be formulated as follows: Does this text claim that Jews are in fact offspring of the devil, and if so in what sense? In this text, do "the Jews" refer to actual people or do they carry some symbolic meaning? What function does this evaluative claim regarding the Jews serve in relation to the other evaluative claims of the gospel?

The reason for the evaluative claim

A final question which can be posed to the text seeks to uncover the reason for the evaluative claim. Why is a particular evaluative judgment toward Jews or Judaism being made? This approach seeks to align the evaluative claims of the gospel with a particular historical situation out of which the biblical author is presumed to have written. For example, if the particular community out of which the author wrote can be shown to have been composed primarily of Gentiles or Jews, or if the community's relationship to the synagogue of its day can be characterized by persecutions or friendly interchange, then these factors can be used to explain the cause of the evaluative claims in the text. The "historical situation of the community" is of course a hypothetical construct derived from certain indications in the text. Nevertheless, the various historical reconstructions of scholars have done much to throw new light upon the writings of the New Testament. An attempt to locate the reason for the claims expressed in John 8 would pose questions such as the following: Is John's community a Gentile, Jewish, or mixed Christian community? Is the strength of the polemic in these verses present because the community of John has been thrown out of the synagogue? Did specific persecutions of the community by Jewish authorities contribute to the negative picture of Judaism in the text?

The focus of this book will be primarily the second type of question. The following pages will center on the evaluative claims of the biblical text, examining the negative evaluative judgments which the canonical gospels espouse regarding Jews and Judaism.

It is, of course, impossible to separate the evaluative claims of the text from issues of historical accuracy and motivation. The issue of historical accuracy must, therefore, be addressed. The biblical scholars who will be discussed frequently present arguments which integrate the evaluative claims of the text with judgments regarding both the motivation for the claim and the historical accuracy of the text. A book such as this which proposes to survey the opinions of scholars cannot simply dismiss aspects of research which do not fit a particular line of inquiry. Therefore, as we work our way through the four canonical gospels, historical questions of accuracy and reasons for the evaluative claims will be duly noted. Nevertheless, the primary focus of this book will be to expose and clarify the evaluative claims of the texts themselves.

CLASSIFYING VARIOUS TYPES OF EVALUATIVE CLAIMS

In assessing the evaluative claims of the various writings of the New Testament, it will become clear that the assertions of different writings are far from identical. We must adopt some method of classification to distinguish among them. There is, however, no one system of classifying anti-Jewish polemic which is satisfying to all interpreters. Apt categories by which to classify negative scriptural evaluations of Judaism have been hampered by a lack of consistent divisions and terminology. In the present state of confusion, therefore, the most that I can presume to accomplish is to state as clearly as possible the rationale for and scope of the categories I will employ.

Anti-Semitism or anti-Judaism?

It is best to begin by explaining the use of the term "anti-Judaism." This use follows a growing trend among biblical scholars to prefer the term "anti-Judaism" to "anti-Semitism." There are at least two reasons why "anti-Semitism" fails to describe adequately the phenomenon we are seeking to locate within the New Testament. First, the word is inaccurate in regard to its extension. Arabs are as much Semites as Jews. Yet the evaluations we will be discussing in the New Testament refer only to Jews and Jewish beliefs. Therefore, to use the term "anti-Semitism" would be to adopt an expression which could literally refer to a much wider issue than the one this book attempts to discuss.

Second, the term "anti-Semitism" as employed commonly today is seen primarily as a racial designation. This is especially due to its association with the program of Nordic superiority as promoted by the Nazis during the Second World War. Not only is this type of racial prejudice lacking in the New Testament, but even the negative evaluations of Jews by pagans in the ancient world never employed a theory of race as a weapon of attack.[3] The term "anti-Judaism" avoids a racial evaluation. As commonly employed within the literature today, "anti-Judaism" is "a purely theological reality; it rejects Judaism as a way to salvation but not Jews as a people."[4] For these reasons, "anti-Judaism" is to be preferred to "anti-Semitism" in reference to the New Testament.

Nevertheless, the issue is not so simply resolved. With appropriate nuance, there remain a number of scholars who would still champion the use of "anti-Semitism" in referring to New Testament polemic.[5] The reason for their choice should not be passed over in silence. When the history of Jewish-Christian relations is surveyed, it is an indisputable fact that the negative evaluations of Judaism present in the New Testament (however they may be termed) have shaped a theological tradition hostile to Judaism. This tradition has in turn fostered an attitude toward Jews which has in no small way contributed the underpinnings of beliefs and actions which are racial and can properly be called "anti-Semitic." It is impossible to deny the disastrous effects which have flowed from the polemic against Jews and Judaism in the New Testament. Lest this disastrous potential of the scriptural writings be overlooked, some scholars argue that "anti-Semitism" or a nuanced form such as "theological anti-Semitism" is the most honest term to describe the polemic.[6] Even though I have opted not to employ these expressions, I am in sympathy with the concerns of scholars who argue for them. Furthermore, I trust that the use of "anti-Judaism" in the following pages will in no way be seen as a denial of the serious anti-Semitic *potential* which these scriptural texts do indeed possess.

The evaluative claims of the canonical gospels which we will be discussing do not arise out of racial prejudice. Rather, they arise out of varying degrees of religious and theological dispute. "Anti-Judaism" will be used in this book as the term to describe such religious-theological polemic within the New Testament.

Douglas Hare: types of anti-Judaism

The polemic of the New Testament is not homogeneous. Douglas Hare has suggested a useful threefold classification which divides the polemic of the gospels into three types of anti-Judaism. Because his categories have been accepted and adapted by others, let me present them briefly here.[7]

Hare's first category of classification is *prophetic anti-Judaism*. By this term he intends to identify a critique of Judaism which comes from within Judaism itself. This kind of critique is part of a long-respected tradition within Israel. On many occasions the prophets felt obliged to criticize the Jewish people for their failure to live as God had commanded. Hare believes that this kind of anti-Judaism was characteristic of Jesus himself who, as a leader of a conversionist sect within Judaism, sought to reform Israel and criticized at least some of the religious leaders of his day for their failure to do so.

Hare calls his second category *Jewish-Christian anti-Judaism.* This kind of anti-Judaism criticizes the Jewish community for failing to accept the new belief of the Christian community that Jesus' death and resurrection are central to a correct response to God. Hare chooses the qualifier "Jewish-Christian" because he connects this type of critique with the work of Jewish-Christian missionaries attempting to convert unwilling Israel to receive the Christian gospel. What characterizes this type of anti-Judaism is the willingness of the Jewish-Christian missionaries to alter, redefine, or discard certain key symbols of Judaism in light of the Christian message. Thus, in this type of anti-Judaism, Israel is called to accept Christ and at the same time to negate certain aspects of the temple, Torah, or ritual commandments. Hare believes that it was this redefinition of key Jewish symbols which was most threatening to Jewish identity and which eventually caused the parting of the ways between the Christian sect and Judaism.

Both prophetic anti-Judaism and Jewish-Christian anti-Judaism seek to move the Jewish community to conversion and therefore demonstrate a concern for Israel by calling Israel to repentance. Hare's final category moves beyond these efforts for conversion and holds that Israel's refusal to believe is fatal and that God has rejected the Jewish community. Hare calls this final category *Gentilizing anti-Judaism.* This type of anti-Judaism is most characteristic of Gentiles. Hare has, however, used the qualifier "Gentilizing" instead of "Gentile," because he recognizes that Jews and proselytes who rejected their Jewish identity could employ this kind of polemic as well. Gentilizing anti-Judaism holds that Jews have been rejected as God's people and replaced by a new community—those who follow Christ.

Adjustments to Hare's terminology

Hare's threefold division is valuable and the substance of the division will be adopted as the basic categories for classification in this book. However, I feel that the titles Hare has chosen to name his categories carry implications which might unintentionally support a misleading picture of Judaism and the early Christian movement. Therefore, even though I hesitate to introduce yet further terminological refinement into an area already saturated with proposed classifications, I will employ new terminology in this book. I believe that the adjustment of terminology will more precisely describe the various types of polemic within the New Testament. In order to explain the reasons for this shift in language, let me raise two concerns which I have regarding Hare's titles and then suggest my alternatives to them.

ANTI-JUDAISM AND THE PROBLEM OF NORMATIVE JUDAISM

The first concern applies to the use of "anti-Judaism" as the basic term within these categories. "Anti-Judaism" presumes we have a clear understanding of what was normative for Jewish identity in the first century. In recent years, however, it has become increasingly doubtful that a stable norm for Jewish identity existed before the fall of the temple in 70 C.E. — or at least it seems rash to claim that we are able to determine what that norm was. After the fall of the temple, the rabbis were instrumental in solidifying Judaism around certain principles which continue to characterize it to this day. It is unlikely, however, that the same clarity of self-definition can be assumed as normative before the rabbinic ascendancy. Judaism in the first half of the first century is best seen as an assemblage of sects and tendencies whose wide diversity has only recently come to light. Luke T. Johnson summarizes the growing recognition of Jewish diversity succinctly:

> So-called normative Judaism was not normative in the period of the NT. The question Who is a real Jew? was then an open question, debated fiercely and even violently by rival claimants. Even if we agree to define Judaism in the first century as an adherence to certain central symbols such as Torah or Temple, the most cursory review of the extant literature reveals that these symbols in particular were open for debate: Which Torah? Consisting of how many books? In which translation? Interpreted from which standpoint? Which temple? Run by which priesthood?[8]

As Judaism in the first century is viewed as more diverse and flexible, polemical statements regarding the scope and normative value of Jewish belief become more difficult to classify as "anti-Judaism." "Anti-Judaism" implies a normative Judaism from which to deviate. John Gager has already suggested that Hare's first category, "prophetic anti-Judaism," is misleading because it implies a negative attitude toward what is best seen as an internal debate. Gager renames the first category "intra-Jewish polemic," thereby highlighting the nature of the polemic as an internal affair.[9] When the diversity of first century Judaism is seriously appreciated, however, the same critique can be leveled against the use of anti-Judaism in Hare's second category. It seems quite probable that discussions over the validity and extension of central Jewish symbols could themselves be understood as an intra-Jewish debate. Before the ascendancy of the rabbis, strong debates over central Jewish symbols need not be read as a deviation from a universal norm. Using "anti-Judaism" to describe the polemic of this period could, therefore, give the false impression that such polemic was a marginal exception to an otherwise monolithic Judaism. It is more likely that such polemic should be situated within the diverse Jewish dialogue of the first century.

What term, then, can be suggested to replace "anti-Judaism"? I believe we can make progress by claiming less. Precisely because the negative evaluations classified within Hare's first two categories are less clearly challenging values which are "normative" for all Jews of the first century, I prefer to replace the term "anti-Judaism" with the simple term "polemic." Therefore, in this book, I will consider Hare's first two categories as kinds of "polemic" rather than kinds of "anti-Judaism." I will retain the term "anti-Judaism" only for Hare's third category in which the Jewish people as a whole are seen to be rejected by God.

THE PROBLEM OF THE JEW-GENTILE DISTINCTION
IN THE NEW TESTAMENT

The second concern I would raise regarding Hare's choice of terminology is his use of the Jew-Gentile distinction in describing the polemic of the New Testament. As we have seen, Hare himself admits that "Gentilizing" has been chosen because "Gentilizing anti-Judaism" need not be limited only to Gentiles. Nevertheless, the use of the Jew-Gentile distinction in these categories continues to give the impression that the identification of a specifically Jewish or Gentile point of view is possible through an examination of the New Testament texts. Such an identification, however, is highly problematic. Again the diversity of the New Testament period complicates our ability to determine what are Jewish or Gentile stances within the texts we possess.

Judaism of the first century was greatly influenced by Gentile or Hellenistic ideas and values. Easy compartmentalization between Judaism and Hellenism has been challenged among scholars for decades. As early as 1964, W. D. Davies could write,

> While there is an unmistakable difference between figures such as Hillel and Philo, this difference must not be made absolute. The lines between Hellenism and Judaism, by the first century, were very fluid.[10]

Nevertheless, despite this recognized fluidity, commentators of the New Testament continue to argue that documents containing "Gentile points of view" were written by Gentiles and those containing "Jewish characteristics" were authored by Jews—as if Jews of the first century only thought and argued in typically Jewish ways and Gentiles could have no understanding or use of such approaches. What a particular Jew believed and how he or she vocalized that belief depended on what type of Judaism the person espoused and to what extent that type of Judaism was influenced by Gentile values. The diversity of first century Judaism permitted a wide range of Hellenizing tendencies, and Hellenistic characteristics within a text cannot be automatically used to argue against the Jewishness of the text.

This is particularly important to remember when interpreting Christian documents. The fluidity and diversity of the early Christian movements paralleled the diversity of first century Judaism from which they sprang. I again quote Luke T. Johnson.

> Christianity was quite literally a new invention every place it appeared. The mission was not centrally controlled with respect either to structure or ideology. . . . There was no long period of stability during which self-definition could be consolidated. The messianists made it up as they went along. For at least the first fifty years of its existence, there was no one thing which could be called "Christianity" as a standard by which to measure deviance. There was rather a loose network of assemblies on the fringe of synagogues and in

lecture halls down the street, whose boundaries of self-definition were vigorously debated.[11]

Amid this diversity of early Christianity, the mixture of Jewish and Gentile values which comprised a particular community was in large part dependent upon the type of Judaism out of which the Christian community evolved. To speak, therefore, of Jewish Christianity or of Gentile Christianity in order to differentiate theological stances of the New Testament period becomes increasingly dubious. Raymond Brown has cogently argued that the labels "Jewish Christianity" and "Gentile Christianity" are inadequate for determining what a particular community believed. He suggests that one should rather speak of varying types of "Jewish/Gentile Christianity."[12] What Brown would hold regarding types of Christianity, I would hold regarding types of polemic in the New Testament.

What would comprise a "Jewish" or "Gentile" attitude is increasingly difficult to determine from the texts which are available to us. When classifying the types of polemic in the New Testament, such qualifiers do not prove helpful. Therefore, rather than associating the various evaluative claims of the New Testament texts with the Jew-Gentile distinction, it seems preferable to me that the title given to the type of polemic reflect the particular thrust of the polemic itself. This avoids the impression that there was a unified viewpoint on the part of Jewish Christians or Gentile Christians regarding Jews and Judaism. It also respects the wide diversity of both Judaism and early Christian communities within the New Testament period. A descriptive term which identifies the polemic's function and evaluative claim within the text would label the type of polemic without necessarily associating it with a supposed Jewish or Gentile identity on the part of either its author or the community from which it emerged.

Therefore, in this book I shall avoid the use of the Jewish-Gentile qualifiers in Hare's second and third categories and replace them with terms which describe the function of the polemic itself. Instead of "Jewish-Christian anti-Judaism" I shall speak of "subordinating polemic." Instead of "Gentilizing anti-Judaism" I shall employ the expression "abrogating anti-Judaism." The basic contours of Hare's categories remain substantially the same. By retitling the categories, however, more nuance will be introduced into his classification and less opportunity will be present to obscure the diversity of first century Judaism or of the early Christian movement itself. Whereas Hare speaks of *prophetic anti-Judaism, Jewish-Christian anti-Judaism*, and *Gentilizing anti-Judaism*, this book will employ the terms *prophetic polemic, subordinating polemic, and abrogating anti-Judaism*. By way of summary and clarification, let us now review what will be intended by each of these three categories.

PROPHETIC POLEMIC

Every religious tradition manifests at times certain disagreements among its members. These internal debates can become very emotional and violent. Yet even in their harshest expressions, the evaluation of the other position does not necessarily amount to a criticism of the religion as such. It usually remains as an internal polemic which intends to call those who will hear to conversion. The biblical prophets provide good examples of this kind of polemic within Judaism. Isaiah (29:13–14) speaks the following words in the name of Yahweh:

Because these people draw near with their mouths
    and honor me with their lips,
    while their hearts are far from me,
and their worship of me is a human commandment
    learned by rote;
so I will again do amazing things with this people,
    shocking and amazing.
The wisdom of their wise shall perish
    and the discernment of the discerning shall be hidden.

There is clearly polemic here. It is not, however, polemic against Judaism itself or of the law. What Isaiah is attacking is the failure on the part of Israel to follow the true terms of the law devoutly. This is prophetic polemic which negatively evaluates the practice of Judaism without rejecting any of Judaism's central symbols. The law, the temple, and even the ritual practices of Judaism remain intact. Furthermore, it is often the intent of prophetic polemic to move Israel towards conversion. This is the case in the above passage from Isaiah. Despite the failure of Israel to adhere to true devotion, Yahweh will reform the false wisdom and understanding of Israel and lead Israel to a genuine response. As devastating as the polemic may sound, its purpose is not to criticize *Judaism* but the *practice of Judaism* so that a renewed Judaism may emerge.

It is possible that the criticism of Judaism by the historical Jesus and some of the negative evaluations of Jews and Judaism by New Testament communities are best classified as prophetic polemic. When New Testament authors see themselves and their communities as a part of Judaism and employ polemic to criticize recognized abuses of the central Jewish symbols of Torah, temple, and ritual practice without subverting the symbols themselves, this can be properly called prophetic polemic.

SUBORDINATING POLEMIC

A second category of New Testament polemic includes evaluative statements which not only criticize the meaning and use of the central symbols of Judaism but in fact subordinate those symbols to another value. What is involved in this type of polemic is not only a critique of the practice of Judaism but an actual redefining or re-symbolizing of what Judaism is about. The group that would use this kind of polemic would seek to convince those who were not of its company to accept the overriding importance of the new value and its corresponding redefinition of God's intention.

The distinction between prophetic polemic and subordinating polemic is particularly difficult to determine. As we have seen, the diversity of Jewish groups in the first century, together with the paucity of accurate information regarding these groups, makes it very problematic to establish what would be common or "normative" for all Jews. Therefore, it is often unclear whether a particular polemic is best classified as a call to conversion or a call to redefinition. The reader is, therefore, warned of the delicacy of the distinctions between these two categories.

Nevertheless, I will continue to hold in this book that most Jews of the first century would have accepted the centrality of the Torah and of the temple until its destruction in 70 C.E., and most would have recognized the importance of circumcision and dietary requirements. Thus, when a particular Christian text subordinates these central symbols to Christ, that text would be understood by most Jews as a kind of subordinating polemic. This understanding of what was important to most Jewish groups of the first century may indeed have to be reevaluated in the light of new discoveries or insights. At the present time, however, it remains the most viable way to distinguish what I have called prophetic polemic from subordinating polemic.

As defined here, subordinating polemic is closely connected within the New Testament to the supreme importance its authors place upon the death and resurrection of Jesus. For the early church the centrality of this saving action quickly rose to the center of its proclamation. Since the majority of the first generation of believers in Jesus were Jewish, the value of the Torah, the temple, and the ritual practices were generally retained. However, rather soon after the resurrection, these central symbols of Judaism began to be subordinated to belief in Jesus himself as the one God had sent. By this process the various early Christian communities were in fact emerging as separate entities from the symbolic system which held the various types of Judaism together. As the risen Jesus became the central symbol of faith, the major symbols of Judaism were subordinated and adapted. From the point of view of the early Christian communities, such realigning of symbols was reasonable and directed by God. From the point of view of many non-Christian Jews this subordination of Torah, temple, and ritual practice tampered with the God-given terms of the covenant and challenged their self-identity as a people.

The refusal of Judaism as a whole to accept the subordination of its central symbols to the risen Christ occasioned many negative evaluations of Judaism within the New Testament. Precisely because the early church believed so deeply that the centrality of the risen Christ was the good news for the entire people of Israel, the failure of the majority of Israel to adopt the new Christian understanding of God's will was seen by many Christian groups as opposition to the very will of God. In prophetic polemic, Jewish groups are criticized for a failure to live up to the terms of the covenant which they themselves profess to accept. In subordinating polemic, Jewish groups are criticized for failing to accept what they would see as a redefinition of that covenant. Whereas prophetic polemic attacks Jews and Judaism for refusing to convert to genuine faith practice within a system of agreed symbols, subordinating polemic depreciates Jews and Judaism for refusing to accept a new alignment of those symbols in which the common symbols are subordinated to belief in the person of Jesus.

Although one is perfectly able to understand why early Christian communities would blame many Jews for refusing to accept what they as Christians believed was the will of God, it is likewise easy to appreciate why large numbers of Jews—perfectly content with their own relationship to God—would have no desire to accept a redefinition of their beliefs or symbols. The disagreement is over the appropriateness of the subordination. The determination of subordinating polemic does not in itself pass judgment on this appropriateness. It only attempts to identify polemical statements in Christian texts which criticize Jews and Judaism for failing to accept the subordination of the Torah, temple, and ritual practices to the risen Christ. It is important to note that subordinating polemic does not involve a belief in the rejection of Israel by God. It was, in fact, the intention of the polemic of these statements to convert recalcitrant Jews into accepting the new definition of belief which early Christian communities proclaimed. Subordinating polemic as found in the New Testament refuses to accept as complete a Jewish stance which would not subordinate central Jewish values to Christ. Yet it also recognizes a privileged position for Israel and lives in the hope that Israel will come to accept the Christian redefinition of God's will.

ABROGATING ANTI-JUDAISM

The final category in the classification of New Testament polemic is simple to explain. It accepts all the assumptions of subordinating polemic but adds the conviction that Israel has been rejected by God because of the refusal to accept the subordination of all to Christ. Abrogating anti-Judaism would hold that Israel retains no special status as a people. God has instead ordained a "new" Israel which replaces and eliminates the "old" Israel. Whereas subordinating polemic seeks to convert Israel precisely because it recognizes the special value that Israel holds as God's people, abrogating anti-Judaism brushes Israel aside, claiming that value is found only in redefined Israel which is the Christian community.

As I have already stated, it is only in this last category that the term "anti-Judaism" has been retained. This is appropriate because only here does the polemic claim that the Jewish people as a whole have been disenfranchised. Without the specific claim that the Jewish people have been rejected, even polemic which would seek to redefine what many Jews would hold as central to their belief can be safely situated within the intra-Jewish discussion. When a clear claim of Jewish disenfranchisement is present, however, "anti-Judaism" can be usefully employed.

The advantages of the proposed system of classification

Every system of classification is to some extent arbitrary. Each system, as it reveals certain connections in the material under discussion, will at the same time conceal other aspects of the subject. The proposed classification of polemic adopted in this book is no exception. I believe, however, that the proposed categories do carry certain advantages which should be enumerated.

For the reader who appreciates the rationale behind the divisions, the complexity of polemic within the New Testament will be understood in ways which may provide benefits beyond the boundaries of biblical scholarship. Not only does this proposed system of classification promote a fuller appreciation of the historical and literary dimensions of the text, but it also may encourage progress in the contemporary dialogue between Jews and Christians.

This possibility can be illustrated by referring to three dimensions of the proposed classification. First, the category of prophetic polemic reminds the reader that at its roots Christianity was in fact a type of Judaism. Indeed, it suggests the possibility that most examples of polemic deriving from the time of Jesus of Nazareth would be best classified as an intra-Jewish dispute. Second, permitting both prophetic and subordinating polemic to be seen as kinds of intra-Jewish debate underlines the diversity and flexibility of both first century Judaism and the early Christian movement. This challenges us to refrain from reading back into the New Testament period our modern understandings of Judaism and Christianity. Third, distinguishing between subordinating polemic and abrogating anti-Judaism highlights the possibility that a belief in the abrogation of Judaism is not necessary for Christianity to maintain its own self-identity either in the first century or in our own. Those writings which are classified in the category of subordinating polemic will therefore give ample testimony to the many witnesses in the New Testament which do not manifest a belief in the rejection of Judaism by God.

Now that both our terminology and system of classification have been stated and explored, the stage is set to begin a survey of the canonical gospels. In approaching each gospel, we will first note significant representations of fact which may be historically inaccurate and derogatory towards Judaism. We will then proceed to locate within the text where the negative evaluative claims regarding Judaism occur. The brunt of each chapter will be to offer the scholarly discussion regarding the interpretation of such polemical passages. In guiding the reader through such a diversity of opinion, I will use the threefold classification of polemic outlined here as a means of organization and consistency. As the reader will soon realize, in some cases the proper classification of a particular work will be far from clear, and no consensus among scholars will emerge. Nevertheless, I will not end the discussions in the following chapters without venturing my own opinion on the proper classification for the gospel in question.

There is, of course, no presumption that this book will somehow resolve the conflict of opinions regarding the polemic of the canonical gospels. Its intention is much more modest—simply to raise the awareness that there are in fact polemical evaluations of differing types against Jews and Judaism within our Christian scriptures. At the same time, this book wishes to demonstrate how much scholarly discussion has centered on this problem in the last fifteen years. Perhaps, if the awareness of polemic within the New Testament begins to spread among Christian believers, then soon we may be ready to face the next logical question. What do we who profess a gospel of truth and love intend to do about it?

1
THE GOSPEL OF MARK: SUBORDINATING POLEMIC AND SILENCE

The first canonical gospel which we will examine is the gospel of Mark. Although neither the date nor origin of this gospel can be established with certainty, there is wide agreement among biblical interpreters that Mark is the earliest of the four canonical gospels and that it serves as a source for both Matthew and Luke. The date of the gospel is usually placed between 65–75 C.E., thus locating its completion slightly before or after the destruction of the temple by the Romans in 70 C.E. It is impossible with our present information to determine whether the temple still stood when Mark reached its final form. I am inclined, however, to accept the argument that had the events of 70 C.E. already occurred, much stronger traces of these events would be discernible within the gospel—especially in chapter 13. Therefore, for our purposes in this chapter, I will examine Mark's polemic presuming that the temple in Jerusalem still functions as a part of Jewish life.

In the introduction, we have already noted the distinction between historical accuracy and evaluative claim. This chapter on the gospel of Mark will therefore be divided into two parts. The first will examine the historical accuracy of certain aspects of Mark's narrative which present Jews or Judaism in a negative light. The second will attempt to determine the evaluative claims which Mark makes regarding non-Christian Jews and their status as God's people.

HISTORICAL ACCURACY IN MARK'S
PRESENTATION OF JEWS AND JUDAISM

Different kinds of narrative place different values on the historical accuracy of the events they relate. A scholarly history of the final days of Richard Nixon's presidency will place a high value on the accuracy of the events that are presented and will carefully discuss the ramifications when various historical witnesses conflict or are incomplete. A political satirist's presentation of the same events will place a lower priority on such accuracy. Facts will be bent and dialogue will be created to serve the impact of the satire and to enhance the point of view which the satirical narrative strives to promote. Between such literary forms, narratives with more of a mixed concern for historical accuracy can be found. For example, an historical novel or television docudrama will certainly seek to hang the narrative on accurate historical events. Yet the nature of these narratives allows considerable flexibility in shaping the story so as to heighten its entertainment value and aesthetic impact.

In regard to historical accuracy, the gospels of the New Testament are best located in the category of such mixed narratives. Historical accuracy is not given as high a value as it is in works of historical research, nor is it treated as casually as it might be in political satire. While attentive to certain clear historical facts, the narratives of the gospels are open to considerable shaping and rearrangement of materials in order to achieve the effect which the evangelists wish to achieve. The effect is neither entertainment nor aesthetic success but rather the proclamation of the good news of the risen Lord as it is perceived by the community which produces a particular gospel.

In other words, what the community believes will often shape how the narrative is told. Within such narratives, faith-belief is central, and the proclamation of what is believed may be given priority over an objective rendering of what precisely occurred. When the nature of the gospel narrative is properly understood, such a priority should not be seen as a deception or as a violation of the truth. As a literary form, the gospel allows for flexibility in historical accuracy when it presents its message. The gospel writers were not eyewitnesses. They received and adapted the stories of Jesus which were passed down to them. Historical precision was not an overriding concern. All aspects of the narrative were meant to serve the primary goal of faith proclamation.

DETERMINING HISTORICAL ACCURACY WITHIN A LITERARY GOSPEL

Even though the literary nature of a gospel allows flexibility in historical accuracy, it is still possible to ask how historically accurate a particular scene or characterization may be. When we ask such questions, however, it must be understood that we are seeking information which the gospel narrative may not be able to provide. The authors of the gospel do not expect us to approach the text focused on historical questions, any more than the authors of a docudrama would expect us to ask in each scene, "Did he really look out the window in just that way?" or "Did she really respond in exactly those words?" In reading a gospel, we are expected to enter the world of the narrative as it is presented to us and experience the particular way in which it proclaims the good news.

Nevertheless, there are times in which it can become vitally important to determine whether a particular aspect of the gospel story is in fact an accurate representation of history, or rather a creative reshaping of the event which is meant to achieve a particular effect within the narrative world. One of those times is when a presentation of a specific person or group is derogatory and accuses them of unjust or self-serving activity. In such cases it becomes crucially important to determine whether such characterization is historically accurate or whether it has been created out of polemic to serve the purpose of the gospel writer.

Several aspects of the narrative in the gospel of Mark picture Jewish characters and their actions in such a negative light. It is an important theological and pastoral problem to determine to what extent these negative descriptions within the gospel narrative can claim historical accuracy. A book which attempts to discuss the presence of anti-Judaism in the canonical gospels cannot pass over these characterizations without comment.

Determining the historical accuracy of these or any other scenes in the gospels, however, is no easy enterprise. The only testimony to most of the events of Jesus' life is found in the gospels themselves, and the gospels contain no clear criterion by which to separate historical accuracy and imaginative artistry. As creations of the early

church, the gospels simply did not tie themselves to the historical
rigor which we would at times wish from them. This leaves us with
a disconcerting realization which A. E. Harvey expresses forcibly.

> If the reports about Jesus in the gospels are the creation of
> the church, rather than the testimony of eye-witnesses to the
> original events, then it follows that it is no longer possible to
> regard any New Testament statement about Jesus as histor-
> ically reliable.[1]

The key word in this sentence is "reliable." Harvey is not saying that
the reports about Jesus in the gospels are historically inaccurate. He
is emphasizing that the nature of our sources simply does not provide
us with a reliable method by which to determine what is historically
exact and what is not. Even after extensive research and deliberation
on the part of competent scholars, a wide range of opinion continues
to exist over what aspects of the gospel narrative can claim historical
accuracy.

It is beyond the scope of this book to present an adequate discussion of the varying views on the historical Jesus or on his relationship to Judaism. All I will attempt in this section is to highlight
two aspects of the gospel of Mark in which an historically inaccurate
picture of Jews and Judaism is likely to exist: (1) the presentation of
Jesus' opponents and (2) the presentation of Jesus' passion and death.
My aim is not to convince the reader that there is irrefutable proof
that such passages are in fact a distortion of history. Only in very
limited cases will the gospel narratives permit that level of certainty.
My aim is to remind the reader that the gospel narratives should not
be naively accepted as historically reliable accounts and that serious
questions can be raised regarding many of the characterizations of
Jews and Judaism within such narratives.

JESUS' OPPONENTS IN THE GOSPEL OF MARK

Throughout the gospel of Mark, Jesus is presented in conflict
with various leadership groups within Judaism. In the first thirteen
chapters of the gospel, Jesus is opposed primarily by scribes and
Pharisees with whom he argues over questions of the law and the
validity of his messianic credentials. In the thirty-two times scribes or
Pharisees are mentioned within Mark's narration, neither group is

ever presented positively with the one exception of a scribe in 12:28–34.[2] Within the gospel, these disputes are clearly connected to a conspiracy on the part of Jesus' opponents to kill him. How accurate is this presentation of conflict between Jesus and the Jewish leadership? How much of Mark's description would be recognizable to the historical Jesus, and how much has been colored by the interests and issues of the early church after the resurrection? Three aspects of Mark's presentation of Jesus' opponents raise questions regarding the historical accuracy of the narrative.

Segregation of leadership groups

In Mark, Jesus is shown to be in conflict with chief priests, scribes, elders, Pharisees, and Herodians. However, within the text these five Jewish leadership groups do not easily mix with each other. Instead, they appear segregated into two separate camps. The chief priests, scribes, and elders form one camp; the Pharisees and the Herodians form another. Except in two places where the scribes and Pharisees appear together (7:1–5 and 2:16), there is no interaction between these groupings.[3]

This segregation of leadership groups is difficult to explain, especially since segments from different camps show a common purpose. Within the gospel, every group of Jewish leaders desires to put Jesus to death, yet only the chief priests, scribes, and elders actually carry that desire to fruition. As early as 3:6, the Pharisees and the Herodians plot together on "how to destroy" Jesus. However, in the actual account of the passion, neither the Pharisees nor the Herodians are mentioned. The passion account is the exclusive domain of the other camp. Are we to assume that this segregation of opposition is reflective of the historical situation during Jesus' lifetime, or are other factors at work?

A strong argument can be marshaled to suggest that the segregation of leadership groups within Mark is the result of the development of the gospel tradition after the death of Jesus. Michael J. Cook has examined this aspect of the gospel in great detail and argues that the segregation of leadership groups is best explained through Mark's use of different sources.[4] Cook theorizes that Mark and the evangelists who follow him are themselves unclear regarding the historical distinctions between Jewish leadership groups at the time of Jesus. "They did not adequately define or describe them or adequately dis-

tinguish among them because they *could* not."[5] They were dependent
upon their sources. Cook's explanation possibly clarifies why these
groups remain so distinct within Mark's gospel and why Mark does
not seem to assist the reader in understanding the differences among
them. It seems very possible that Mark's failure to clarify the differences did not result from a lack of good will but from a lack of
knowledge. The picture of Jewish leadership groups in the gospel
seems to be shaped by literary factors rather than by historical information, and the way in which such groups are presented in Mark
cannot be taken as a reliable indication of their relationship to Jesus
during his public ministry.

Generalization of leadership groups

A second concern regarding Mark's historical accuracy in treating Jesus' opponents is the notable tendency to generalize and ste-
reotype the groups which are presented. Frequently Jesus is not
presented in debate with only a few members of certain leadership
groups, but seemingly takes on the groups as a whole.

Of the five groups which Mark mentions, scribes are given the
most nuanced treatment. Although Mark frequently speaks generi-
cally of "the scribes," he is often more specific, presenting "some of
the scribes" (2:6, 7:1), "the scribes of the Pharisees" (2:16), or simply
"scribes" (9:14). This concern for precision, however, does not seem
to extend to the other Jewish groups. Except in two places where
some qualification can be read (10:2, 12:3), Mark always talks of "the
Pharisees" and "the Herodians." "The chief priests" usually act as a
group; "the elders" never fail to do so.

The clear tendency in Mark to generalize the opponents of Jesus
into groups raises serious questions regarding the accuracy of the
picture presented in the controversy stories. In Mark's narrative, every Jewish group (often *as* a group) is opposed to Jesus. The situation
during the actual ministry of Jesus would certainly be less universal.
The historical Jesus probably disagreed with *some* scribes and *some*
Pharisees. But it is also likely that he *agreed* with others. Even Mark
betrays an indication that Jesus can agree with a leadership group. In
the one place in Mark where the Sadducees are presented (12:18),
Jesus argues against them by adopting a Pharisaic position favoring
the resurrection from the dead. This one exception only emphasizes
the normal pattern of generalized opposition.

It is improbable to imagine that the historical Jesus was facing opposition in the generalized form which Mark presents. There was more likely a tendency on the part of the evangelist to draw the opponents of Jesus in an over-simplified manner, allowing them to serve as a stereotypical foil to his central character. Concrete details about the opponents of the historical Jesus do not seem to have been preserved by the tradition and were not necessary for Mark's purposes. Therefore, it is probable that what we receive in Mark's presentation of Jesus' opponents is not an accurate reflection of the scope and issues which Jesus debated during his ministry, but rather a generalized picture of "the opponent" in which specific descriptions are not considered important.[6] What Michael Cook describes as a prejudiced portrait of the Pharisees within the gospel can be extended to Mark's treatment of all the Jewish leadership groups.

> In the gospels, the Pharisees most often emerge more as the foil for Jesus than as persons of whom the Evangelists are concerned to convey an objective description. While the Evangelists may have been describing the Pharisees as they themselves saw or knew them, at the same time their concern was a presentation of Jesus, not of the Pharisees. Very likely, therefore, the Gospels afford us only a partial picture of the Pharisees—highlighting those aspects of Pharisaism with which Christianity came *into conflict*, not those elements which the Pharisees may have had *in common with* Jesus. The resulting image is not simply disparaging, but incomplete, disproportionate, and virtually a caricature.[7]

The stereotypical presentation of Jewish groups within Mark's gospel reminds us again that the gospel is meant primarily to proclaim the good news of salvation as perceived by the evangelist, rather than to attain historical precision. This leads us to our third consideration regarding Mark's presentation of the opponents of Jesus. How do these Jewish leadership groups function within the gospel to serve Mark's theological purposes?

Theological concerns and the presentation of Jesus' opponents

The simple fact that a gospel is primarily a narrative work of proclamation does not necessarily preclude historical accuracy. However, when clear theological concerns are seen to direct certain aspects of the narrative, the question of historical accuracy naturally comes into focus. No summary of Mark's theology will deny his emphasis on the cross. The climax of the gospel occurs in the account of the passion where the true identity of the Son of man is revealed in his suffering and death. A closer analysis of the historical accuracy of the passion narrative will be offered in the next section. Here I will limit my comments to the manner in which Mark's theological emphasis on the cross influences his treatment of the Jewish leaders in the first thirteen chapters of the gospel.

The widely quoted dictum of Martin Kahler that Mark can be seen as "a passion narrative with an extended introduction" captures an essential truth. The events of the passion anchor the gospel of Mark, and indeed all the gospels. Most likely the account of Jesus' death was the first part of the tradition to be shaped into a narrative. As the events of Jesus' ministry, birth, and even preexistence were also given narrative shape within the four gospels, their characterization was significantly colored by the events of the passion. This process of formation carried with it a very specific influence upon the presentation of the Jewish leadership in the gospels. It would be difficult to find a more eloquent statement of this influence than these words of Paul Winter:

> The gospel grew in the shadow of the cross. . . . The nucleus around which the gospel material accumulated consisted of a bare report of Jesus' arrest and trial, of his crucifixion. . . . Hence there was a report of a clash between Jesus and the Jewish authorities, a conflict that was set in the story of his arrest. The preaching grew and the gospel expanded. When it came to include recollections of happenings before Jesus' arrest, when the starting point of the gospel was set back to the time of his baptism, or his birth, the motif of Jewish enmity was also retrojected. When, still later, the story was expanded even more and now took as its point of departure the creation of the world, the theme of Jewish hostility was shifted back yet more: the Jews of the Fourth Gospel are by nature the enemies of the World Savior, determined to destroy him. . . . In this respect, the Fourth Gospel only gives a bizarre exaggeration to a notion

that is already present in the Marcan outline: *the Jews are ab initio* [from the beginning] *the enemies of Jesus.*[8]

It is, then, the literary and theological nature of the gospel itself, building to its climactic assertion in the passion and resurrection, which explains the violent and seemingly unwarranted opposition which Jesus experiences from the Jewish leaders even in the opening chapters.

This perspective can clarify many problematic passages in Mark. For example, when we read in Mark 3:6 that after Jesus healed the man with the withered hand on the sabbath, "the Pharisees went out, and immediately conspired with the Herodians against him, how to destroy him," we might well be perplexed. How can we make sense of this extreme and unexpected reaction? Why would Pharisees travel from Jerusalem to Galilee early in Jesus' ministry to observe him and his disciples and begin at once to plot his death? Historically, a sensible explanation is difficult to establish. It seems more likely to assume with Winter that the sudden and violent opposition by the Pharisees in this scene fulfills Mark's literary need to connect the early events of the ministry with the passion, emphasizing the centrality of the cross even as the ministry begins.

In this sense the violent opposition from the Jewish leaders which greets Jesus from the start is similar to the predictions of the passion which Mark has carefully situated in his gospel. The purpose is not to present an historical report of what Jesus said and how he was received in his ministry, but rather to key the reader into the significance of the cross and prepare the reader for the theological climax which will emerge at Calvary.

Summary: the accuracy of presenting Jesus' opponents in Mark

When one considers the segregation and generalization of leadership groups, and the theological emphasis of Mark's gospel, serious doubts are raised about the historical accuracy of Mark's presentation of the Jewish leaders within the controversy stories of the gospel. It seems likely that these stories reflect times and issues which are subsequent to the historical Jesus. The disputes regarding sabbath rest, dietary prescriptions, and the messianic identity of Jesus would loom much larger in the postresurrectional, ever-more-Gentile church than they would in pre-Christian Judaism. It is, therefore, not unlikely that later disputes between early Christians and the synagogue were read back into controversies of the historical Jesus.[9] Doubts can be raised concerning not only the issues of the debate but the participants as well. Possibly Mark did not know who the leadership groups were at the time of Jesus and filled in the picture with Jews whom he did know or those who might be opposing his own community.

None of these factors lead to firm conclusions. They do, however, raise a healthy skepticism. The possibility must be entertained that in many of the conflict stories neither the issues nor the opponents genuinely reflect incidents at the time of Jesus. When aspects of literary and theological shaping are factored in, it becomes ever more clear why the presentation of Jesus' opponents in the gospel of Mark should not be accepted as "reliable" history.

THE PRESENTATION OF JESUS' PASSION AND DEATH

A second aspect of Mark's gospel in which historical inaccuracies regarding Jews and Judaism are likely to exist is the presentation of the events of Jesus' passion and death. The passion narrative in Mark's gospel recounts, of course, a series of events by which Jesus is led to his death. The passion narrative, however, is no less theological than any other part of the gospel. In fact, Mark's emphasis on the cross places even more theological weight upon this particular section. In the second half of this chapter, we will examine some of the theological claims which this narrative makes. Here, our purpose is to pose again the question of the historical accuracy of the story.

The historical factors which led to Jesus' death have been extensively debated. It is unnecessary to present here the various attempts to uncover the reasons for Jesus' execution, since complete and readable treatments are available elsewhere.[10] My purpose is only to bring to the attention of the reader how the same skepticism which we found appropriate in evaluating the historical accuracy of Mark's treatment of the Jewish leaders also applies to Mark's treatment of Jesus' death.

The night trial in Mark

The issues of historical accuracy in Mark's passion account can be quickly illustrated by examining one scene: the night trial of Jesus (14:53–65). The power of this scene in which the full Jewish Sanhedrin condemns Jesus to death for the blasphemy of claiming to be "the Christ, Son of the Blessed" cannot be denied. Furthermore, because the night trial so clearly attributes the death of Jesus to the official leadership of Judaism, the need to assess its historical accuracy is particularly strong.

Today a vast amount of literature addresses the night trial in Mark. An examination of that literature renders the historical accuracy of the trial particularly suspect. The conflicts among the gospel accounts themselves first introduce the question. Only Mark and Matthew (who follows him) present a night trial of Jesus. Luke reports what seems to be only a hearing without any verdict (Luke 22:66–71). This hearing in Luke takes place not at night but in the morning. John recounts only an inquiry before Annas and Caiaphas, the high priest (John 18:12–14, 19–24). This inquiry ends without any official decision other than to hand Jesus over to Pilate. Which of these scenarios is closest to the historical fact? Consensus seems to be moving toward the simple sequence of John's narrative, and this is in no small part the result of the significant historical problems which the night trial in Mark poses.[11]

Donald Juel provides a convenient summary of these problems in eight points.[12] (1) The entire account of the trial is sandwiched between the account of Peter's denial. This gives a strong indication that Mark has a literary desire to contrast the weakness of Peter with Jesus' confident strength. In this way Jesus is clearly presented to the reader of the gospel as a model for imitation in time of trial. The purpose of the scene is, therefore, primarily hortatory. (2) The trial violates almost every known regulation given for Jewish trials in the Mishnah. Some of these regulations direct that capital trials could not be held at night, nor on the eve of a sabbath or festival, nor could a verdict of conviction be given on the same day as the trial itself. (3) The trial before Pilate which begins in Mark 15:1 gives no indication that the night trial has taken place. This seems to indicate that the trial scene has been inserted into an earlier narrative by the evangelist. (4) Jesus is condemned in the night trial for the religious charge of blasphemy. This is a Jewish religious offense, the punishment for which would be death by stoning. Yet Jesus is crucified. Crucifixion would result from a Roman process rather than the formal decision of the Sanhedrin which Mark presents. (5) According to our best reading of the Jewish legal sources, a blasphemer must pronounce the divine name itself. This Jesus does not do in Mark's narrative. (6) There is

another charge in the trial account: that Jesus threatened to destroy
the temple. It is not clear, however, how this charge is related to the
blasphemy charge, nor to Jesus' ministry where Mark does not
present him making such a threat. (7) Although Jesus is said to be
silent before his accusers, when asked by the high priest about his
identity he answers openly. He thereby reveals something which
throughout the entire gospel he has jealously kept hidden. The impact
of this revelation seems to indicate a literary and theological purpose.
(8) Between the high priest's question and Jesus' answer three separate titles and at least two scriptural references are employed. The
relationship between these titles is unclear and seems to be the result
of theological reflection rather than historical reporting.

Even with this long list of historical incongruities, we cannot
conclude with certainty that the night trial of Mark is devoid of valid
historical remembrances. What we can conclude is that the night trial
is a particularly weak candidate to be seen as reliable history. All the
inconsistencies which Juel offers make it more probable that Mark has
aesthetically shaped or even created this scene of the passion in order
to express his theological concerns.

SUMMARY: HISTORICAL RELIABILITY IN MARK

Where has the examination of Mark's treatment of Jesus' opponents and Jesus' night trial led us? It may have provided more questions than clear conclusions. Nevertheless, there are certainly reasons
to question the historical reliability of Mark's narrative.

To the believer who desires a reliable historical account upon
which to found faith assertions, the inconclusive nature of this historical inquiry may lead to frustration. Yet I believe that to settle for
historical probability rather than certainty should be seen as an advantage. It is better to recognize the limits of our sources than to
presume that they provide more than they can deliver. We do not
assist our faith nor the spread of the gospel by claiming a certainty
which is in fact questionable. What the gospels promise to provide us
is not scientific history but the assertions of faith-belief.

Having briefly surveyed the historical reliability of Mark's account, it is now time to examine these assertions of faith-belief.
Among such assertions are found the evaluative claims which reveal
the evangelist's stance toward Jews and the Jewish people. The re-

mainder of this chapter will attempt to review and classify those evaluative claims.

EVALUATIVE CLAIMS REGARDING JEWS AND JUDAISM IN THE GOSPEL OF MARK

When we move from a concern for historical accuracy to the question of Mark's beliefs about Jews and Judaism, we move into an inquiry which is more compatible with the intentions of the gospel narrative itself. Regardless of how accurately the narrative may reflect history, the gospel asserts certain beliefs within the narrative which the evangelist espouses and which the reader is meant to espouse as well. In this section we will ask what evaluative claims regarding Jews and Judaism can be located in the final form of Mark's gospel, and how these claims can be classified according to our categories of polemic. Three aspects of Mark's gospel will be examined: (1) the evaluation of legal traditions in Mark 7:1–23, (2) the anti-temple polemic, and (3) the parable of the wicked tenants. By discussing the possible interpretations of these dimensions of the text, we should be able to gain some insight into the gospel's evaluative stance toward Judaism.

MARK 7:1–23 AND THE VALIDITY OF THE JEWISH LAW

The extended controversy narrative between Jesus and the Pharisees over the traditions of the elders (7:1–23) provides the clearest statements within the gospel on the question of the Jewish law. The narrative is complex, including several abrupt shifts in the issues which are discussed. This complexity provides a rich resource for form critics who wish to reconstruct the tradition history of the text. Since our concern, however, is to understand the claims of the gospel in its final form, let us review the narrative as it now stands.

The Pharisees and scribes approach Jesus' disciples whom they see eating with defiled hands (vv 1–2a). This leads the narrator to explain that "defiled" should be understood as "unwashed" (v 2b), and then add that such practices are the custom of "the Pharisees and all the Jews" who follow the tradition of the elders (vv 3–4). The Pharisees and scribes then ask Jesus why his disciples do not follow the tradition of the elders (v 5), and Jesus responds by calling the questioners hypocrites who call down on themselves the reproach of Isaiah (vv 6–7). Jesus then hurls a counatercharge that their practice of

following the tradition of the elders does not respect the commandment of God (v 8). Suddenly a new charge emerges. Jesus accuses his
questioners of the practice of "Corban" which is presented as a way
of evading the responsibility of supporting one's parents (vv 9–13).

With an apparent new beginning, Jesus is then said again to
address the people. In that address he gives them a general
principle—nothing outside a person can defile by going in, but what
defiles is that which comes out of a person (vv 14–15). The scene then
shifts to the inside of a house where Jesus' disciples ask him to explain
what he meant (v 17). Jesus responds with a physiological argument,
insisting that food cannot defile because it does not enter the heart but
the stomach from which it passes out into the sewer (vv 18–19a). The
narrator then announces that Jesus has just declared all foods clean
(v 19b). The narrative ends with another response—this time an ethical one—in which it is stated that defilement comes from the evil that
lies within the heart (vv 20–23).

The evaluative claim of Mark 7:1–23

The present shape of the narrative is clearly the work of the
evangelist who moves us (although abruptly) from handwashing, to
tradition in general, to the specific tradition of Corban, to the food
laws, to a concluding ethical statement. Despite the complex nature
of the text, one basic evaluative claim of the text in its final form is
clear. The food laws have no further validity. The explanation provided by the narrator in verse 19b removes any uncertainty from this
claim.[13]

Furthermore, the narrative tends to generalize the opposition to
the food laws so that it extends to a wider rejection of Jewish cultic
practices. The explanation of the narrator of the handwashing in
verses 3–4 presents the practice as representative of "many other traditions" of "the Pharisees and all the Jews." The concluding comment
of Jesus in the discussion of Corban presents this custom as representative of "many things like this" (v 13).[14]

It is also clear that the text attempts to distance the reader from
Jewish practices, which are treated with sarcasm. The cultic practices
are presented as *Jewish* practices (vv 3–4) with which the reader is not
meant to identify. When speaking to the Pharisees, Jesus terms such
practices as "your" traditions (v 13) which distances both Jesus and
the reader from association with them. The physiological argument

against the food laws is sarcastic—literally a "gutter argument" in which the image used presents the religious practice with about as much value as the food which is evacuated.[15] Overall, then, the text argues that the cultic food laws of the Jews no longer have validity and have been superseded by ethical responsibilities.[16]

Mark 7:1–23 in light of the whole gospel

When the invalidation of the food laws found in Mark 7:1–23 is situated in the context of the whole gospel, confirmations of further rejections of Jewish cultic practice can be located. The present form of the controversy narratives in 2:23–28 and 3:1–5 shows that Jesus claims for himself an authority which surpasses the sabbath law. The downplaying of common Jewish practice as opposed to God's real intention is asserted, not only in regard to food laws and sabbath practice, but also in regard to divorce, 10:1–12.

By contrast, there are a few places in Mark where the continuing validity of the law is affirmed. The ten commandments are accepted as valid in 7:10 and 10:17–22; the two great commandments of love of God and neighbor are adopted as central in 12:28–34. The general impression in the gospel, however, is that aside from the continuing validity of these key requirements, the binding character of the Jewish law has ended—even for Jews.[17] This opens Mark's gospel to the charge of subordinating polemic in which widely-accepted requirements of the Jewish law have been redefined as unimportant in light of Christ.

It should be noted, however, that the polemic in Mark 7:1–23 does not move into an abrogating anti-Judaism. This is true even though there is a ready opportunity for such a claim to be made. When Jesus employs the quotation from Isaiah, the charge is that "this people" worships God in vain (7:6–7). As we saw in the introduction, this passage was originally directed by Isaiah against Israel as intra-Jewish polemic. Mark's gospel uses it here to subordinate certain parts of Jewish cultic practice to Christ. The quotation, however, could have been easily pushed further. The scope of the charge has the potential of being turned into a rejection of the Jewish people as a whole. Yet in the gospel of Mark this is avoided. The rejection is directed to Jesus' questioners. They alone seem to be the hypocrites who fall under the judgment of the prophet. Therefore, although the text asserts that many legal requirements are not of God, only the leadership who teach such practices are rejected. The people as a whole are not indicted.[18] Mark 7:1–23 conspicuously avoids an abrogating anti-Judaism.

THE ANTI-TEMPLE THEME IN MARK

When we turn from Mark 7:1–23 to examine other passages which might betray negative evaluations of Judaism, our way is less clear. As we have seen, Jesus' controversy with the Pharisees over handwashing contained a number of direct comments by the narrator which imparted a definite direction to the interpretation of the passage. In the sections of the gospel which shall be examined in the remainder of this chapter, we possess no such advantage. Instead we are presented with symbolic scenes and parables which stand on their own within the narrative. The precise reference any of these sections might have toward Judaism is unclear because direct interpretative comments by the narrator are minimal or lacking altogether.

A good example of this interpretative challenge is a chain of narrative scenes within the gospel which concern a negative attitude toward the temple. Before Jesus arrives in Jerusalem, there are already indications within the gospel of an opposition toward the holy city. The journey to Jerusalem with its three passion predictions (8:27–10:52) is a journey into opposition and suffering. Early controversies with Pharisees and scribes "from Jerusalem" (3:22; 7:1) point in the same direction.[19] Since cultic purity is directly tied to access to the temple, Jesus' negative evaluation of cultic practices which we have just discussed in Mark 7:1–23 hints that Jesus' attitude toward the temple in Jerusalem will be no less negative.

That subtle indication comes into full light once Jesus enters the holy city. From chapter 11 of the gospel forward, a series of scenes focuses on a specific opposition between Jesus and the temple. Mark has framed Jesus' driving of buyers and sellers out of the temple (11:15–18) with a narrative about a withered fig tree (11:12–14, 20–25). After this there follows a series of controversy stories between Jesus and the temple authorities. During the eschatological discourse of chapter 13, Jesus foretells the destruction of the temple (13:2, 14). During the interrogation in the night trial, Jesus is charged with claiming to destroy the temple and build another not made by hands (14:58). Those who deride Jesus as he hangs on the cross again bring up his threat to destroy the temple (15:29). Finally, at the moment of

Jesus' death, "the curtain of the temple was torn in two, from top to bottom" (15:38).

This chain within the narrative clearly sets Jesus and the temple in opposition. How shall this opposition be interpreted? Does the temple stand within the text as a symbol for all of Israel? Does it refer to a particular aspect of Jewish worship? Does it function as a locus for criticism of those who hold authority over the temple? All of these possible understandings of the anti-temple theme have been suggested. I will offer a representative survey of these opinions by examining one scene within Mark's narrative: Jesus' cleansing of the temple (11:12–25).

The cleansing of the temple/cursing of the fig tree

Mark frames Jesus' cleansing of the temple with the narrative of the fig tree which does not produce (11:13), is cursed (11:14), and withers away (11:20). By doing this, the gospel clearly intends that the cleansing of the temple and the cursing of the fig tree should interpret each other. The non-productivity and destruction of the fig tree is associated with the temple scene. What, however, is being rejected? At least three different referents are possible.

THE WHOLE JEWISH PEOPLE ARE REJECTED

T. A. Burkill and Lloyd Gaston are representative of the most encompassing interpretation: the destruction of the fig tree/temple symbolizes the rejection of Israel as God's people. Reading the Markan narrative in light of the fig tree in Luke 13:6–9, Gaston argues that, for Mark, the fig tree stands for Israel whose time has run out. Although Mark's framing technique ties the fig tree specifically to the temple, Gaston argues that the curse and destruction spread wider than this one institution of Israel. For Mark, Israel itself has been cursed and will perish.[20] Burkill adopts the same understanding which must be seen as abrogating anti-Judaism:

> St. Mark's sympathies are primarily on the side of the masses as distinct from those of high estate, and yet it remains that *in toto* his contemporaries constitute an adulterous and sinful generation (8:38), ordinary folk being only too easily misled by the nefarious machinations of their political leaders (10:42; 15:10f). As for the chosen race, its

doom is sealed; the cursed fig tree inevitably perishes (11:21). . . .[21]

Burkill's and Gaston's decision to interpret the destruction as applying *"in toto"* — extending to the whole people — is contested by other interpreters. A second way of reading the fig tree/temple scene would restrict the opposition and consequent destruction only to the religious leaders. Douglas Hare points to the verse immediately after the action in the temple: "When the chief priests and the scribes heard it, they kept looking for a way to kill him; for they were afraid of him, because the whole crowd was spellbound by his teaching" (11:18). Hare argues that Mark sees a distinction between the Jewish people and their leaders. The crowd responds positively to Jesus. It is only the Jewish leadership which opposes him, and it is upon that leadership that the curse and destruction symbolized by the fig tree falls.[22] Donald Juel summarizes this position:

> The cleansing of the temple must in some sense imply the rejection of the official representatives of Israel, the leaders of the temple establishment. Some care is necessary at this point. It is perhaps inaccurate to suggest that the events point to the rejection of Israel. Jesus' opponents in the last chapters of the Gospel are clearly the leaders of the temple establishment, the scribes, the high priests, and the elders. . . . it is at least possible to say that the cleansing, interpreted by the cursing of the fig tree, points to the rejection of a particular group within Israel. Those in charge of the temple have borne no fruit; they have perverted God's intentions and will thus be rejected.[23]

To the extent that this understanding of the scene is adopted, the polemic does not attack a central symbol of Judaism but is rather a critique of those who exercise a particular position within the temple structure. Such an opposition to the temple would be best understood as prophetic polemic.

THE TEMPLE CULT IS REJECTED

A third possibility for understanding the significance of the fig tree/temple scene reads the text as opposing the cultic significance of the temple. Paul Achtemeier argues that for Mark the cleansing of the temple is an event which goes beyond any simple protest against abuses by the money-changers or by the temple leadership. For Achtemeier, Jesus' action indicates that the value of the temple has come to an end. This is true not only because of the abuse present in its functioning, but also because the temple could not serve for Mark as a locus where Gentiles, as well as Jews, could worship. Of the evangelists, only Mark states that the temple should be "for all the nations" (11:17). The temple is the fig tree which has not borne its proper fruit. Therefore, its value has ended. The locus of God's salvation is no longer to be found in the temple or its sacrifices. Jesus replaces the temple as the way to God.[24]

In what is perhaps the most extensive treatment of the anti-temple theme in Mark, John Donahue understands the cleansing of the temple in a manner similar to Achtemeier's interpretation. Donahue argues that the key to understanding Mark's purposes can be found in the account of the night trial which is primarily a redactional creation of the evangelist. There in the trial scene, the double charge leveled against Jesus in 14:58 brings the anti-temple theme to its climax. The double charge has been created by Mark to assert that the definitive end of the Jewish cult center has come ("I will destroy this temple") and that the Christian community now forms a new temple ("I will build another").[25] With this understanding of the double charge as an anchor for interpretation, Donahue reads the cleansing of the temple in its light. The cleansing framed by the two fig tree references implies an eschatological visitation on the temple. The prohibition of Jesus against carrying anything through the temple (11:16) abrogates the cultic role of the temple which will be replaced by a house of worship for all nations.[26]

Although Donahue believes that Mark views the Christian community as the replacement for the temple cult, this does not necessarily imply the rejection of Israel by God. While the text is in fact open to such an implication, it does not state it. What has been rejected is the temple cult. The temple was certainly central to Jewish religious life. As already stated, we presume that Mark was writing at a time when the temple still stood. In the interpretations of both

Achtemeier and Donahue, therefore, Mark is involved with reinterpreting a basic Jewish institution in light of Christ.

Because of Christ, true worship must be understood in a new way. If Mark claims that the temple has been replaced by a new Christian community, he is clearly redefining Judaism and thus opening the gospel to a kind of subordinating polemic. Such a claim, however, does not necessarily introduce an anti-Judaism which would abrogate the status of Israel as such.

Summary: A variety of possibilities

As indicated at the beginning of this section, the anti-temple theme in Mark can be understood in a number of different ways. Should the stance against the temple be read as a stance against Israel itself (*in toto*) and therefore a kind of abrogating anti-Judaism? Should it be understood as an opposition against the Jewish leadership of the temple and therefore a kind of prophetic polemic? Or should it be seen as an attempt to assert an elimination of the temple as the center of Jewish cult, and thus as subordinating polemic where the temple is replaced by Christ? The nature of the narrative is open to all these possibilities. Before suggesting which one might hold the greatest probability, one further section of Mark's gospel must be examined—a section in which many interpreters would claim to find the clearest indication of the gospel's stance toward Israel.

MARK 12:1–12: THE PARABLE OF THE WICKED TENANTS

Amidst the series of controversy stories which link Jesus' cleansing of the temple to the eschatological discourse in chapter 13, Jesus tells one parable: the parable of the wicked tenants. This parable is also found in the gospels of Matthew and Luke, thus making it one of a relatively few parables found in all three synoptic gospels. The parable does not refer to the temple specifically. It is, however, told in the midst of the rising anti-temple theme which we have examined in the previous section. The context implies that Mark wishes the parable to address the growing opposition which the narrative has been describing. Because the parable is one of judgment and rejection, it is important to determine exactly what is being rejected and how that rejection contributes to possible anti-Judaism in Mark's gospel.

Much of the research on this parable has sought to determine whether it was a parable actually told by the historical Jesus and how its form may have been altered in the process of transmission. Following our stated approach, we will bypass this valid effort at historical reconstruction and attempt rather to interpret the parable's import as it presently stands in the Markan narrative.

The parable of the wicked tenants (12:1–12) follows a controversy story in which Jesus vies with the chief priests, the scribes, and the elders over the basis of his authority (11:27–33). Jesus then tells this parable about a man who planted a vineyard, leased it to tenants, and went to another country. When the time came to receive the fruit of the vineyard from the tenants, he sent numerous servants to them, but they rejected, beat, and killed the messengers. Finally the man sent his beloved son. The tenants, seeing him to be the heir, killed him and cast him out of the vineyard. Jesus then says that in response the owner of the vineyard will destroy the tenants and give the vineyard to others. This is followed by a quotation from Psalm 118 about the rejected stone which has become the cornerstone according to God's design. In the text, some who hear this parable realize that it is told against them. They want to arrest Jesus but leave him alone because they fear the multitude.

The allegorizing tendency of the parable

What this parable means, of course, depends upon how you read it. Almost every interpreter admits that there is an allegorizing tendency within the parable. The various characters in the story are meant to stand for specific individuals or groups. This understanding is supported by the text itself. After the parable is told, there are some people who perceive that Jesus "told this parable against them" (12:12). The text itself invites us, therefore, to draw some connections between characters within the parable and those who are outside of it. The central interpretive issue of the parable is determining how those connections are to be made.

There is a firm consensus that the owner in the parable is meant to represent God. Because of the strong similarity to the Song of the Vineyard in Isaiah 5, the vineyard in the parable is commonly thought to stand for Israel. Most authors will also agree that Mark intends the "beloved son" to stand for Jesus.

The most difficult allegorization to determine, however, is the one which is the most important for our purposes. To whom do "the tenants" in the parable refer? The anger expressed by those who perceived that the parable was "against them" (12:12) clearly associates "them" with the tenants. But who are "they"? The first verse of the section says "Jesus began to speak to *them* in parables" (12:1). This would at first seem to refer to the last group mentioned within the narrative. In this case it would be "the chief priests, the scribes, and the elders" of verse 11:27.

But this is not as secure a technique of identification as it might seem. For example, in 8:14 Mark says, "Now *they* had forgotten to bring bread." Yet this imprecise "they" cannot be taken to refer to the last group specifically mentioned in the text. That group would be the Pharisees of 8:11–13. Yet in 8:14 it is certainly the disciples and not the Pharisees who are the object of the "they." It seems that Mark is not always exact in his references back within the text.[27]

Taken alone, therefore, the "them" of 12:1 remains uncertain. When linked, however, to the "they" of 12:12, the matter is clarified. Here the text clearly distinguishes "they" from the crowds. Therefore, the only group which would qualify in this context for the referent would be the Jewish leaders previously mentioned in 11:27. However ambiguous the "them" of 12:1 might appear, by the end of the section "they" have been clearly identified by Mark as the chief priests, the scribes, and the elders. These Jewish leaders, therefore, are the tenants of the parable.

The symbolic function of the Jewish leaders

Yet even when it is accepted—as it is by almost all commentators—that the Jewish leaders are the tenants of the parable, one can still continue to discuss whether the Jewish leaders are themselves symbolic of some larger reality. In other words, is the rejection of the tenants limited to the rejection of the Jewish leadership or does it extend beyond them? In order to determine how widely the rejection of the parable should be extended, we need to draw verse 9 of the parable into the discussion. That verse states that the vineyard will be taken away from the old tenants and given "to others." Although the parable does not state the identity of "the others," who these "others" are has a direct bearing on how far the rejection in the parable should be applied. Who or what is being rejected is therefore connected in interpretation with who are "the others" who receive the vineyard. These two interpretative aspects of the parable can be related to each other in at least three possible ways.

THE JEWISH LEADERS: A STRICT INTERPRETATION

The first option is to interpret the rejection in the parable as strictly as possible. Adopting this alternative, one can argue that the Jewish leadership is not symbolic of any larger reality and that the parable is told against the religious leaders and not against anything beyond them. The rejection of the tenants is read, therefore, as a rejection of the present leadership of Judaism. In this understanding, the unspecified "others" to whom the vineyard is given would presumably be another set of Jewish leaders. Aaron A. Milavec adopts this position and adds further that the parable states that this destruction and replacement by others will take place when the owner "comes." This he reads as a reference to the future return of the Lord when full justice will be achieved. At that time the unfaithful leaders will be replaced by others. But it is the Jewish leadership and not the people who will be replaced. Israel remains God's favored people until the end of time. The replacement of unfaithful leadership with better leaders is a sign of God's faithfulness to and love of Israel.[28]

It can be argued, therefore, that in the parable the rejection of the tenants refers only to the Jewish authorities of the temple and envisions a time when Israel will be given to other Jewish leaders who will be more faithful.[29] Such critique is commonplace among the prophets and expresses a kind of prophetic polemic.

THE JEWISH LEADERS: A SYMBOL FOR THE TEMPLE

A second way to interpret the "tenants" and the "others" in the parable begins to extend the rejection in the narrative beyond the Jewish leadership. Here the rejection of the tenants is read in the light of the anti-temple polemic which, as we have seen, some scholars believe colors this section. "The chief priests, the scribes, and the elders" are then seen as the tenants, but the tenants become symbolic of the temple itself. Therefore, the rejection of the tenants in the parable is representative of the rejection of the temple as a place of valid worship.

Donahue, as we would expect, adopts this interpretation. For him the vineyard with its tower is the temple; the tenants are the temple officials; and Jesus is the son. By referring to the quotation about the rejected stone which has become the cornerstone (12:10–11), Donahue argues that Jesus is the new cornerstone of a new temple which is the new community that accepts him. The "others" are therefore the nucleus of this new community which replaces the temple.[30] Donahue thus extends the rejection of the tenants to the rejection of the temple institution. Interpreted thus, the parable would express a subordinating polemic, attempting to replace the centrality of the temple with the new community having Christ as its cornerstone. Donahue does not, however, take the additional step of extending the rejection of the tenants to a rejection of Israel as such.

THE JEWISH LEADERS: A SYMBOL FOR THE JEWISH PEOPLE

This additional step, however, has been taken by others and leads to a third way to read the rejection of the parable. Ernst Best accepts the basic anti-temple understanding of Donahue but pushes it further,

> Mark continually emphasizes judgment on old Israel; new Israel replaces it. . . . The underlying logic is therefore clearer if we take the "others" of v. 9c to be the new Israel rather than either the new rulers for old Israel or rulers for the new Israel.[31]

Lloyd Gaston agrees. Although in its origins the parable may have simply indicated a rejection of those who care for Israel, Gaston believes that in the text of Mark the destruction of the tenants means judgment on all of Israel.[32]

When the extension of the Jewish leadership spreads out to symbolize all of Israel, the parable has been read in a manner that can be characterized as abrogating anti-Judaism. Whether the "others" are said to refer simply to the Markan community or to a larger Gentile church, in this interpretation Israel has been replaced and is no longer God's people.

CONCLUSION: MARK'S EVALUATIVE CLAIM

The limited survey of key passages of Mark's gospel has surfaced a variety of possible understandings of Mark's evaluation of Judaism. Depending on the manner in which the narrative is read, Mark can be seen as a proponent of abrogating anti-Judaism, subordinating polemic, or prophetic polemic. Obviously no conclusive resolution can be adopted which will convince all interpreters. I would suggest, however, that Mark is best understood as professing a kind of subordinating polemic.

Mark 7:1-23 as a crux for interpretation

The starting point and firmest ground upon which to build such a conclusion is the gospel's clear anti-cultic stance which surfaces in 7:1-23. Here in terms that are difficult to refute, the gospel asserts that the food laws no longer have validity. This reformation of an established practice of Judaism demonstrates that the gospel has no reservations about promoting a gospel in which Jewish practice has been significantly redefined in light of Christ. Once this aspect of the narrative is appreciated, it is more likely that the opposition of Jesus toward the temple, which begins in chapter eleven, should be interpreted as opposition against the validity of the temple cult. There is, of course, a jump from purity requirements to the worship of the temple, but the two certainly move in the same cultic sphere. A text which would dispense with the one could easily see the new community as replacing the other. Both adjustments would involve a realignment of central Jewish symbols and result in subordinating polemic.

One can easily question whether a text which would claim to redefine both purity laws and temple would not also propose an abrogation of Israel itself. Does not Mark's redefinition in fact imply that Israel itself has been replaced? This is a serious question, and there are many who would answer in the affirmative, as we have seen. Mark, however, does not seem to push his reformulation that far.

One truly positive view of the Jewish tradition

In at least one case, the gospel contains a very positive picture of Jewish tradition. In the encounter between Jesus and a scribe over the first commandment (12:28-34), we have been given one of the few passages in the gospels where Jesus interacts with a Jewish leader in a positive interchange. Here Jesus discusses the law with a fellow-Jew. In solid camaraderie, they both agree that the greatest commandment is love of God and neighbor. The scribe says, "You are right, Teacher" and affirms that Jesus has spoken "truly" (12:32). Jesus says that the scribe has answered "wisely" and was "not far from the kingdom of God" (12:34). The greatest commandment upon which they would agree represents standard pharisaic teaching, and Jesus' use of the standard Jewish prayer (the *Shema*—"Hear, O Israel") hardly implies an attitude which has rejected Israel's status as God's people.

This single encounter cannot in itself disprove that the gospel might suggest the abrogation of Israel. It does, however, point in a direction which would forestall such a conclusion. And in this particular gospel, even a small indication in such a direction is important.

The silence of Mark

What makes the precise determination of Mark's evaluation of Israel difficult is the lack of any specific statement on the status of Israel as such. There are clear indications that Judaism is being reformulated, but there is no clear statement that Israel is being rejected. As we have seen, certain parables and images can be read in such a way that this conclusion is possible. Yet the same material can be read in a manner in which Israel continues as God's people. This leads to ambiguity about the status of Israel. Juel expresses the dilemma which the interpreter faces:

> The concern for the Gentiles that many have observed in Mark does not necessarily imply a negative view of Jews. Nevertheless, the "rejection" theme is present in Mark, particularly in the parable of the wicked husbandmen in 12:1–11. The destruction of the temple demonstrates that God has rejected at least one segment of the Jewish community. Mark's concern in the trial to heighten the responsibility of the Jewish leaders in Jesus' death are part of this concern. The temple charge suggests that Jesus' death not only brings about the birth of a new community but the rejection and the destruction of another.[33]

Juel seems to say that there is much in the text which might imply the replacement of Israel, but Mark does not actually say it. I think that such an understanding captures the ambiguity of Mark on the status of Israel.

Mark is proposing a redefinition of Judaism in light of Christ. In reading Mark, one receives the impression that should Israel be replaced, it would cause no serious problem for the evangelist. There is not a high investment in Jewish identity as such. Yet for all the themes of rejection and reformulation, Mark never clearly states that Israel's status has been taken away. The silence of the text on this issue is important, especially when there are many places in the narrative where a definitive rejection of Israel could have been easily included.

We must not jump to a conclusion which Mark does not specifically express. Therefore, it seems wisest to understand Mark's evaluative claims regarding Judaism by taking the gospel at its word—and no more. Central aspects of Jewish life will have to be subordinated to Christ and the new community. Israel, however, is not abrogated. Although it may remain so only by the failure to state the opposite more clearly, within Mark's gospel, Israel remains God's chosen people.

2

THE GOSPEL OF MATTHEW: AN ABROGATING POLEMIC WITH VIOLENCE

Compared to Mark, Matthew seems both more Jewish and more anti-Jewish. There is a furious ambivalence in this gospel. On one hand, Matthew is filled with expressions, interests, and attitudes that flow from the traditions of Israel. On the other hand, the gospel contains an astonishing animosity toward certain Jewish groups and institutions—and perhaps even against the nation itself. In order to understand the gospel and its evaluation of Judaism, some account must be given of this venomous incongruity.

Our examination will proceed in three steps. First, we will survey the aspects of the gospel which contribute to its strong Jewish character. Second, we will identify the passages in which the polemic of the gospel occurs. Finally, we will review the evaluative claims of the gospel regarding Judaism, attempting to classify the polemic of the gospel in light of our previously defined categories.

JEWISH FEATURES OF MATTHEW'S GOSPEL

Several characteristics impart to Matthew's gospel a particularly Jewish flavor. John P. Meier notes that the gospel contains:

> . . . echoes of Semitic linguistic usage, use of Semitic words without translation, interest in and controversy over Jewish customs and rites, a use of rabbinic argumentation, a great amount of space given to the question of the Mosaic law,

and a heavy emphasis given to the fulfillment of OT prophecy.[1]

Let us examine a sampling of these characteristics in more detail.

JEWISH EXPRESSIONS AND POINT OF VIEW

Certain Jewish expressions are frequently employed in Matthew. With only four exceptions (12:28, 19:24, 21:31, 43), the gospel changes its sources so that the phrase "the reign of God" becomes "the reign of heaven." It is also common in Matthew to find the phrase "your Father in heaven." Both of these practices seem to indicate typical rabbinic efforts to avoid the direct mention of "God" (*theos*). This approach imparts to the gospel a particularly Jewish deference in addressing the deity. Furthermore, only Matthew refers to Jerusalem as "the holy city" (4:5, 27:53), and the terminology of "binding" and "loosing" which is found in 16:17–18 and 18:18 has a special Jewish background.[2]

Another clue to the gospel's Jewish character is that a Jewish point of view can be frequently discerned in the text. Proper pious practice is contrasted to the practice of the "Gentiles" or the "heathen." In 5:47 followers of Jesus are told that if they greet only members of the community, they would be doing no more than what the "Gentiles do." In 6:7 they are warned that to pray by heaping up empty phrases would be to pray "as the Gentiles." Chapter 18 of the gospel reflects practices of the Matthean community on issues of church life and order. When discussing how a recalcitrant member of the community should be treated, Matthew directs that an offender who refuses to listen to the decision of the church should be cut off from the community. This excommunication, however, is expressed in a manner that reveals a Jewish perspective, directing that the offender "be to you as a Gentile and a tax collector" (18:17).[3]

Matthew is also able to express positive qualities from a Jewish perspective. The true disciple and ideal for this gospel is carried by the image of the "scribe who has been trained for the kingdom of heaven" (13:52). Although we will soon see many statements which seem to contradict it, some valid authority seems to be conceded to the scribes and Pharisees because "they sit on Moses' seat" (23:2). Most importantly, there are several places in the gospel where the priority of Israel is affirmed in the narrative's presentation of the missionary practice of Jesus. When Matthew relates the cure of the Syrophoenician woman's daughter, he adds to Mark's account the reason why Jesus was opposed to granting the mother's request: "I was sent only to the lost sheep of the house of Israel" (15:24). The same idea is present in another saying unique to Matthew. When Jesus sends out the twelve disciples, he charges them: "Go nowhere among the Gentiles, and enter no town of the Samaritans, but go rather to the lost sheep of the house of Israel" (10:5–6). All of these examples seem to betray a point of view which is Jewish in its orientation.

ATTITUDES TOWARD PIETY, SCRIPTURE, AND THE LAW

Matthew exhibits a clear espousal of Jewish piety. The heart of the sermon on the mount is the Lord's Prayer (6:9–14). Matthew has carefully situated the prayer in the center of the traditional Jewish triad of pious practices: almsgiving (6:2–4), prayer (6:5–15), and fasting (6:16–18). Even though there is a clear distinctiveness to the manner in which the followers of Jesus are expected to carry out these practices, the threefold pattern presumes a typically Jewish point of departure.[4]

Matthew's use of scripture adds further to the gospel's Jewish flavor. Scriptural proof texts and prophecies are a part of almost every early Christian text. Nevertheless, Matthew's gospel demonstrates a particularly strong interest in the fulfillment of the Jewish scriptures. At least one hundred twenty-three scriptural quotations and allusions can be located within the gospel. Furthermore, Matthew rarely, if ever, shortens or omits scriptural references which are found in his sources. He rather tends to expand allusions and add quotations.[5] This results in a gospel in which the Jewish scriptures are extensively used and honored.

The gospel is also clearly concerned about the role and authority of the Mosaic law. The law in Matthew is a thorny problem, and we will discuss it more fully later in this chapter. Here it is only necessary to underline how the very strong positive attitude toward the law adds yet another Jewish element to this gospel. The key text in this regard is Matthew 5:17–18 where, during the sermon on the mount, Jesus says:

(17) Think not that I have come to abolish the law and the prophets; I have come not to abolish but to fulfill. (18) For truly, I tell you, until heaven and earth pass away, not one letter, not one stroke of a letter, will pass from the law until all is accomplished.

This statement in Matthew's gospel seems to affirm that the Mosaic law in some sense remains valid, and Jesus' connection with that law only adds to the impression of Matthew as a gospel which grapples seriously with Jewish issues.

MATTHEW VERSUS MARK: THE SABBATH

Matthew uses Mark as a source. In doing so Matthew includes several stories from Mark in which Jesus argues with the Jewish leadership over the proper attitude toward the sabbath. The two gospels, of course, share a common view that Jesus' approach to the sabbath was correct. Matthew, however, is inclined to show more deference toward the sabbath than Mark. When Jesus is arguing about the plucking of grain on the sabbath, Mark gives one justification from the example of David, and then declares that "the Son of Man is lord even of the sabbath" (Mark 2:25–28). In Matthew's version, two more scriptural arguments are added: one relating to the practice of the priests in the temple (Matt 12:5), the other drawn from the prophet Hosea (Matt 12:7). Cumulatively these arguments indicate that, according to Matthew, Jesus' practice is not a rejection of the sabbath nor a violation of it, but rather a way in which the God-given purpose of the sabbath can emerge.

It seems likely that Matthew's gospel would have the reader continue to hold the Jewish sabbath in respect. When Mark describes the flight that the reader will be forced to make in the final days, he advises, "Pray that it be not in winter" (Mark 13:18). Matthew recognizes another unfavorable time for flight and adds it to his gospel: "Pray that your flight be neither in winter nor on a sabbath" (Matt 24:20). This seems to indicate that Matthew's gospel still accepts the sabbath as a religious day on which flight would pose legal problems.[6]

MATTHEW VERSUS MARK: THE DIETARY REQUIREMENTS

Matthew is not only more Jewish than Mark in his approach to the sabbath; he demonstrates a similar inclination in his attitude toward the Jewish dietary requirements. This can be shown by comparing the versions of Jesus' debate over the tradition of the elders. This debate occurs in Mark 7:1–23, and we have already seen how it provides a clear indication that Mark's gospel no longer considers the food laws binding. Faced with such a scene in which Jewish food laws are rejected, Matthew makes several changes in his source which greatly soften Mark's rejection of Jewish dietary restrictions. Matthew accepts Mark's ethical orientation to the food question. He agrees with Mark that what comes out of a person does indeed defile that person. Yet Matthew wants to blunt Mark's claim that all foods are clean. He accomplishes this by making three changes.

First, in the physiological argument, Matthew omits Mark's claim that what is outside a person cannot defile that person. Matthew does this because he most likely still believes that there are food regulations which, if not obeyed, can indeed defile a person. Compare Mark's and Matthew's versions:

Mark 7:18b–19a   Do you not see that whatever goes into a person from outside cannot defile, since it enters not the heart but the stomach, and goes out into the sewer?

Matt 15:17   Do you not see that whatever goes into the mouth enters the stomach, and goes out into the sewer?

Second, Matthew changes the end of Mark's account. Compare again the two versions.

Mark 7:23   All these evil things come from within, and they defile a person.

Matt 15:20   These are what defile a person; but to eat with unwashed hands does not defile.

In Mark's account this closing sentence is intended to finally refute any validity to Jewish dietary restrictions. For Mark it is the ethical issue alone which is important, and this is determined only by what comes from within. One can appreciate the thrust of Mark's last line by making explicit what is implied: "All these evil things come from within, and they defile a person—*not any food requirements.*" Matthew, however, mutes Mark's implied rejection of the food laws by re-introducing the issue of handwashing. Thus, while accepting Mark's ethical stance that evil comes from within, Matthew does not allow the implication that dietary requirements can be ignored. The "outer" practice which can be ignored according to Matthew is handwashing. By this clever alteration of the Markan text, Matthew has diverted the rejection of Mark back against the practice of handwashing and away from any rejection of the food laws.

The third and final change Matthew makes is to simply omit what we have seen is Mark's clearest statement in opposition to the dietary laws. This is the parenthetical comment by the evangelist in Mark 7:19b: "Thus he declared all foods clean." This key phrase is missing from Matthew's account.

An obvious conclusion to be drawn from these three alterations of his Markan source is that Matthew is comfortable with following the requirements of the Jewish dietary requirements and has no desire—as does Mark—to reject them.[7] It seems likely that in Matthew we are dealing with a gospel which still expects the Jewish sabbath to be respected and the Jewish food laws to be followed.

All of the above characteristics which we have noted in this section explain why Matthew emerges as a particularly Jewish gospel. Such a robust appreciation of Jewish expressions, customs, and point of view is, however, only half of the picture. Matthew's gospel is characterized by the awkward ambivalence which we noted at the beginning of this chapter. It not only manifests strong Jewish interests but also contains numerous features which seem to depreciate Jewish values and characters. Our next task will be to review these aggressively polemical traits of the gospel.

FEATURES NEGATIVE TO JEWS AND JUDAISM IN MATTHEW

For all its Jewish flavor, Matthew's gospel is characterized by a vivid polemic against certain Jews and aspects of Judaism. Matthew

reduces Mark's favorable presentation of the Jewish scribe in the debate over the greatest commandment,[8] and increases the negative presentation of Jewish characters during his version of the passion.[9]
Furthermore, Matthew directs his polemic more specifically toward
the Pharisees than Mark does.[10] In material that Matthew shares with
Luke, the polemic is stronger in Matthew's treatment of the saying
about eating in the reign of heaven and in his version of the parable
of the Great Supper.[11]

ANTI-JEWISH POLEMIC IN MATERIAL UNIQUE TO MATTHEW

Not only does Matthew adapt his sources in ways that shift them
toward an increasingly polemical bent against Jews and Jewish
groups, but the gospel also contains polemic in material which is
unique to his gospel.

The infancy narratives

Early in the gospel, polemic unique to Matthew emerges in the
infancy narrative. Raymond Brown has eloquently argued that the
infancy narrative functions as "a gospel in miniature."[12] The infancy
narrative is proclaiming the postresurrectional message shaped by the
early church. In subtle ways, as the infancy narrative describes the
events of Jesus' birth, the form of that description has been influenced by the events of Jesus' passion and resurrection as well as the
issues of Matthew's own community. This applies to the polemic in
the infancy narrative as well, which can be seen as a polemic twice
removed. The polemic of Matthew's own time was first read back into
Matthew's account of the passion, shaping the account of Jesus'
death. Once present in the passion account, that polemic was then
further thrown back into the account of Jesus' birth.

This twice-removed polemic can be recognized in several characteristics of Matthew's infancy narrative. The growing Gentile nature
of the church of Matthew's time is reflected in the magi who come
from the east (Matt 2:1). Although Jesus is identified as "the king of
the Jews" (2:2), it is ironic that in Matthew's infancy narrative only
these non-Jews pay him homage. The use of this title is also significant. The only other place Jesus is referred to as "the king of the
Jews" is in the passion narrative where Pilate will question him con-

cerning the title (27:11), where the soldiers will use it to mock him (27:29), and where it will identify Jesus on the cross (27:37). A similar title, "the king of Israel" is used by the chief priests, scribes, and elders to mock Jesus as he hangs on the cross (27:41–43).

When in the infancy narrative Herod and "all the chief priests and scribes of the people" (2:4) do not recognize the newborn child as "the king of the Jews" but instead try to kill him (2:16), we can recognize a proleptic presentation of Jewish rejection and involvement in Jesus' passion. Matthew's use of the Greek verb "to assemble" (*synagein*) to describe Herod's gathering of the Jewish leadership (2:4) only strengthens this association. Although never used in Mark's passion narrative and used only once in Luke's, Matthew uses this verb five times in his passion narrative to describe the assembling of Jesus' enemies against him.[13] The connection to the passion narrative is further tightened by the comment in 2:3 that when Herod heard of the new birth he was troubled and "all Jerusalem with him." This mirrors what we shall soon see is another unique contribution of Matthew to the gospel narrative—his claim that during the trial before Pilate "the people as a whole" accepted the responsibility for Jesus' blood (27:25).

The beauty of Matthew's infancy narrative and its association with the peace of Christmas has perhaps dulled our awareness of the polemic which has been read back into the account from later events and disputes.

> The dramatis personae may be exotically costumed as Eastern potentates and as a Jewish king and priests, and for that reason they are not easily forgotten. But beneath the robes one can recognize the believers of Matthew's time and their opponents.[14]

Even in the early scenes of Bethlehem, Matthew is already proclaiming the gospel with the polemic edge which typifies his gospel. The Gentile magi accept and pay homage to the newborn king. But the Jewish leaders in Jerusalem and all the people do not believe and instead seek to put the king of the Jews to death.

The blood curse of Matthew

The precise scope and nature of the polemic of the notorious "blood curse" of Matthew 27:24–25 will be discussed when we examine the evaluative claims of Matthew. It is mentioned in this section, however, because only Matthew includes these verses in which "the people as a whole" agree to have Jesus' blood upon them and their children. No other evangelist mentions Pilate's washing of hands or the people's proclamation.

A moment's reflection will produce a number of reasons why this scene should be taken as a polemical addition of Matthew rather than an accurate historical account. First, although it is not inherently impossible that Pilate might have washed his hands to signify his own nonculpability, it is hardly conceivable that he would have made a *public* demonstration of such cowardice before a subject population. Second, considering the potential of mob rebellion that was present during any Jewish festival while Judea was occupied by a foreign power, it would be highly unlikely that Pilate would allow any sizable crowd to gather—much less call one together. Third, even if a sizable crowd were called together, how would it have been possible for "the people as a whole" to speak in unison? Fourth, even if they could speak in unison, why would they ever be inclined to accept "in perpetuity the full responsibility for a death sentence imposed by an oppressive occupation force upon a popular leader from among [their] own people"?[15] Clearly the significance of these verses are to be found in Matthew's theology and literary purpose rather than in historical accuracy.

The plot to deny the resurrection

Another section of polemic and anti-Jewish material unique to Matthew is the supposed plot by the Jewish authorities to cover up the resurrection of Jesus. This material occurs in three places: (1) the request by the Jewish leaders that Pilate set a guard at the tomb to prevent the stealing of Jesus' body (27:62–65); (2) the paralysis of the guard at the tomb at the appearance of the angel (28:4); and (3) the plot of the Jewish leaders and the guard to spread a false story that the disciples have indeed stolen the body (28:11–15). This material obviously colors the Jewish leadership in the most duplicitous terms.

Moreover, as in the case of the blood curse, historical difficulties are apparent in the account. First, it is very unlikely that the Jewish leaders would seek an audience with Pilate on the sabbath (27:62). Second, there seem to be serious problems with the plan for cover-up. The soldiers are told: "You must say, 'His disciples came by night and stole him away while we were asleep' " (28:13). However, if the guards were asleep, how could they know that it was the disciples who took the body? More importantly, to admit that you were asleep while on guard would mean death for any Roman soldier, even if the Jewish leaders had promised to set things right with the governor (28:14).[16] All these factors suggest that this account was an attempt by later Christians to refute attacks upon the truth of Jesus' resurrection. Eduard Schweizer suggests the following development:

> On one hand, non-Christians considered how to account for the empty tomb and suggested that the body had been stolen; on the other hand, the Christians asked themselves how these others could have fallen into such an erroneous assertion, and suggested that there was a Jewish conspiracy against belief in the resurrection of Jesus. This suggestion slowly turned into rumor, and the rumor turned into a narrative to which men gave full credence.[17]

The possibility that the negative view of the Jewish leaders has been influenced by the later polemic of the Matthean community is strengthened by the use of "the Jews" in the editorial comment made by the Matthean narrator: "This story is still told among the Jews to this day" (28:15). This is the first time that "the Jews" is used by anyone other than a Gentile within the narrative. It seems to betray a later perspective in which "the Jews" could in some sense be considered as distinct from the many Jewish disciples in the narrative. The inclusion of the Pharisees as members of this plot (27:62)— although they appear nowhere else in the passion narrative—only further confirms the Matthean tendency to introduce them into material in which we would not expect to find them.[18]

The polemic of Matthew 23:1–36

The mention of the Pharisees in the supposed plot to cover up the resurrection leads us into the last area of uniquely Matthean polemic which we shall examine. Chapter 23 of Matthew has been called "the showcase of Matthean attitudes toward the Pharisees."[19] The polemic in these sections is intense, and the reader is encouraged to read the chapter through to appreciate its full impact. A partial appreciation can be offered, however, by simply listing the accusations and derogatory epithets which are addressed to the scribes and Pharisees. Within this one chapter they are accused of:

—not practicing what they preach (v 3)
—refusing to lift the heavy burdens they place on others (v 4)
—doing all their deeds to be seen (v 5)
—seeking places and titles of honor (vv 5–8)
—shutting others out of the reign of heaven (v 13)
—leading their converts into evil (v 15)
—corrupting the practice of oaths (vv 16–22)
—trivializing the purpose of tithing (vv 23–24)
—being full of extortion and rapacity (v 25)
—being inwardly dead and unclean (v 27)
—being full of hypocrisy and iniquity (v 28)
—killing, crucifying, scourging, and persecuting prophets, the wise, and scribes (v 34)
—being guilty for all the righteous blood shed on earth (v 35)
—murdering Zechariah, son of Barachiah (v 35)

The force of this list is increased by the use of derogatory epithets. In this one chapter, the scribes and Pharisees are called:

—hypocrites (vv 13, 15, 23, 25, 27, 29)
—children of hell (v 15)
—blind guides (vv 16, 24)
—blind fools (v 17)
—blind (v 19)
—blind Pharisee (v 26)
—children of those who murdered the prophets (v 31)
—serpents (v 33)
—brood of vipers (v 33)
—those sentenced to hell (v 33)

This is vehement polemic. What are we to make of it? It is certainly a kind of prophetic polemic directed towards a particular group within Judaism. As such it does not directly address the evaluative claims we will soon discuss regarding Matthew's attitude towards Judaism as a whole. The intensity of the polemic, however, is of such a strength that some comment should be made regarding its accuracy and rhetorical function.

HISTORICAL ACCURACY IN MATTHEW 23:1–36

Matthew 23:1–36 is certainly not a balanced picture of the Pharisees as such. That the scribes and Pharisees should inherit responsibility for "all the righteous blood shed on earth" (23:35) demonstrates this point clearly enough. Moreover, the stereotypical charge which would lead the reader to believe that such traits and attitudes can be applied to *all* "the scribes and Pharisees" only reinforces the position that what is being presented to us is no accurate description of these groups as they existed. There is no reason to believe that there was any greater amount of hypocrisy, iniquity, or other negative traits among the scribes and Pharisees than there was among other religious groups of the time. Something else is being served in this polemic other than an accurate presentation of these historical groups.

THE FUNCTION OF THE POLEMIC IN MATTHEW 23:1–36

Attention to the function of such polemical rhetoric among religious groups can take us some distance towards explaining the presence of such virulent language in Matthew. Sean Freyne has emphasized the importance of the social function of such polemic. The efforts of Matthew to vilify the scribes and Pharisees attempt to set the Matthean community apart from such groups and thus establish its own identity. The scribes and the Pharisees are presented as those who are outside of the Matthean community—as "the other." The purpose of describing them in strongly negative terms is to ensure that the reader of such polemic is thrust away from the group of "the other" and all its religious claims. This draws the reader back more tightly into the community which has composed the polemic and assures the reader that to identify with *this* community is what is best to do. Freyne has noted that it was a part of normal rhetorical techniques to disparage the identity of "the other" so as to reaffirm one's own identity. This rhetorical effort (technically called *vituperatio*) sought to destroy the social presence (or *persona*) of one's adversary.[20]

Such polemic did not aim to influence the opponents who were being attacked but rather to ensure that the members of the community which wrote the polemic might not be drawn towards "the other." It was not the purpose of the polemic to describe "the other" as they actually existed, but primarily to define them as the opponent. Luke T. Johnson describes such polemic as it was used in the ancient world:

> The main thing such slander signified, therefore, was that someone *was* an opponent. This did not detract from its seriousness. Just because commitments were taken seriously could others so systematically be slandered. The slander was not affected by facts. A particular Platonist may be a good person, but that does not affect the way that Platonists as such are to be described. The purpose of the polemic is not so much the rebuttal of the opponent as the edification of one's own school. Polemic was primarily for internal consumption.[21]

To the extent that this sociological use of rhetoric has correctly located the purpose of the polemic in passages such as those found in chapter 23 of Matthew, one can argue that what we find out about the scribes and Pharisees in chapter 23 is only that they are the opponents of the Matthean community. How they are described informs us that they are opponents, but it cannot be used to derive any reliable information about how they acted or what they actually believed.

Such an understanding of the rhetoric helps to clarify certain inconsistencies among the many charges leveled against Matthew's opponents. One of Matthew's favorite charges is that of hypocrisy. As normally understood, this characteristic describes a lack of correspondence between what is said and what is actually done. In a few places within chapter 23 this charge is appropriate to the activity which is being described (vv 3, 25–27). Most of the descriptions of the scribes and Pharisees do not, however, fit this understanding of hypocrisy. For example, it is unclear how misusing converts (v 15) or excessive concern for tithing (v 23) can be properly termed hypocrisy. A credible explanation of this discrepancy is to understand such epithets as "hypocrite" and "blind guide" not as a critique of the other's practice but rather simply as a means to tag the other as an opponent. Therefore, charges of hypocrisy, culpable blindness, and false interpretation of the tradition are all related because they share the purpose of asserting that it is not "they" but "we" who have the truth and identity which is valid.[22]

Matthew's polemical assertions against other definable groups can be most consistently understood as a rhetorical effort to characterize such groups precisely as the opponents and thus draw the reader into a closer bond with the author's community whose practices and beliefs are thereby both identified and sanctioned. It is likely, therefore, that Matthew's vilification of the scribes and Pharisees is meant primarily to encourage the members of Matthew's own community to glory in the validity of their own beliefs and practices and to warn against straying from them.

Such contextualizations of the polemic in chapter 23 of Matthew do not eliminate the shock of finding such language in our sacred scriptures, nor do they absolve us from the responsibility of preventing such language from fostering violent attitudes towards religious groups in our world today. Such contextualizations can, however, help us to understand what this type of language was attempting to accomplish. It can also provide a foundation upon which to argue that name-calling and stereotyping should not be accepted as part of the gospel or somehow be understood as approved by God.

SUMMARY: POLEMIC UNIQUE TO MATTHEW

This section has tracked the increased polemic which can be found in material unique to Matthew. We can only conclude that the gospel stands as a document carrying significant vituperation against certain Jewish groups and their practices. Whether the sociological reasoning of establishing self-identity is accepted or not, it remains clear that the gospel presents these Jewish groups in an unflattering and judgmental manner which may be inaccurate as well. The strong polemical edge of Matthew's message cannot be denied.

However, strong polemic does not correlate directly to the type of evaluative claim which the gospel might profess. Matthew's frequent polemical stances do not necessarily imply that the gospel has adopted a particular position on the status of Israel. Matthew's harsh and violent statements do not automatically allow us to conclude that Jewish traditions and promises have been subordinated or abrogated. In fact, the exact opposite can frequently be the case. Violent arguments often occur between those who are closest, and they do not necessarily indicate that what binds the parties together has been altered or lost. Family arguments are often the most heated; civil wars spill the most blood. The intensity of the rhetoric is not the gauge by which we judge the closeness of the bond.

This insight is one way to explain the ambivalence within Matthew's gospel which we noted at the beginning of this chapter. What at first blush seems problematic or contradictory can be understood as characteristic of a family dispute. The reason Matthew can at the same time seem both so Jewish and so anti-Jewish is precisely because both tendencies can be part of an argument occurring within bonds of kinship. Among those who share common traditions both love and hate run deep. Strong polemic is not incompatible with close ties.

Precisely because strong polemic and strong bonds can coexist, we cannot from the degree of polemic alone draw any immediate conclusions regarding the type of evaluative claims which the gospel espouses. Our catagories of classification are not based on the intensity of polemic. Admitting that Matthew is characterized by violent aspersions, we are still free to determine—as a separable issue—what is the scope and intent of Matthew's evaluative claims toward Jews and Judaism. It is to that determination that we now turn.

EVALUATIVE CLAIMS REGARDING JEWS AND JUDAISM IN THE GOSPEL OF MATTHEW

To the extent that the gospel of Matthew does not subordinate any of the central Jewish symbols to another value and does not abrogate the status of Israel as God's people, the polemic of the gospel can be classified as prophetic polemic. As harsh as the polemic of chapter 23 is seen to be, it is clearly directed against a specific group within Judaism. It is possible, therefore, to approach the classification of the polemic in Matthew by examining whether Matthew's polemic remains on the level of prophetic polemic or whether signs of subordination or abrogation within the text force us to classify the polemic in other categories. In this section, we will survey the arguments about the classification of Matthew's evaluative claims. Yet before that is done, we must pause and apprise ourselves of the crucial historical event of 70 C.E. which forever altered Jewish and Christian history and left its imprint on the gospel of Matthew.

THE DESTRUCTION OF JERUSALEM
AND THE ENSUING CRISIS

In the first half of the first century of the common era, Judaism in Judea was a thriving religious community. The very variety of religious groups or sects which have come down to us testify to its fertility. We are aware of Pharisees, Sadducees, Essenes, Haberim, as well as several other Jewish movements which centered around popular leaders. Among these were those who followed Jesus of Nazareth, John the Baptist, Judas the Galilean, Theudas, and a certain man whom both Luke and Josephus call "the Egyptian." It is very difficult to establish the beliefs and purposes of most of these groups because only some groups endured and were able to preserve their traditions. It is probable that there were other Jewish movements whose names have not come down to us. However much these groups might disagree with each other, most could recognize each other as fellow Jews united under the central Jewish symbols such as monotheism, temple, and Torah.

Furthermore, all these Jewish groups lived in a country which was under the domination of the Roman empire. Jews were united in the belief that the land had been given to them by God and that therefore it could not be validly governed by the Gentile Romans. This general discontent with Roman rule came to full expression in the Jewish revolt which began in 66 C.E. and culminated in the destruction of Jerusalem by Titus in 70 C.E. With the destruction of its cultic center and the devastation of its holy city, Judaism was thrown into a crisis over its very existence. The shape of Judaism was drastically altered.

Only two Jewish groups successfully survived the events of 70 C.E.: pharisaic Jews and Christian Jews. Both developed their own strategies to insure the continuance of their beliefs. Pharisaic Jews under the leadership of Yohanan ben Zakkai centered their survival plan around the study of the Torah. It is from these pharisaic roots that Rabbinic Judaism and therefore modern Judaism trace their lineage.[23] Christian Jews placed increasing emphasis upon the central role of Jesus as the Christ (the Messiah) and developed their own survival plan under the influence of a growing number of Gentile converts.

Before 70 C.E., a diversity of Jewish groups coexisted around the common symbol of the temple. After 70 C.E., two basic Jewish groups vied with each other over the direction of the tradition in intensely critical circumstances. By the turn of the century, Christian Jews had become the minority in a growing Gentile-Christian church which was step-by-step losing its Jewish identity. In the years after the destruction of the temple, however, the struggle between pharisaic and Christian Jews over the traditions of Israel remained strong, and it was during these years that much of the New Testament including Matthew, Luke-Acts, and John reached their final stages of composition. The issue of the destruction of Jerusalem and the struggle with those of pharisaic lineage has therefore left its mark upon much of the Christian scriptures.

This is the reason why the Pharisees emerge within our gospels as the foremost opponents of Jesus. There are many reasons for believing that the historical Jesus shared much in common with the Pharisees. However, there is a clear tendency by Matthew to introduce the Pharisees as Jesus' enemies. This tendency is present to a lesser degree in the other gospels.[24] The ongoing struggle in which the gospel writers themselves were engaged with the successors of the Pharisees after the destruction of the temple has shaped both the form and the intensity of New Testament polemic.

A moment's reflection will allow us to appreciate how this new state of affairs after the destruction of Jerusalem complicates our category of subordinating polemic. Subordinating polemic has been defined as the evaluative claim which subordinates a central symbol of Judaism to another value. The destruction of the temple, however, removed one of Judaism's central symbols and therefore necessitated a realignment of Jewish belief and practice on the part of all Jewish groups. In the midst of this crisis of realignment, it was much more difficult to determine how the central symbols of Judaism should be defined. When we look at the modern day descendants of pharisaic Jews and Christian Jews, it is clear that differences between Judaism and Christianity have been clearly drawn. A variety of historical circumstances has moved modern Christianity through a significant process of de-Judaization. In the aftermath of the Jewish revolt, however, as pharisaic Jews and Christian Jews struggled over the direction of a common tradition, such clear lines of demarcation had not yet developed. In those times the struggle was much more clearly a struggle among Jews, and it was out of that struggle that Matthew seems to have written.

Therefore, the effort to determine whether Matthew contains subordinating polemic will of necessity be highly nuanced. The reader is to be warned of the tentative nature of this discussion as the question of subordinating polemic in Matthew is now pursued.

SUBORDINATING POLEMIC IN MATTHEW

Because subordinating polemic involves the redefinition of a central symbol of Judaism, in this subsection we will attempt to ascertain the evaluative position of the gospel of Matthew toward widely-accepted Jewish symbols. Earlier in this chapter, as the Jewish nature of the gospel was discussed, we were able to conclude that Matthew continues to hold the sabbath and the dietary requirements in respect. Unlike Mark's gospel, which seems to dispense with such practices in light of Christ, Matthew appears to maintain such practices as part of an appropriate response to the gospel. Therefore, the realignment of these values does not serve as a basis for subordinating polemic in Matthew.

We shall now examine Matthew's evaluative claims towards two other central symbols: the law and the Messiah.

Matthew and the law

We have already noted the high opinion of the law which can be found in Matthew's gospel and which gives to it a particularly Jewish flavor. The question we are to take up here is whether Matthew's high regard for the law includes the willingness to subordinate parts of the law to the new teaching of Christ. The reason this question is often entertained is that there are several sections of the gospel in which it seems that Jesus is setting aside the requirements of the Torah. It is often suggested that this is the purpose of the so-called "antitheses" of the gospel which occur in Matthew 5:21–48.

The antitheses will serve us as a focus around which to discuss Matthew's attitude to the Jewish law. These pithy mandates treat six different issues: murder, adultery, divorce, oaths, retaliation, and love of neighbor. In treating these issues, Jesus seems to be contrasting what was decreed in the law ("you have heard that it was said") to what he teaches ("but I say to you"). What are we to make of this contrast? Does Matthew present Jesus as changing the Torah by subordinating parts of it to his own teaching? Or is Jesus offering his own new interpretation of the Torah, while leaving the demands of the Torah intact? Both avenues of approaching the antitheses, and thus Matthew's attitude to the entire law, have been suggested.

In order to determine whether subordinating polemic is present, the key question is whether Matthew rejects part of the Mosaic law. Every Jewish group from the Pharisees to the Essenes had their own particular interpretation of what the law meant and demanded. These varying understandings of the law were far from harmonious. Nevertheless, what was held by all was that the law was given by God and authoritatively binding. Although interpretations of the law could be debated, the importance of the law was secure. There is no doubt that the gospel of Matthew promotes its own interpretation of the Mosaic law as a new revelation, given by Jesus, which is binding upon the Matthean community. To say this, however, does not necessarily imply that the law in whole or in part could now be dismissed.

TWO REPRESENTATIVE INTERPRETATIONS OF LAW IN MATTHEW

In order to simplify our discussion of this very complex question, we will focus on two representative interpretations which illustrate the disagreement over Matthew and the law. John P. Meier's understanding of Matthew will be used as an example of an interpretation in which parts of the Mosaic law are seen to be set aside by Jesus.[25] The work of W. D. Davies and Dale C. Allison will represent the opposite view, arguing that Matthew intends no devaluation of the demands of the law.[26]

Both of these approaches recognize the importance of giving an adequate explanation of the section which introduces the antitheses, Matthew 5:17–20. We have referred to these verses earlier in this chapter as an indication of the Jewishness of Matthew, and rightfully so. Note how they seem to state rather clearly that no part of the Mosaic law can be set aside.

(5:17) Do not think that I have come to abolish the law or the prophets; I have come not to abolish but to fulfill. (18) For truly I tell you, until heaven and earth pass away, not one letter, not one stroke of a letter, will pass from the law until all is accomplished. (19) Therefore, whoever breaks one of the least of these commandments, and teaches others to do the same, will be called least in the kingdom of heaven; but whoever does them and teaches them will be called great in the kingdom of heaven. (20) For I tell you, unless your righteousness exceeds that of the scribes and Pharisees, you will never enter the kingdom of heaven.

For someone arguing that Matthew does in fact set aside certain parts of the Mosaic law, these verses pose a major problem.

Meier faces this problem in the following manner. He argues that Matthew's understanding of the law is related to his understanding of history. There was a period of time when the letter of the law remained in full force, but this period ended with the death and resurrection of Jesus which Matthew sees as the eschatological turning of the ages. The interpretation of verse 5:18d, "until all is accomplished," is crucial to Meier's argument. By reading this phrase as a reference to the death and resurrection of Jesus, Meier is able to understand the phrase as placing a temporal limit upon the unchangeable nature of the law. Thus, with the death and resurrection of Jesus, the command that nothing in the law can be set aside no longer holds true. Meier argues that by adding this phrase, Matthew has adapted an earlier saying stringently upholding the Mosaic law to his own "economy" of salvation.[27] At the apocalyptic event of Jesus' death and resurrection, the law becomes subordinated to the teaching of Jesus.

Davies and Allison do not accept the reading of 5:18d which Meier proposes. They would argue that "until all is accomplished" refers not to Jesus' death and resurrection but to the final consummation of the world. Thus 5:18d stands in synonymous parallelism with 5:18a, "until heaven and earth pass away."[28] In this interpretation the entire section of 5:17–20 is read as asserting that every aspect of the Mosaic law will remain in effect until the end of time. According to Davies and Allison these verses are specifically intended to introduce the six antitheses which follow. Their precise purpose is to prevent readers from drawing the wrong conclusion that the antitheses set aside any part of the law. As a preamble, the section of 5:17–20

. . . plainly states that the six subsequent paragraphs are not to be interpreted—as they have been so often by so many—as "antitheses," "antitheses" that, in at least two or three instances, set aside the Torah. Instead Jesus upholds the law, so that between him and Moses there can be no real conflict.[29]

Davies and Allison then proceed to read each of the six antitheses as demanding more than the law might require but in no way setting aside or contradicting what the law demands. In their view, Matthew promotes Jesus' interpretation of the law as authoritative and demanding without setting aside or altering any of the demands of Moses.

Meier, of course, reads the six antitheses differently. He argues that Jesus' teaching does set aside parts of the Mosaic law. While admitting that three of the antitheses (murder, adultery, and love of neighbor) do not go so far as to revoke the letter of the Torah, Meier claims that those which discuss divorce, oaths, and retribution do in fact set the law aside.

MATTHEW'S JEWISHNESS AS A CRITERION

Both Meier and Davies-Allison marshal strong arguments for their positions. How does an interpreter choose between these two very different explanations of Matthew's attitude towards the law? Can a criterion be found to decide between them?

Don T. Smith has suggested an aspect of the gospel which could function as such a criterion. It is one which we have already identified as a pole in the furious ambivalence of this gospel and examined earlier in this chapter: the Jewishness of Matthew. The more that one appreciates the overall Jewishness of this gospel, the more one is attracted to the Davies-Allison reading of the text. Smith highlights Matthew's Jewish character and notes the absence of issues which could be identified as Gentile concerns.

There are no questions about circumcision, dietary laws (cf. Mark 7) and the like. And the absence of these types of issues would appear to argue for a genuine degree of continuity with the past traditions of the community much more than a decisive shift of orientation. . . . Therefore, we propose that it seems most plausible to see Matthew's community as holding tightly to their Jewish Christian past, and perceiving no real reason why they should change.[30]

Although any secure conclusions on this issue are impossible, I find Smith's appeal to the Jewish character of Matthew persuasive. The Jewish nature of the gospel which we have surveyed at the beginning of this chapter leads naturally towards agreement with the Davies-Allison view of Matthew and the law. The overall conservative stance of the gospel and its strong attachment to Jewish values renders the position that Matthew is in fact setting parts of the law aside less convincing.

THE POLEMICAL SIDE OF THE ANTITHESES

If drawn to such a reading of Matthew and the law, an interpreter must still explain the presence of such seemingly strong polemic in the antitheses. We have spoken of an ambivalence within the gospel—manifesting Jewish and anti-Jewish characteristics at the same time. If the Jewish side of the ambivalence is used to argue continuity with and respect for the law, what sense is to be made of the polemical side? Why, after all, are the "antitheses" set in such an over-against manner if there is not some opposition to the law? The very form of the "antitheses" seems to indicate that Matthew is over-against something. If the newness of Jesus' teaching is not presented against the law, what is it over-against?

One possible response to this question can be found in recalling again the sociological approach to polemics which we examined in our treatment of Matthew 23. If the primary purpose of polemic is to reaffirm the identity of the group using the polemic over-against other groups which the polemics attack, then it is possible that here as elsewhere the polemical edge of Matthew is sociological rather than ideological. In other words, the over-against nature of the antitheses need not be read as a polemic against the law but as a polemic which functions to distinguish Matthew's community from other communities.

This possibility gains support by focusing on the last verse of the preamble to the antitheses: "For I tell you, unless your righteousness exceeds that of the scribes and Pharisees, you will never enter the kingdom of heaven." (5:20). The over-against nature of the antitheses might well serve as a polemical effort to distinguish the Matthean community from the scribes and Pharisees. The new teaching of Jesus is meant to serve this purpose. Matthew wants to claim that "our" interpretation of the law is better than "theirs." Jesus is thus presented as increasing the demands of the law in order to achieve this distinction. The over-against thrust of the antitheses need not be directed against the law, for it can be seen to be directed against other interpretations of the law by those outside the community.

In this understanding, the "content" of what Matthew teaches is free to remain thoroughly Jewish and even conservatively so. Indeed, we need not presume that in actuality the "content" of the teaching is that much different than that of the scribes and Pharisees. What is important is that the polemic find a basis—however strained—on which to assert the distinctiveness and superiority of Matthew's teaching. It asserts "we" are not "they."

Lloyd Gaston suggests that a clarifying and even comical example of the way this kind of polemic functions can be drawn from the *Didache*, a noncanonical work written probably in Syria during the second century of the common era. Gaston quotes 8:1 of the *Didache*,

> "Let not your fasts be with the hypocrites, who fast on Mondays and Thursdays; rather you should fast on Wednesdays and Fridays" (8:1). Here perhaps is the real parallel with the antitheses of the Sermon on the Mount; one could almost paraphrase: "You have heard that it was said to the men of old, 'You shall fast on Mondays and Thursdays,' but I say unto you. . . ."[31]

Gaston's suggestion warns against interpreting polemical statements as secure indications of theological differences. One must be careful not to assume that the presence of polemic automatically reveals significant ideological disagreement either with the opponent or with the common tradition. The presence of strong polemic can be explained simply by the need to establish a separate self-identity.

MATTHEW AS BOTH POLEMICAL AND RESPECTFUL OF THE LAW

It is therefore possible to argue that Matthew's gospel demonstrates *both* a polemical need to claim superiority over the scribes and Pharisees *and* an attitude which does not revoke one letter, not even one stroke of a letter of the law. In fact, I am persuaded that such a combination fits the text of Matthew rather well. Though initially problematic in our minds, the ambivalence between strong Jewish identity and forceful polemic against Jews can make sense when one accepts both the Davies-Allison understanding of the antitheses and the sociological function of polemic. Matthew is advocating additional requirements to fulfill the law, but the law itself remains intact. The validity of the law is not challenged. What is offered is a definitive interpretation of the demands of the law, aimed with polemical accuracy to ensure that those who follow the Matthean Christ will in righteousness surpass the scribes and Pharisees. Matthew's stance on the content of the Mosaic law itself does not demand an alteration of its demands. If subordinating polemic is to be found in Matthew, it need not be located in Matthew's claim that the demands of the law have been set aside.

This conclusion regarding the law does not, however, eliminate the possibility of subordinating polemic in Matthew. For even if the requirements of the Mosaic law are respected, it is still possible that the importance of the law as a whole is subordinated to another value. It is with this possibility in mind, that we turn to examine Matthew's understanding of Jesus as the Messiah.

Matthew and the Messiah

Matthew's christological claims are central to his gospel. It is clear from the first verse of the gospel that Jesus is presented as the Messiah of Israel: "The account of the genealogy of Jesus the Messiah, the son of David, the son of Abraham" (1:1). Whereas Luke will trace the genealogy of Jesus back to Adam (Luke 3:38), thus giving Jesus' origins a more universal thrust, Matthew begins his genealogy with the patriarch, Abraham (1:2). In this way it is Jesus' Jewish origins and his role as the Messiah of Jewish expectations which are stressed. As the angel tells Joseph, "You are to name him Jesus, for he will save his people (*laos* = Israel) from their sins," (1:21).[32]

The claim that Jesus is the Messiah is not necessarily to be seen as a realignment of Jewish symbols. The wide range of expectations concerning the Messiah gave Matthew a good deal of room in which to make his claims about Jesus. Matthew's description of the person of Jesus need not be seen as offensive to Jewish sensibilities. Douglas Hare would argue that there is nothing in the identity of Jesus as drawn in Matthew which would place Matthew outside of Jewish expectations.

Matthew . . . presents Jesus in such a way that it is not
necessary for a Jew to cease being a Jew in order to accept
the martyred prophet from Nazareth as the one appointed
by God to perform the yet-to-be-fulfilled functions of the
Messiah. That is to say, Matthew does nothing to shock
Jewish monotheistic sensitivities by depicting Jesus as a god
dressed up in human clothes. His christology is functional,
not ontological.[33]

As far as the description of Jesus' person, Matthew can be seen as
working within the accepted limits of Jewish beliefs.

When we examine the way in which Matthew relates his idea of
the Messiah to other Jewish symbols, however, we run into claims
which, from a Jewish perspective, are more problematic. The role of
the Messiah in Matthew presents Jesus as superior to the Torah. We
have adopted an opinion in the previous section that the teaching of
Jesus in Matthew does not alter the prescriptions of the Mosaic law.
To follow Jesus' teaching would not require a Jew to violate any of the
laws of the Torah. Yet, without contradicting the Mosaic law, Jesus
increases the demands for the one who will follow him. This new
teaching of Jesus is placed by Matthew on a level which is equal and
even superior to the demands of the Torah. In other words, Jesus is
not presented in Matthew as simply the definitive interpreter of the
Torah but as a teacher whose instruction is given weight beyond the
Torah itself. The Mosaic law, then, without being contradicted, is
nevertheless subordinated to the *person* of Jesus who claims an authority which surpasses it.

Functionally, this is shown most clearly in Matthew's antitheses
where the words of Jesus are placed in tension with what "was said
to those of ancient times." This phrase refers to what was said by God
in the very giving of the law and thus sets Jesus' word on the same
level of authority. Without setting aside what the law requires, Jesus
adds to the law requirements which are given weight equal to those
which God had established. Jesus is not comparing his interpretation
of the law to other interpretations, but claiming an authority which is
equal to the law itself. He speaks in his own name (*egō*) without
reference to other scriptural texts. Jesus is not engaging in rabbinic
argument over the Torah but speaking on a level equal to the Torah.[34]

This same supreme authority in regard to his teaching is indicated in the very last scene of the gospel where Jesus claims that "all

authority in heaven and on earth has been given to me" and that all nations should be baptized and taught to "obey everything that I have commanded you" (28:18–19). The basic claim of this gospel is that it is now Jesus' teaching which is normative. Jesus' teaching fulfills the law. Although the precepts of the law are not set aside, what is definitive in regard to the law is the teaching of Jesus. This teaching, which includes the Torah but surpasses it, is the ultimate norm by which to discover the will of God. The Mosaic law, without being contradicted, is in fact subordinated to the person of Jesus as the risen Messiah.

> He who fulfills the law and the prophets displaces them in so far as he must become the center of attention: the thing signified (Jesus) is naturally more important than the sign (the law and the prophets) pointing to it. That is why Matthew's book is firstly about Jesus, not about the law and the prophets.[35]

This shift in emphasis, by which the person of Jesus claims authority beyond that of the Torah, displaces the Torah as a central symbol. Even though the presence and authority of the Torah is maintained, it is now subordinated to the teaching of Jesus. For other Jewish groups, Matthew's claim for Jesus as Messiah need not be seen as an assault on a central tenet of Judaism. They could simply disregard the claim as belief which they do not accept. The presentation of Jesus as having authority which exceeds that of the Torah, however, begins to tamper with the centrality of the law. To that extent the very identity of Jewish understanding would be at stake. Setting Jesus above the law begins to redefine the central place of the Torah in Jewish tradition. Possible opposition to Matthew's claim would, of course, be much more intense if Matthew was in fact setting aside concrete provisions of the law. However, even if this were not the case, the very elevation of Jesus' role to one above the law could be seen as an attack on a basic Jewish symbol. From this perspective, it would not be the claim of Jesus as Messiah, but the functional superiority of Jesus over the law which can be read as a kind of subordinating polemic.

Summary: subordinating polemic in Matthew

Examining Matthew's attitude on the provisions of the law, we did not find secure evidence that Matthew sets himself against the law. His claim that the followers of Jesus have a distinct teaching need not be read as a new teaching which sets aside aspects of the Torah, but can be understood as a teaching intended to enhance the Torah by pressing beyond its demands. By means of the "greater righteousness" which this new teaching demands, Matthew is able to affirm a self-identity distinct from and (in his conviction) superior to the scribes and Pharisees. Although the reader can clearly recognize the tentativeness which the nature of this kind of reconstruction necessitates, it is possible to argue that Matthew contains no subordinating polemic in regard to his view of the concrete provisions of the law.

When the position of Jesus as the Messiah is examined, however, a different conclusion must be drawn. The functional superiority of the exalted Christ over the law realigns the Mosaic law by subordinating it to the person of Christ. Matthew's claims for the Messiah promote an arrangement of religious symbols in which the Messiah Jesus and his teaching are presented as superior to the Torah. Matthew is content and convinced that the Jewish symbols of sabbath, food laws, and Mosaic prescriptions remain in effect. There is no need to ask any Jew to reject any of them. Matthew's basic attitude is Torah *plus*.[36] Yet it is the *plus* which is the real concern of the gospel. For it is by this *plus* both in the person of Jesus and in the "greater righteousness" which his teaching provides that Matthew's community is able to establish its unique identity.

The view that has been adopted here reads Matthew's gospel as one fully devoted to the traditions of Judaism. At the same time, however, this gospel is convinced that in Jesus a new configuration of God's plan has been realized. Even though the new configuration tampers very little with the basic Jewish symbols that survived the destruction of Jerusalem, the subordination of all those symbols to the person of Jesus the Messiah gives to the gospel a distinctive character. That character would have been seen by other Jewish groups as a devaluation of the law even as the prescriptions of the law were retained. In this limited sense, Matthew can be seen to contain subordinating polemic.

ABROGATING ANTI-JUDAISM IN MATTHEW

Finally we take up the question of whether the gospel of Matthew contains abrogating anti-Judaism. Does Matthew claim that the Jewish people as such are now rejected by God? This might seem a strange question after surveying the significant attachment which Matthew shows toward the symbols of Judaism. Yet the reader is reminded that the manner in which Jewish emphases and types of polemic interact cannot be simplistically drawn. The presence of strong Jewish elements within the gospel does not in itself eliminate the possibility that the gospel could see the position of Israel as abrogated. In fact, the rejection of Israel as God's people is a claim which is frequently associated with Matthew. Our discussion thus far has emphasized certain qualities of this gospel. Beginning with what has already been established, we will now take up Matthew's evaluation of the Jewish people as a whole.

Matthew's absolute claims

We have already noted that the claims made by Matthew throughout the gospel are asserted with strength and emotional vigor. The desire to distinguish Jesus' teaching from the teaching of the scribes and Pharisees and to demonstrate its superiority is a theme which pervades the gospel. Matthew does not present his understanding of Jesus' teaching as one among possible interpretations of the Jewish tradition. Jesus' teaching alone reveals the will of God. The centrality and necessity of Jesus as the exclusive way to God is asserted in Matthew 11:25–30.

(25) At that time Jesus said, "I thank you, Father, Lord of heaven and earth, because you have hidden these things from the wise and the intelligent and have revealed them to infants; (26) yes, Father, for such was your gracious will. (27) All things have been handed over to me by my Father; and no one knows the Son except the Father, and no one knows the Father except the Son and any one to whom the Son chooses to reveal him. (28) Come to me, all you who are weary and are carrying heavy burdens, and I will give you rest. (29) Take my yoke upon you, and learn from me; for I am gentle and humble in heart, and you will find rest for

your souls. (30) For my yoke is easy, and my burden is
light."

These words indicate that Jesus alone determines access to God.
God's will and identity are mediated only through Jesus. Verses 28–30
are unique to Matthew. It was customary among the rabbis to speak
of the "yoke" of the Torah. Jesus presents *his* "yoke" as the means to
attain God's favor. In so doing this he draws an implicit comparison
between his yoke and that of others who would teach God's will.
Connected as it is with the preceding verses (25–27) which are drawn
from Q, it is clear that Matthew would allow only Jesus' yoke as the
means to do God's will.

Sean Freyne has argued that Matthew's gospel asserts "absolute
claims." Although it is clear that he is using the language, piety, and
scriptural instruction which was the common property of other Jewish
groups of his time, Matthew "wishes to make absolute claims for his
Jesus figure and the community which is linked to him in his teaching
mission."[37] Much like the approach of the gospel of John, the absolute claims made for Jesus and his teaching render those who do not
accept Jesus or who refuse to take up his yoke bereft of salvation.

Third race or true Israel?

According to Matthew's absolute claims, individuals who fail to
accept this gospel's message would certainly be judged as rejected by
God. It is still possible, however, to ask whether Matthew extends
this rejection to the Jewish people as a whole. In other words, are
there specific places within the gospel where Matthew claims that
Israel has been rejected as God's people? Such polemic would open
the gospel to the charge of abrogating anti-Judaism. In order to address this question, the remainder of this chapter will examine several
passages in Matthew's gospel where interpreters have suggested that
the status of Israel has been abrogated.

In examining these passages, we will find that two schools of
thought emerge. One school will read the passages as examples of
abrogating anti-Judaism. They will see Matthew's claim as an assertion that Israel is no longer God's people. Israel is now replaced or
superseded by another reality. This reality is usually seen as the
Christian church which is a new grouping of both Jews and Gentiles.
Although the expression is never used by Matthew, Justin Martyr's

phrase calling the church the "third race" can be adopted as an appropriate parallel to Matthew's point of view. Interpreted from this "third-race" perspective, Matthew views his community as a new entity which is distinct from Judaism, and the absolute claims for his own community abrogate Israel's status as God's people.

A second school will insist that Matthew does not claim the abrogation of Israel. Rather the polemic which is present in the gospel is part of an intra-Jewish struggle over who will control the tradition of Israel. Ben Viviano has used the image of the Jewish Christians of Matthew's community and the pharisaic Jews of the Jamnian synagogue "fighting over the family tablecloth, as in a family quarrel over inheritance."[38] When the polemic of Matthew is read in this way, Matthew is not claiming that Israel has been abrogated, but rather relocated in his own community. Matthew's subordinating polemic has redefined Israel around the person of Christ, and Matthew's absolute claim will insist that the true inheritance of Israel can only be found in his redefined community. To use another term not found in Matthew, the Matthean community is not so much a "third race" as the "true Israel." When key passages of Matthew are read from this "true-Israel" perspective, Matthew does not espouse abrogating anti-Judaism. From his perspective Judaism is not rejected but redefined, and his community has the absolute claim on the new definition

As we found in Mark, interpreters will tend to read all relevant passages together. Opting for either the "third race" or the "true Israel" paradigm, arguments are marshaled to read all the passages one way or the other. Those who wish to demonstrate that Israel as a whole has been abrogated will emphasize terms and scenes in which rejection seems to extend beyond any subgroup of Judaism. Those who wish to argue that the polemic is an intra-Jewish debate will attempt to find indications that the rejection extends to only part of the people of Israel, most commonly the Jewish leadership. The text of Matthew is flexible enough that both of these interpretations can be credibly maintained. In order to judge between these two possibilities, we will examine two key texts which have often been seen to assert the abrogation of Israel: the parable of the wicked tenants and the blood curse.

Matthew's parable of the wicked tenants (21:33–46)

Within chapters 21–23 of Matthew, three sections are frequently seen to indicate the abrogation of Israel. The first of these is the parable of the wicked tenants. In treating Mark's version of this parable, we have already seen how the parable itself is open to a variety of interpretations. Here we will limit our discussion to Matthew's version of the parable, and specifically its connection to evaluative claims regarding Judaism.

There are four changes which Matthew makes over his Markan source which are relevant to establishing his evaluative claims.

TWO INTENSIFICATIONS OF MARK'S ALLEGORIZATION

The first two alterations by Matthew heighten the allegorization of the parable which was already discernible in Mark and imply a connection between the death of Jesus and the destruction of Jerusalem. In 21:39 the Markan order of events is inverted. Whereas Mark reads "they seized him, killed him, and threw him out of the vineyard" (12:8), Matthew reads "they seized him, threw him out of the vineyard, and killed him" (21:39). This is best understood as an effort by Matthew to rearrange the details of the death of the son in the parable so that they conform more closely to the details of Jesus' death. Jesus was first taken out of Jerusalem (here the "vineyard" is read to refer to the holy city) and then killed on Calvary.

The second alteration of Mark is an intensification of the destruction of the wicked tenants. Whereas Mark reads that the owner "will come and destroy the tenants" (12:9), Matthew reads, "he will put those wretches to a miserable death" (21:41). This intensification can be understood as a reference to the disastrous destruction of Jerusalem by the Romans, which was an accomplished fact at the time of Matthew's writing.

These two alterations by Matthew, when taken together, indicate a belief that Jerusalem was destroyed because of the rejection of Jesus. The wicked tenants are, of course, those who have rejected the son (Jesus). However, as in Mark's version, the identity of the tenants is not specifically stated and must be determined from the context. Two other alterations by Matthew have direct bearing on the identity of the tenants. Unfortunately they seem to pull in opposite directions.

THE DEBATE OVER THE TERM *ETHNOS*

Matthew's version of the parable of the wicked tenants includes a verse which is unique to him. Matthew follows Mark by asserting that the vineyard will be given to others and by providing the quotation from Psalm 118 about the rejected stone. Then Matthew inserts the following verse: "Therefore, I tell you, the kingdom of God will be taken away from you and given to a people (*ethnos*) producing the fruits of it" (21:43). Suddenly we are no longer talking of "the vineyard" but of the "kingdom of God." Matthew is clearly attempting to draw out in this verse the meaning of the parable as he sees it. What is said about "the kingdom of God" is that it will be taken from "you" and given to "a people" (*ethnos*). The referent of the "you" is not clear, and various interpretations exist to determine its meaning.

Abrogating interpretations. The "you" can be read to refer to the Jewish nation. Matthew's use of the term *ethnos* (usually translated "nation") opens the possibility of reading the "you" as one nation (Israel) which has lost the reign of God to another nation (*ethnos*). In fact, this verse is often used as the most conclusive proof that Matthew intends the rejection of Israel.

This position can be argued in two variations, depending on how one chooses to translate *ethnos*. *Ethnos/ethnē* can be translated "Gentiles," which refers to a group of nations other than Israel. When this option is chosen, it is possible to read the verse, "the reign of God will be taken from you and given to *a Gentile nation* producing fruits of it." [39] When this translation is adopted, the Gentile nature of the nation receiving the reign of God is explicit in the term itself.

Ethnos need not, however, be translated in a way which identifies the term solely with Gentiles. The word can also be translated as simply "a people." Adopting this less explicit translation, "the people" who will receive the reign of God can now be read as the new people of the church, composed of both Jews and Gentiles who now stand in the place of Israel. This interpretation is the most common approach today, and it understands Matthew's community as a "third race" which has replaced Israel. [40]

Whether *ethnos* is translated "Gentile nation" or "people," the position of Israel has been abrogated. The Jewish people as such have been left behind. A new, discontinuous entity has superseded them as God's people. Lloyd Gaston expresses this view of abrupt replacement.

The rejection of Israel freed the way for the Gentile mission, but the connection is not direct. . . . The church is not the new Israel, not the true Israel, not the heirs of Abraham's faith or the grafted branches, not the inheritor of the promises. Insofar as there is continuity, it lies in the concept of the gospel of the kingdom, preached by the Messiah to Israel, the sons of the Kingdom, and then taken away from them and made available to non-Israel.[41]

The identification of the "you" of 21:43 with the people of Israel has made this verse the keystone in the argumentation that Matthew holds a discontinuous replacement of Israel. Whether *ethnos* is understood as the Gentiles or as a third race, Israel has lost its status as God's people.

A non-abrogating interpretation. Matthew's use of *ethnos* need not, however, be read as an abrogation of Israel. Daniel Harrington has recently suggested yet another translation of *ethnos*, taking it to refer to "a group of people."[42] The translation "group" makes less extensive claims than a "nation" or a "people." The "group" which Matthew claims has received the reign of God is still, of course, Matthew's Christian community. However, the less extensive scope of "group" allows Matthew's community to be envisioned as a "group" within Judaism. Therefore, the polemic of this passage need not be read as a rejection of the "nation" or "people" of Israel. It can be understood as a claim that Matthew's community now holds the true authority in Israel. Matthew could well be asserting that the care of Israel has been given to his community and taken from another "group" previously entrusted with its care.

Within the gospel of Matthew this group would certainly be identified with the scribes and Pharisees. Matthew's addition to the parable of the wicked tenants could thus be read as a rejection of the leadership which the scribes and Pharisees provide for Israel in favor of the leadership which Matthew's community feels it is now called to provide. The Matthean version of the parable emerges as part of the struggle over the direction of Judaism after the destruction of the temple. Matthew's claim is a claim to be the "true Israel" guided by the understanding of God's plan which the Matthean community espouses. Such a reading of the parable of the wicked tenants to Matthew can certainly be challenged. It should be noted, however, that the last alteration of the Markan source by Matthew speaks in favor of its acceptance.

MATTHEW'S SPECIFIC REFERENCE TO THE
CHIEF PRIESTS AND PHARISEES

Matthew ends his version of the parable with a fourth and final divergence from his Markan source. In Mark the parable ends by saying that "they" perceived that the parable was told against them (Mark 12:12). In our treatment of Mark's gospel, we concluded that the "they" of this verse was best understood as a reference to the Jewish leadership. Mark's reference in this verse, however, was indirect. Matthew does not leave us in doubt. As he concludes the parable he makes explicit what was only implied by Mark: "When the *chief priests and the Pharisees* heard his parables, they realized that he was speaking about them" (21:45). By adding this specific reference, Matthew seems intent on making it clear that the parable is to be interpreted in reference to the Jewish leadership.

One can, of course, claim that the Jewish leadership is meant to stand for the whole nation. The addition of the explicit mention of these leadership groups, however, tends to support the reading that the "you" from whom the reign of God is taken are the Jewish leaders. They are being replaced by another "group"—the Matthean church which now claims the authority to direct the Jewish tradition.

If this interpretation of the parable is adopted, the claim that the Jewish people have been rejected appears too simple. Rather than seeing the discontinuous replacement of the Jewish "people" by another entity, we are called to envision a more complex situation of two Jewish groups vying for control of a common tradition. Matthew's claim in the parable is that because one group has in fact rejected the authority of the "son," the care of the vineyard has been given to another group—the Matthean church. Israel is not abrogated, its leadership is. Israel has been redefined by the new teaching of the Matthean community. The precise struggle between that community and other Jewish groups is over whose view of Israel is correct. Matthew, of course, believes it is his. "True Israel" is found in his community. What is rejected is any other view of Israel. Davies and Allison would adopt this view when they claim that in Matthew's gospel,

... both Jew and Gentile are assumed to belong to the Christian church; Matthew's animus is not directed against the Jewish people as an indivisible whole but against its Jewish counterparts, who mislead others down the wrong path, away from the Christian church door (cf. T. Levi 10:2). The Pharisees and Sadducees do not simply stand for all Israel. They stand for its non-Christian leaders. Our gospel [Matt] nowhere excludes faithful and fruitbearing Jews from the ecclesia; and there is still hope for the nation as a whole.[43]

Despite the alterations that Matthew has made in the Markan version, the parable of the wicked tenants need not be read in a way which adopts an abrogating anti-Judaism. In fact, it is particularly noteworthy that so strong an argument can be made against the abrogation of Israel in this parable. For it is this parable which is most often cited as the clearest indication that the status of Israel has been overthrown.

The blood curse of Matthew

We turn now to the notorious blood curse of Matthew 27:24–25.

(24) So when Pilate saw that he could do nothing, but rather that a riot was beginning, he took some water and washed his hands before the crowd, saying, "I am innocent of this man's blood; see to it yourselves." (25) Then the people as a whole answered, "His blood be on us and on our children!"

Earlier in this chapter we discussed the problems of historical accuracy concerning these verses. Our conclusion was that it is unlikely that these verses, unique to Matthew, report actual events of Jesus' trial, but that they rather serve the evaluative views of the evangelist. Here it will be our task to examine the various possibilities of understanding those views.

THE MEANING OF "HIS BLOOD BE ON US"

The statement of 27:25 which requests that Jesus' "blood be on us" is most frequently read as an acceptance of the responsibility for

Jesus' death. In the scene which Matthew presents, Pilate washes his hands. Frank Matera expresses the majority opinion on this gesture, relating it to the prescription in Deuteronomy 21:1–9 which asks the elders of the city to wash their hands upon finding a slain body outside their walls. They are to say, "Our hands did not shed this blood, nor were we witnesses to it" (Deut 21:7).[44] If the text from Deuteronomy is understood as the context for the saying of the blood curse, the issue is one of responsibility for a slain person. Thus, when Pilate disavows responsibility for Jesus' death by washing his hands, the Jewish people are presented as taking that "blood" (responsibility) upon themselves and upon their children. Read in this manner, the reference to blood is understood as an attempt to situate the guilt for Jesus' death.

There is, however, a way of reading the reference to blood differently. Frederick Niedner has argued that the reference to blood should be read in the context of the choice which Pilate offers between Jesus and Barabbas. Niedner believes that the atonement ritual prescribed in Leviticus 16 is the interpretive key for this choice. In Leviticus a choice is prescribed between two identical male goats, one to be released, the other to be killed in order to make atonement for the people. This sets up an interpretive context in Matthew where Barabbas is released and Jesus is killed. Niedner argues that by this association with Leviticus, Matthew gives expression to his soteriology which claims that Jesus "will save his people from their sins" (Matt 1:21). Thus when the people say, "His blood be on us and on our children," the comment should be read not as an acceptance of responsibility but as an appropriation of atonement. The "blood" is the blood of forgiveness. "Matthew does not leave the Jews cursed, but rather forgiven by what has occurred in the death of Jesus."[45]

I believe that the gesture of handwashing in Matthew 27:24 argues in favor of the Deuteronomy reference and thus makes it more likely that blood should be related to responsibility for a slain person. Nevertheless, Niedner's argument for blood as atonement again demonstrates how the context in which the verse is placed is often determinative for interpretation.

THE EXTENSION OF "THE PEOPLE AS A WHOLE"

The most crucial phrase for the interpretation of the blood curse is "the people as a whole" (*pas ho laos*). Frank Matera interprets this phrase as a direct reference to the Jewish people as a whole.

> In 27:24 Matthew says that Pilate washed his hands *before the crowd*, and in 27:25 he reports that *all the people* answered "his blood be upon us and on our children." Matthew's shift of language, from "crowd" to "people" is not without significance. The Greek word for people (*laos*) is the way Matthew usually refers to the covenant people of God. In effect, the evangelist is saying that it was more than a mob which rejected Jesus on Good Friday; it was the covenant people of God.[46]

Matera's view is illustrative of the majority opinion which reads "blood" as responsibility for Jesus' death, "all the people" as the Jewish people as a whole, and then further links both phrases to the destruction of Jerusalem as divine punishment for the Jewish rejection of Jesus.[47] There are, however, at least three other interpretations of the phrase which adjust the impact of the verse. These three adjustments all claim that the blood curse does not extend to the whole people of Israel.

The historic adjustment. A simple alteration is to read "the people as a whole" in a more historic sense. Rather than referring to the Jewish people as a whole, this phrase can be understood as denoting "all the people" who were standing before Pilate in the scene in question. Davies and Allison point out that we must leave room in Matthew for overstatement. They note that when Jesus tells his disciples in 24:9 that they will be "hated by all the nations (Gentiles)," no one would conclude that Matthew is asserting that every Gentile would reject the gospel message.[48] When "the people as a whole" is read in a way which limits it only to the particular crowd which has been incited by the high priests to ask for Jesus' crucifixion, the scene in 27:24–25 makes a much less troublesome claim. Matthew is then seen as placing the responsibility for Jesus' death on a specific crowd rather than on the entire Jewish people.[49]

The temporal adjustment. The import of the blood curse can also be reduced by limiting its temporal extension. Normally the responsibility for Jesus' blood is seen as following those who are cursed through all generations. Although many would see the destruction of Jerusalem in 70 C.E. as illustrative of this curse, the guilt has traditionally been understood as following the Jewish people ever after. It is possible, however, to read the extent of the curse as lasting only *until* the destruction of Jerusalem.

O. Lamar Cope contends that the blood guilt accepted by the crowd need not be extended to all future generations. In fact he can find no usage in scriptural or rabbinic sources where the phrase "our children" refers to anything other than the present generation.[50] Within this context Cope argues that with the destruction of Jerusalem the effects of Jesus' death have been repaid:

> Mt 27:25 . . . utilizes the Jewish concept of blood guilt for the illegal execution of an innocent man. This concept is Jewish, not Roman or Greek. It places that guilt on precisely two generations of the inhabitants of Jerusalem and their leaders. Thus it is firmly in accord with the Jewish-Christian explanation of the catastrophe that the destruction of Jerusalem represented for all Judaism. Jerusalem fell because of the crucifixion of Jesus. In her destruction and burning the penalty for that blood guilt was exacted.[51]

When this viewpoint is adopted, the effect of the curse is terminated by the destruction of Jerusalem. Matthew 27:25 does not carry ongoing responsibility. It can be read as an explanation of a specific historical event in 70 C.E.

The theological adjustment. One final reading of this verse moves its import away from ethnic categories and more into theological ones. It is possible to understand the "blood guilt" of the crowd as symbolic not of Jews, nor even a particular crowd in Jerusalem, but rather of any group which refuses to accept what Matthew holds as the good news. Benno Przybylski points out that the phrase "the people as a whole" cannot refer to all Jews because there were certainly some Jews in Matthew's community who by accepting Jesus would be excluded from the scope of this guilt.[52] Therefore, the group which is being rejected here is not Jews in general but those who would not accept what the Matthean community would claim as essential for God's plan. Rather than identifying the rejected group according to any ethnic category, those who bear the responsibility for Jesus' death are those who refuse to accept the truth of the Christian message as proclaimed by Matthew's community. This approach offers yet another interpretation of Matthew 27:25. It is a way of reading this verse which meshes rather well with Matthew's tendency to express his claims in absolute terms.

The polemic of the blood curse can be read as part of an intra-Jewish debate in which Matthew claims to speak for "true Israel." As one among other Jewish groups, Matthew presents the blood of Jesus as falling on "the people as a whole" not in their Jewishness but rather in their rejection of who the Matthean community believes Jesus to be. The crowd that is responsible for Jesus' death is indeed composed of Jews. It is not their ethnic Jewishness, however, which calls forth rejection and the destruction of Jerusalem but their non-Christian and specifically non-Matthean character. The true response to God is found in the Matthean community which claims to possess the authentic tradition of Israel. Those who do not accept Matthew's teaching are responsible for the blood of Jesus. In this light the blood curse in Matthew is not directed against Jews specifically but against whoever will not agree to the absolute claims of Matthew's community.

Does Matthew espouse abrogating anti-Judaism?

Throughout this chapter we have examined a number of positions which would hold that the strong polemic of Matthew promotes what we have defined as abrogating anti-Judaism. In contradistinction to those views, it has been my intention to suggest that another reading of the gospel is possible.

AN INTRA-JEWISH POLEMIC

From the beginning of our discussion of Matthew, the ambivalent nature of the gospel's stance towards Judaism has been noted. I am persuaded that this tension is best explained by reading Matthew's polemic as part of an intra-Jewish debate over the direction of the Jewish tradition after 70 C.E. Even though the gospel subordinates the position of the law to the person of Jesus, I have attempted to show that Matthew still holds a strong and even conservative stance in favor of the sabbath, dietary requirements, and the content of the Torah. These stances all argue for a gospel which is heavily invested in a Jewish identity.

Furthermore, as we examined two key passages of the gospel which have been used to argue Matthew's rejection of Judaism, in both cases it has proved possible to read the text as claiming not the abrogation but the redefinition of Judaism according to the teaching of Matthew's community. Rather than reading the rejection of the wicked tenants as a discontinuous replacement of the Jewish nation, we saw that the parable can also be understood as supporting a transfer of leadership from the Pharisees to the Matthean community. The claims of the blood curse did not necessarily assert an abrogation of the Jewish people. They could also be interpreted as efforts to present the reason for the destruction of Jerusalem, while leaving open the question of the final status of Israel. Neither of these texts so specifically expresses the rejection of the Jewish people that we are forced to accept such a rejection as the position of the gospel.

When this realization is factored into Matthew's high investment in Jewish issues, the intra-Jewish nature of the polemic becomes very probable. Returning to a distinction I have employed throughout this section, I believe that the polemic of Matthew is better read in light of a claim to be the "true Israel" rather than a "third race." I agree with the position of Przybylski:

> Matthean anti-Judaism deals with the problem of the correct interpretation of Judaism. Jewish Christians insist that the acceptance of Jesus as the Messiah is part of true Judaism. What is at stake is this interpretation of what is Jewish, not the wholesale rejection of Judaism or Jews.[53]

Rather than attacking Judaism from without and setting itself against what is Jewish, Matthew argues that his community is true Israel. The polemic addresses other groups claiming Jewish identity and argues that Matthew's community possesses the authentic right to direct the Jewish tradition.

A POLEMIC WITH ABSOLUTE CLAIMS

The polemic of Matthew is not, however, a discussion open to other points of view. We have already discussed how Matthew espouses absolute claims for his position. The gospel believes that its teaching alone carries on the authentic Jewish tradition which has been fulfilled by the new revelation of Jesus. Other claimants to the tradition have validity only to the extent that they agree with Matthew. The Matthean community is the true Israel.

The absolute claims of Matthew give to his polemic an abrogating nature which is directly related to a struggle for rights over a common tradition.

> The language of annihilation not denigration is called for as the community seeks to establish its exclusive claims on the Jewish inheritance that its opponents also claim. Both want to appropriate the law and the prophets (seen both as the story of God's history with his people and the revelation of his will).[54]

There can be only one true inheritor of the tradition, and Matthew fully intends to claim that position as his own. All other claims are dismissed.

MATTHEW'S COMMUNITY AS A MINORITY SECT

In this light Matthew emerges as the text of a minority group within Judaism whose minority status only heightens the intensity of the polemic. Graham Stanton has argued that Matthew's community should be seen as a "somewhat beleagured minority 'sect'."[55] Stanton's argument supporting the sectarian nature of Matthew's gospel is convincing. However, Stanton also concludes that Matthew's community was a "separate and distinct entity over against Judaism" and that the gospel asserts that "Judaism as a whole is rejected."[56] I believe that these conclusions are separable from those which argue Matthew's minority status. Stanton's insight into the sectarian nature of Matthew can just as convincingly be interpreted as part of an intra-Jewish struggle, wherein Judaism is not abrogated but appropriated. Although a minority group, Matthew still strives to claim the rights to the entire Jewish tradition, rejecting with increasing intensity all other claims.

To support his sectarian argument, Stanton has drawn a persuasive parallel between Matthew and the Qumran community.

> We need look no further than Qumran for a parallel: there we find a minority group which has cut itself off from mainstream religious life, a group which indulges in fierce po-

lemics against unfaithful Israel and which lives on apocalyptic fervor, a group much concerned about internal discipline. Alongside these features of the Qumran community which are broadly similar to the features of Matthew's gospel to which I have tried to draw attention, there is also, as in Matthew, a keen interest in and 'scholarly' approach to the re-interpretation of Scripture for the new circumstances in which the community believed itself to be living.[57]

This parallel to Qumran, to my mind, not only supports Stanton's argument that Matthew should be understood as a minority group armed with absolute polemic, but at the same time undercuts his view that Matthew believes in the rejection of Judaism. His reference to Qumran actually provides a parallel for a kind of polemic which can be seen more "intra-Jewish" than "anti-Jewish." The argument that Qumran professes "anti-Jewish" polemic would not win many supporters. This is because Qumran is too clearly seen as a Jewish sect which claims that the true interpretation of Judaism is found in its own community.[58] Matthew appears to me as a minority group along much the same lines. Matthew's gospel is not so much rejecting Judaism as attempting to appropriate Judaism to itself. Outnumbered by the size and scope of other Jewish and Christian groups, the Matthean community only asserts more strongly that it alone possesses the true understanding both of Jesus and of Israel.

CLASSIFICATION AND POINT OF VIEW

When Matthew's Jewish identity, sectarian nature, and absolute claims are drawn together, they conspire to produce a particular kind of abrogating polemic within the gospel. If Matthew's community sees itself to be true Israel, all other claims to be Israel are abrogated. Is it proper to classify such an orientation as "abrogating anti-Judaism"? I believe that such a classification is problematic. It inherently implies a stance against Judaism, and this would not apply to a community which saw itself to be true Judaism.

Not that this charge is entirely without validity. To another group believing itself to be the only true possessor of the Jewish tradition, Matthew's polemic against it would easily be seen as an attack upon Judaism itself. In the eyes of the rabbis at Yavneh, for example, Matthew's claim that his community was true Israel and theirs had been rejected might well be perceived as abrogating anti-Judaism. However, when the perspective is shifted to Matthew's intention, the polemic of the gospel is not intended to abrogate Israel but to assert that Israel is only to be found within Matthew's community. Again, much like other absolutist sects such as Qumran, Matthew is not so much rejecting Israel as promoting the claim that Israel is to be found within his interpretation alone.

In other words, the issue of proper classification depends upon whose perspective is adopted. An illustration using a more contemporary context might prove helpful here. From the perspective of a third-party observer, it would prove inappropriate to classify polemics between a group of Catholics and a group of Lutherans as "anti-Christian." The third-party observer would be inclined to accept both the Catholic and Lutheran groups' self-identification as Christian and seek a more specific category by which to identify the attacks. In the eyes of a third-party, "anti-Christian" would be seen to be misleading by lack of specificity. A more precise term, such as "anti-Lutheran" or "anti-Catholic," would be deemed more accurate.

The case might appear very different, however, when the perspective is shifted. If both the Catholic and Lutheran groups were to believe that they alone could be called Christians, if they had concluded that the truth of Christianity resided in their community alone, then they would judge the appropriateness of the term "anti-Christian" along quite different lines than those of the third-party observer. To such groups holding absolute claims over the tradition, "anti-Christian" would be appropriate to describe polemic addressed toward their own group, but inappropriate as a description of their attacks on other groups. "Anti-Christian" would be judged inappropriate as a classification of their polemic toward outsiders, because as believers with absolute claims they would not accept "Christian" as a true designation of any group other than their own.

To the extent that Matthew can be shown to be a minority group holding such an absolute claim regarding the Jewish tradition, it is difficult to argue that it was *his intention* to engage in "anti-Judaism." Matthew would not perceive his polemic against other Jewish groups as an attack upon Judaism because he would believe that only his community was true Judaism. Precisely because Matthew believed that his polemic was meant to protect "true Israel" as it was to be found in his own community, his attacks upon other Jewish groups were not intended to abrogate Israel but rather to abrogate groups who were promoting what Matthew believed were false claims to be Israel.

ABROGATING POLEMIC IN MATTHEW

We are left then with some choices to make. Whose perspective shall we adopt—that of Matthew, that of those whom Matthew attacks, or that of a third-party observer? To allow comparisons with the other gospel writings which this book examines, I shall opt here for Matthew's perspective. From Matthew's viewpoint, the charge of abrogating anti-Judaism would not be appropriate. In his eyes the polemic of the gospel would not be directed against Jews or Judaism specifically, but against the authenticity of any claim other than that of his own. Believing his community to be true Judaism, Matthew would not see himself as attacking Judaism. It is for this reason that I suggest that "anti-Judaism" should not be used of Matthew. A less specific term such as "abrogating polemic" would better capture the nature of Matthew's claims. "Abrogating polemic" identifies the absolutist orientation of the gospel without implying that Matthew is specifically opposed to Judaism.

What is emphasized by "abrogating polemic" is Matthew's exclusive stance. There is reason to believe that any teaching which would not correspond to the absolute validity of Matthew's claims would be rejected. For example, although we have no evidence of how Matthew might react to another Christian group which would disregard the Torah or food laws, there is reason to believe that such Christian groups would be rejected with just as strong a polemic as Matthew uses to discredit the "scribes and Pharisees." The phrase "abrogating polemic" captures the absolute nature of Matthew's claims without forcing us to see the polemic as an attack on Judaism.

Of course, neither the recipient of Matthew's attacks nor a third-party observer would necessarily accept the absolute claims of his polemic. Having suggested that the polemic of Matthew can be validly termed "abrogating polemic," I do not intend to deny that a real kind of anti-Judaism can be connected to the text when it is read from other perspectives or in other contexts. This is in fact what happened rather soon to the gospel of Matthew. Taken up by Christian groups who were increasingly more Gentile, the gospel was interpreted by those who wished to see themselves distinct from Jews and Judaism. The high Jewish identity of this gospel was therefore overlooked, and the abrogating polemic was read as a specific thrust against Judaism as "the other."

We will take up again the issue of shifting interpretations of the New Testament in the conclusion to this book. For now let me only restate my conviction that the polemic of the gospel is best understood as part of an intra-Jewish debate, wherein, from the perspective of Matthew, all positions which do not correspond to his own understanding of Jesus and Judaism have been abrogated. The commitment which Matthew holds towards his community's Jewish identity renders "abrogating anti-Judaism" a misleading classification. The attacks of Matthew against all outside groups are better seen as a kind of "abrogating polemic."

3
LUKE-ACTS: ABROGATING ANTI-JUDAISM WITH SOPHISTICATION

The gospel of Matthew is not the only New Testament document which exhibits an ambivalence regarding Jews and Judaism. Luke-Acts demonstrates a similar tension in this area, giving voice to an ambivalence which is all its own. The approach of Luke-Acts to Jews and Judaism is complex and often pulls in different directions. Flattering images and evaluations commingle with harsh programmatic statements. The interpreter is left baffled by such contradictory signals. At the same time, the polemical force of the ambivalence appears more muted than the polemic in Matthew, and its emotional expression seems reduced both in pitch and in volume. If Matthew's ambivalence is furious, Luke's is controlled and even deliberate. Some conscious purpose, clothed in the graceful sophistication which is typical of Luke's writing, seems to be directing the unfolding of this uncomfortable admixture—even though the identification of that purpose is far from clear.

This chapter will examine the varying perspectives through which the gospel of Luke and its accompanying history of the early church, the book of Acts, can be read. It will survey the diverse attempts to uncover the purpose of the refined ambivalence of Luke-Acts and try to classify the evaluative stance of Luke according to our categories of anti-Jewish polemic. The presentation will be divided into two parts. First, we will discuss two characteristics of Luke-Acts which are peculiar to this work and relevant to a judgment regarding Luke's stance toward Jews and Judaism. Second, we will attempt to determine what evaluative claims Luke-Acts actually promotes. As in our previous discussions of the gospel writings, the conclusions reached may be far from secure. Nevertheless, it is hoped that the journey taken to reach them may illustrate the complexity of Luke's writing and identify the possible angles from which the polemic of Luke-Acts may be viewed.

DISTINCTIVE CHARACTERISTICS OF LUKE-ACTS PERTAINING TO JEWS AND JUDAISM

Having already examined in some depth the characteristics of Mark and Matthew, we are now in a position to highlight rather expeditiously the qualities of the gospel of Luke which distinguish it from the other synoptic gospels. Again, as in the case of Matthew, we will accept the commonly held hypothesis that both Mark and Q are sources for Luke's gospel. We must limit the review in this section to two distinctive aspects of Luke-Acts which will have direct bearing on determining Luke's anti-Jewish polemic: the overall literary structure of Luke-Acts and its use of the term, "the Jews."

THE LITERARY STRUCTURE OF LUKE-ACTS

Luke-Acts is more than a gospel. It is the only work of the New Testament which provides us with a narrative concerning the development of the early church. Among other things, this unique literary structure allows the author of Luke-Acts to present the theological convictions of his work in a series of phases or periods of salvation history. The historical periodization of Luke-Acts was first championed by Hans Conzelmann, whose divisions, the "Period of Israel," the "Period of Jesus," and the "Period of the Church under Stress" still serve as the touchstone for more recent interpretations.[1] Because the range of the narrative extends beyond the life and resurrection of Jesus, Luke has more narrative time in which to express his central beliefs. Moreover, those key convictions can be expressed as a development through the temporal stages which Luke-Acts contains.

The presence of historical periodization gives to Luke-Acts a decidedly chronological dimension which must be taken into account as the evaluative claims of the work are determined. We have already seen how Mark and Matthew have read back issues of their own time into the events of Jesus' ministry. For example, Mark's belief that "all foods were clean" is expressed as part of Jesus' debate over the tradition of the elders in Mark 7:19, and Matthew's negative valuation of the Pharisees substantially colors Jesus' description of them in Matthew 23. Luke certainly adopts this same procedure when he allows some of his own judgments to be expressed in the words and deeds of Jesus' ministry. However, the unique literary structure of Luke-Acts also provides him with another option. Because Luke is aware that the narrative of Acts will follow the gospel, he is able to locate his ultimate valuations in the period of the church, allowing the images and claims of Jesus' ministry to stand as a preparatory phase for the evaluations which Luke-Acts finally wishes to adopt. In other words, Luke has the option of postponing important convictions until he relates the events of church life which follow the resurrection. As we shall see, there is reason to believe that Luke frequently exercises this option.

In attempting to interpret Luke-Acts, therefore, the entire sweep of the narrative must be taken into account. Simply comparing the gospel of Luke with another gospel is insufficient. In Luke-Acts all that is asserted does not have to be expressed within the gospel narrative. In fact, the final and most complete convictions can be most naturally located in the period of the church when God's truth was being clarified through the guidance of the Spirit. Therefore, the chronological dimension of Luke-Acts will prove important in our discussion of Luke's evaluative claims. Any adequate interpretation of Luke-Acts must give full respect to the progression of the narrative throughout the entire work.

"THE JEWS" IN LUKE-ACTS

The second distinctive feature of Luke-Acts which we shall examine is the use of the expression, "the Jews" (*hoi Ioudaioi*). This term seems to carry a technical sense. The significance of the term for Luke is highlighted by a sudden increase in usage after the martyrdom of Stephen in Acts. "The Jews" occurs in Luke-Acts seventy-four times. Of these only eight occur before the martyrdom of Stephen in Acts 6:8–8:1. These eight occurrences all seem to be used in a neutral and practical sense. In Luke 7:3 "the elders of the Jews" are distinguished from other leaders. In Luke 23:3, 37, 38 the "King of the Jews" is distinguished from other kings. In Luke 23:51 Arimathea is called "a city of the Jews" for further designation. In Acts

2:5, 10, 14 the term is used to stress that Peter's Pentecost sermon was delivered to Jews from Jerusalem and elsewhere.[2]

After the martyrdom of Stephen certain neutral usages of "the Jews" still occur (Acts 10:39; 14:1; 17:1; 18:4; 19:10; 24:18). However, with increasing frequency the term is used in a decidedly negative sense which identifies the term with the enemies of Paul. Often used in conjunction with "the people" (*laos*), the repetition of the term gains the cumulative reference of "the Jews in general." Moreover, the term consistently places "the Jews" in a negative light. D. Slingerland has noted that according to these negative usages "the Jews" are jealous (13:45; 17:5), liars (18:12; 24:9; 25:7), treacherous (14:2; 23:12, 20), clamorous (17:5), inciters of riots (13:50; 14:2; 17:5, 13; 21:27), and plotters of violence and murder (13:50; 17:5; 21:11; 23:30).[3] Gaston lists thirty-eight occasions in which some sweeping negative reference to "the Jews" or "the people" is used from Acts 9:22 forward.[4]

Something very deliberate seems to be occurring here. "The Jews" as a group are becoming the enemies of Christianity. This hostility reaches a clear focus in the trial of Paul in Acts. As J. T. Sanders argues:

> It is "the Jews" who arrest Paul and who denounce him to the temporal authorities. It is "the whole city" and "the people" (Acts 21:30) who apprehend Paul and "the multitude of the people" (21:36) that demands his death. "They" called for Paul to be "remove[d] from the face of the earth" (22:22), he is brought before the Sanhedrin because he has been "accused by the Jews" (22:30), and it is "the Jews" (23:12) who plot to ambush and kill him. Luke thus makes clear that Paul is done in, not by the religious authorities alone, not by the Diaspora Jews alone, and not by Jerusalem alone, but by THE JEWS. Jewish opposition to Christianity is now universal and endemic.[5]

What is so devastating about the overall use of "the Jews" in the latter parts of Acts is that the term seems so biased and so universal. Tyson has pointed out that the use of the word in the singular (*Ioudaios*) which is found only ten times in Acts is usually employed to refer to a specific person: Timothy's mother (16:1), Aquila (18:2), Apollos (18:24), Alexander (19:34). In its singular form the term does not carry any pejorative value. This positive sense, however, only highlights the technical sense in the plural where "the Jews" are characteristically seen as opponents.[6] Taken at face value, it would seem that Acts has shifted into a decidedly anti-Jewish stance.

Attempts to mollify Luke's use of "the Jews"

There are of course a number of efforts made by interpreters of Luke-Acts to mollify this sweeping negative use of "the Jews." Most efforts seek to find within the term some way to reduce its universal extension by limiting it to only *part* of the Jews. D. L. Tiede has admitted that the term is "a conundrum," and suggested that it be translated "the Judeans."[7] M. Lowe, however, who argues that "the Judeans" is the best translation for *hoi Ioudaioi* in John's gospel (as we shall see in the next chapter), does not believe that this translative option can be applied to Luke-Acts.[8] Lowe's opinion on this matter is reflective of the majority of scholars, and this leaves Tiede unsupported in his attempt to restrict the universal extension of "the Jews" in Luke-Acts by translating them as "the Judeans."

Lowe himself has suggested another way to soften the impact of "the Jews" in Luke-Acts. He argues that "the Jews" should be read as an abbreviation for "the Jews who disbelieved." Lowe cites Acts 14:1-2, 4 to support his contention (emphases added):

> (14:1) The same thing occurred in Iconium, where Paul and Barnabas went into the Jewish synagogue and spoke in such a way that a great number of both Jews and Greeks became believers. (2) But the *unbelieving Jews* stirred up the Gentiles and poisoned their minds against the brothers. . . . (4) But the residents of the city were divided; some sided with *the Jews* and some with the apostles.

Lowe argues that "the Jews" as it occurs at the end of the quotation is just a shorthand way of saying "the unbelieving Jews" which is stated earlier (v 2).[9] Lowe wishes to extend this same qualification to other negative usages of "the Jews" in Acts. Thus it is not the Jewish people as a whole but only the Jews who disbelieve who are under attack by the author of Luke-Acts. Although Lowe's argument carries some weight in the passage of Acts 14:1-2, 4, his extension of the same reading to all the uses of "the Jews" is far from secure. Only in

Acts 14:2 are "the Jews" specifically qualified as unbelieving. The overwhelming number of instances in which the term remains unqualified argues that it should be read in exactly that unqualified sense.

A similar but less technical attempt to mollify the negative and universal nature of "the Jews" is offered by M. Salmon. Salmon reads Luke-Acts as a document written by someone who is a part of Judaism and therefore an "insider." Luke-Acts is intended for other "insiders" who share a common knowledge of persons and events. This allows Salmon to argue that "the Jews" in Luke-Acts are indeed restricted to only part of the whole people:

> . . . if he [Luke] did not mean the Jews, all the Jews, then why did he not say so? I think he did not say so because he did not need to say so. It would have been obvious to him and to his audience which Jews he meant. They knew which Jews were guilty. We place too great a burden upon our narrator to expect him to clarify for outsiders what is obvious to insiders.[10]

Perhaps so. Yet Salmon's comment is based on the presupposition that Luke is an insider—a position that her article must go to some length to argue. Her very point can be turned around. With even greater probability, the literal and universal extension of the term can be used to argue that Luke is writing from a perspective which sees "the Jews" from the outside. Therefore, contrary to Salmon, the use of "the Jews" seems to argue that Luke-Acts is willing to speak of the Jewish people in a universal and negative sense.

The sudden shift in the frequency of "the Jews" after Stephen's martyrdom, the consistent negative thrust it carries thereafter, and the universal connotation it carries on a literal level all argue that Luke's use of "the Jews" is both distinctive and important in determining the claims of Luke-Acts. These characteristics argue that the term should be read as a literary device which gains its impact as part of a larger literary pattern. Luke's particular use of "the Jews" will prove significant as we now examine the evaluative claims of Luke-Acts.

THE EVALUATIVE CLAIMS OF LUKE-ACTS
REGARDING JEWS AND JUDAISM

The sophistication and nuance of Luke-Acts greatly complicates the attempt to determine its evaluative stance toward Jews and Judaism. Gaston's summary of the problem is appropriate.

> Luke's is in many ways the most complex of all the gospels. On the one hand, he is unsystematic enough as a theologian and author that no statement about his work can stand without qualification. On the other hand, he is creative enough as a theologian and author to be able to assert contradictory motifs simultaneously and throughout his two-volume work.[11]

For these reasons, at least initially, the task of examining Luke's evaluative claims might seem discouraging. Our task, however, is greatly simplified by the existence of two distinct streams of interpretation which can be located within the scholarly literature pertaining to Luke-Acts. Luke's writing is indeed complex, and, as Gaston says, it does contain contradictory motifs. Interpreters, however, have tended to associate themselves with one of two overarching paradigms which arrange the relevant data of Luke-Acts into two distinct and differing patterns. What interpreters say about Luke's view of Jews and Judaism can generally be situated within one or the other of these two paradigms. We shall, therefore, begin this section on the evaluative claims of Luke-Acts by outlining the contours of these two distinctive interpretive approaches.

CONTINUOUS AND DISJUNCTIVE PARADIGMS FOR
ISRAEL IN LUKE-ACTS

Two paradigms for understanding Luke's stance toward Israel will serve as a foundation for our discussion of Luke-Acts throughout the rest of this chapter. Each suggests a particular way to understand Luke's view of salvation history and Israel's role within it. At this time I will only attempt to identify each of them in a foundational way. As we continue to discuss the claims of Luke-Acts, the full implication of each paradigm will be more fully appreciated.

The continuous paradigm

The first paradigm argues for the centrality of Israel within Luke-Acts and insists upon the continuous presence of Israel within history, if God's plan is to be effective. I will call this paradigm "the continuous paradigm" because it asserts the continuing validity of Israel for the life of the church. Although this paradigm is held by many scholars, the name most closely connected to this understanding is that of Jacob Jervell. A brief exposition of Jervell's position will therefore establish the basic contours of this interpretative approach to Luke-Acts.

Jervell bases his interpretation upon three theses. First, Luke does not describe a Jewish people who have as a whole rejected the Christian message. Rather, the proclamation of the gospel has divided Israel into two groups: repentant Israel (i.e., Christian Israel) and unrepentant Israel. The strong theme of rejection is of course known to Jervell, but he is able to use his view of divided Israel to associate the rejection and its consequent polemic only with the unrepentant part of Israel. Jervell emphasizes several sections in Acts where Luke clearly presents great success in the Christian mission to Jews. Conversions of Jews are reported in Acts 2:41; 4:4; 5:14; 6:1, 7; 9:42; 12:24; 13:43; 14:1; 17:10, 12; 21:20. Jervell reads this constant repetition of positive Jewish response as Luke's way to underline the presence of a repentant Israel. The constant pattern found in the reports of missionary activity outside of Jerusalem is that some Jews are converted, some become opposed to the gospel, and persecution results. This is not read by Jervell as the wholesale rejection of the gospel by Israel. Israel has not rejected the gospel but has become divided over the issue.[12]

Jervell's second thesis is that repentant Israel remains the essential link by which the Christian church can claim to be God's people. "Israel" remains for Luke the Jewish people. This term is not taken over in Luke-Acts to refer to a church made up of Jews and Gentiles but refers only to the repentant portion of "empirical" Israel. Jervell finds in Acts a strong attachment to this Jewish identity: the earliest Jerusalem Christians live as pious Jews. Unrepentant Israel has forfeited its membership in the people of God. Repentant Israel, however, forms an essential link which allows the people of God to continue.

Luke is unaware of a break in salvation history. The point of view "Israel first and after that the Gentiles" is, therefore, not to be understood as an unsuccessful proclamation to the Jews, which thereby compelled the proclamation to the Gentiles so that the Gentiles form a substitute for the lost people of God. The continuity of salvation history does not lie exclusively in the history of Jesus but also in the people who represent Israel.[13]

Rather than saying that the Jews rejected the gospel and the way is now open to the Gentiles, Jervell would insist that for Luke it is only when (repentant) Israel has accepted the gospel that the Gentiles can also enter in.[14]

This leads to Jervell's third and final thesis. For Gentiles salvation is gained by having a share in the promises to Israel. The successful mission to the Jews is an essential stage of salvation history through which salvation then proceeds from a restored Israel to the Gentiles. Jervell certainly recognizes that for Luke the Gentiles are included in salvation without the necessity of circumcision. Nevertheless, even though they are freed from this rite which remains in force for Jews, their status is possible only through a relationship with Israel. Gentiles are saved only by their association with empirical Israel.[15]

Jervell's approach presents Luke-Acts as one of the most favorable works of the New Testament toward Jews and Judaism. In this view the repentant portion of empirical Israel becomes the essential link through which salvation is open to the Gentiles. All of the negative polemic is diverted to unrepentant Israel which has given up its right to be God's people. Jervell's interpretation has persuaded many scholars, including J. Fitzmyer, D. L. Tiede, D. Juel, and R. L. Brawley.[16] Positive presentations of Jews within the gospel, especially those of the pious Jews of the infancy narratives, are cited to support Jervell's positive interpretation.[17] The overall result is a paradigm for understanding Luke-Acts in which Luke emerges as an enthusiastic champion for continuity: the Christian church can claim to be God's people only through the continuing presence of repentant Israel.

The disjunctive paradigm

Luke-Acts can, however, be interpreted through a radically opposed paradigm. I have chosen to call this paradigm "the disjunctive paradigm" because it builds its interpretation upon the claim that there is a break in salvation history. The Jewish people as a whole have rejected the proclamation of the gospel and have been themselves rejected. The Gentile church thus replaces the Jews as God's people. Although some Jews did respond and became Christian, Luke is understood to claim that it is now a new (primarily Gentile) people in whom salvation is found. Jews are saved insofar as they choose to join this people, but their status which held validity before Christ has now been revoked. This view is in many ways the traditional reading of Luke-Acts, championed by scholars such as F. Overbeck and E. Haenchen. In recent times, however, its fullest expression can be found in the work of J. T. Sanders whose arguments will serve us as the counterpoint to those of Jervell.

Sanders agrees with Jervell that some Jews accepted the gospel and some did not. He also agrees that the term "Israel" refers only to Jews. But whereas Jervell argues that Israel serves as a point of continuity, Sanders believes that Israel has been rejected and replaced— thus marking a disjunctive step in salvation history.

> Luke understands that he is shifting the pre-Christian understanding of people of God as people of Israel to the Christian understanding of people of God as Christians.[18]

Sanders' basic strategy is to interpret Luke-Acts according to a division between its speech and narrative material. This approach separates what is said about Jews from what Jews in fact do and say. When he examines the speech material of Acts and of the gospel, Sanders finds a consistent attitude toward the Jewish people as a whole. In that speech material the Jews are always willfully ignorant of God's will, rejecting of salvation, and responsible for Jesus' death and the persecution of Christian missionaries. According to Sanders, the sayings and speeches of Luke-Acts assert that Luke has written the Jews off.[19]

The narrative material of Luke-Acts portrays a more developmental pattern. Sanders argues that throughout the narrative material a basic literary pattern is repeated. This pattern is first signaled in the

Nazareth scene that all commentators recognize as crucial for understanding Luke's purposes. First, *all* in the synagogue in Nazareth speak well of him (Luke 4:22), and then by the end of the scene *all* turn against him and seek to kill him (4:28–29).

Sanders reads this same acceptance-rejection pattern throughout the rest of Luke-Acts. In the gospel the Jewish people are favorable to Jesus until suddenly in chapter 23 they turn and call for his death.[20] Chapters 1–7 of Acts are understood as a "Jerusalem springtime" during which the Jews in Jerusalem respond favorably to the gospel. But with the death of Stephen they again turn and oppose the mission of the church. Jewish opposition grows in intensity during the mission activity of Paul, during which the basic pattern keeps repeating: initially favorable, the Jews eventually reject and oppose the gospel. This pattern carries through to the end of Acts.[21]

Whereas Jervell has taken the mass conversions of Jews and the positive images of Jews throughout Luke-Acts as an indication of the abiding validity of the repentant portion of a divided Israel, Sanders reads the same material as part of a literary pattern whereby Israel is rejected after an initial, though partial, acceptance. It is of the essence of Sanders' argument that Luke makes his points by *historical progression*.[22] Thus, what Luke really claims as important is to be found, not in the scattered positive statements regarding Jews and Judaism, but in the ending of that historical progression. Within the pattern of the narrative material of Luke-Acts, that ending is not one of acceptance but of rejection, and this is what the speech material has been asserting from the start.

> By the end of Acts the Jews have *become* what they from the first *were*; for what Jesus, Stephen, Peter, and Paul say about the Jews—about their intransigent opposition to the purposes of God, about their hostility toward Jesus and the gospel, about their murder of Jesus—is what Luke understands the Jewish people to be in their essence.[23]

When Sanders' approach is adopted, Luke-Acts contains one of the most negative evaluations of Jews and Judaism within the New Testament. The line of salvation history is broken with the refusal of the Jews to accept the gospel, and the Christian (and largely Gentile) church replaces Israel as God's people. The positive images of Jewish piety and practice are meant to support the claim that the Christian church did indeed grow from Jewish roots. However, the negative polemic is primary. It refers to the Jews as a whole who have rejected the truth of the gospel message and ruined themselves in the process. Although Sanders' separate analysis of speech and narrative material is unique to him, and not all scholars would agree with him that the rejection of Israel is final, he serves as an excellent model for the disjunctive paradigm in which the line of salvation history has been broken by Israel's rejection of the gospel. With varying adjustments, scholars such as J. B. Tyson and S. G. Wilson hold to the disjunctive paradigm and claim that Luke would no longer see Israel as God's people.[24]

It is important to note the radically different readings of Luke-Acts which are present in these two paradigms. We will discuss the variations of these paradigms in more depth when we examine the possibility of abrogating anti-Judaism in Luke-Acts. Now, however, we take up the question of subordinating polemic within Luke-Acts, and, as we shall see, the overall paradigm which the interpreter adopts is not without influence upon this question as well.

SUBORDINATING POLEMIC IN LUKE-ACTS

The question we now address is to what extent does Luke-Acts exhibit subordinating polemic regarding Jewish practices and beliefs? As in our treatment of Mark and Matthew, the approach will be to center upon certain texts which seem to claim that a major Jewish symbol has been rejected or redefined. Our discussion will center upon an examination of Luke's view toward the Jewish law. The previous section has highlighted two overarching paradigms by which to understand Luke's attitude towards Jews and Judaism. I will therefore begin this section by outlining the understanding of the law which those two paradigms provide, together with a third intermediary position. Once these overall approaches to the law have been discussed, we will then proceed to examine the specific issues of Luke's evaluation of the sabbath and the dietary laws. Finally, the section will conclude by drawing together a judgment regarding the relationship of Luke-Acts and subordinating polemic.

Three views of the law in Luke-Acts

When it comes to the question of Luke's attitude to the Torah, the positions of Jervell and Sanders are predictable. Jervell who wishes to show the strong continuity provided by empirical Israel will argue that the Jewish law continues to apply to both Jewish and Gentile Christians. Sanders, wishing to present a radical break between Israel and the Christian church, will argue that the law has no real value for either Jews or Gentiles. We will examine these two positions below. We will also examine the position of S. G. Wilson which will serve as an intermediary understanding between those of Jervell and Sanders. In all three positions the interpretation of the apostolic decree in Acts 15 will serve as a common touchstone in understanding Luke's evaluative claim concerning the Torah.

J. JERVELL: THE LAW FOR ALL

Jervell believes that Luke's approach to the law is both conservative and Jewish. For Jervell what is most important for Luke is not the moral aspects of the law but rather its ritual and ceremonial dimensions. This is because the law is the mark of distinction between Jews and non-Jews and therefore the sign of Israel as the people of God.[25] As we have seen, Jervell sees empirical Israel as the essential means of continuity in God's plan. It is precisely by following the law that repentant Israel extols its identity as God's people and can thus serve as this connective.

This does not mean that the law is a way of salvation for Luke. Salvation comes only through the grace of Jesus (Acts 2:38, 4:12). Yet Jervell argues that this grace is never opposed to adherence to the law. The purpose of the law is not to save but to identify the particular people who provide continuity to God's plan of salvation. This people follows the entire law and provides the Jewish Messiah who is now come in Jesus.[26] For Jervell there is no salvation outside of repentant Israel. "Luke's view of salvation is bound up with his ecclesiology; it is a sign of the identity of the church."[27]

This positive view of the law explains to Jervell why observant Jews play such a prominent role in Luke-Acts. The infancy narratives present Jesus' parents fulfilling the ritual prescriptions of the law (Luke 2:21, 22, 24, 39). Indeed, their observance of the law includes the circumcision of the Messiah. Jervell claims that Jesus avoids any criticism of the law during his ministry. In the early chapters of Acts the church is characterized by universal adherence to the law, and the Pauline section is structured as defense of Paul against the charge that he is unfaithful to the law.[28] D. Juel agrees fundamentally with Jervell's position.

> His [Luke's] narrative assumes that if there is a people of God, they will live by the law. Zechariah and Elizabeth, Joseph and Mary, Jesus, Peter, and Paul are all portrayed as observant Jews.[29]

In what way, then, do the Gentiles relate to the law? As we have already seen, Jervell understands that the Gentiles are saved through a connection with repentant Israel. Does their association with the Jewish people also involve an adherence to Jewish law? Jervell would answer in the affirmative. No interpreter of Acts, including Jervell, would claim that Luke feels that Gentiles should be circumcised. The decision made by the apostles in Jerusalem (Acts 15:1–12) too clearly rejects circumcision as a requirement for them. Yet after agreeing that circumcision should not apply, James convinces the council to adopt certain further requirements for Gentile converts (Acts 15:19–21):

> (19) Therefore I have reached the decision that we should not trouble those Gentiles who are turning to God, (20) but should write to them to abstain only from things polluted by idols and from fornication and from whatever has been strangled and from blood. (21) For in every city, from generations past, Moses has had those who proclaim him, for he has been read aloud every sabbath in the synagogues.

How should one understand this imposition of James and the council upon the Gentiles? Jervell argues that it is an imposition of the Torah. He sees in the requirements of Acts 15:20 a reference to Leviticus 17–18 which enumerates the law's demands for "strangers" who sojourn among the Israelites. Thus, although the Gentiles need not practice circumcision, it is not true to say they are free from the law. They are in fact required to follow those portions of the law which apply to Gentiles. Thus, the apostolic decree of Acts 15 enjoins the Gentiles to keep the law. As an associate people, the Gentiles are connected to repentant Israel by following that part of the law which applies to them.

Luke labors to prove that the salvation of the Gentiles occurs in complete accordance with the law; no transgression has taken place; the law is not invalidated, abridged, or out-moded.[30]

For Jervell the law remains binding on both Jew and Gentile, though in different ways for each. Following the law identifies Israel as the people of God and the Gentiles as an associate people.

S. G. WILSON: THE LAW IS FOR JEWS

S. G. Wilson does not believe that Jervell has understood Luke-Acts correctly. Wilson begins his analysis by admitting that the view of law in the gospel is not consistent. There are indeed the many positive images of the law which Jervell mentions. There are as well several scenes in which the law is undermined. (We will discuss these below.) The ambiguity is most pointed in passages where potentially contradictory sayings on the law are closely juxtaposed without any effort to resolve them.[31] The prime example of this is Luke 16:16–18, the only notable discussion of the law in Luke's gospel:

(16) The law and the prophets were in effect until John came; since then the good news of the kingdom is pro-claimed, and everyone tries to enter it by force. (17) But it is easier for heaven and earth to pass away, than for one stroke of a letter in the law to be dropped. (18) Anyone who divorces his wife and marries another commits adultery, and whoever marries a woman divorced from her husband com-mits adultery.

Verse 17 seems to hold the continuing validity of the law; but verse 16 seems to limit its authority only until John; and verse 18 appears to give a concrete example of an alteration of the law. Wilson exam-ines various interpretations at length only to conclude that the am-biguity of these verses epitomizes the ambiguity of the gospel as a whole, wherein the law is both upheld and challenged.[32]

For Wilson, however, the testimony of Acts is much clearer, and it is here that he expresses his disagreement with Jervell. Wilson argues that the requirements imposed on Gentiles in Acts 15:20 should not be seen as an imposition of part of the law. The demands

of Acts are at best an incomplete list of what the law would require
of sojourners and should not be connected with Leviticus 17–18.
Rather, they should be read as an apostolic decree imposed upon the
Gentiles for the purpose of order within the Christian community.[33]
This view of Acts 15:20 allows Wilson to argue that the Gentiles are
free from any relationship to the law. They follow the apostolic decree, not the Torah. Their salvation is not connected to Israel.

> If it is true, as seems to be the case, that Luke viewed the
> Church as the inheritor of the promises to Israel, as the true
> or renewed Israel, there is no evidence that he considered
> Gentile participation to depend upon a successful renewal of
> the old Israel or that the Church was thereby obliged to keep
> the law in all respects. Luke's view of the law and his view
> of the Church and Israel are developed in different ways and
> for different reasons and, as far as I can see, the one has
> nothing much to do with the other.[34]

Thus, for Wilson, the law does not apply to Gentiles. Even so,
his evaluation of the role of the law for Jews remains rather benign.
He would agree with the common opinion that salvation does not
come from the law for either Jews or Gentiles. Nevertheless, the law
remains "the proper and peculiar possession of the Jews, appropriate
to the expression of Jewish and Jewish-Christian piety."[35] Jewish
Christians would not have to keep the law, but Wilson seems persuaded that it would be valuable for them to do so. The next position
we shall examine will not view the law so positively.

J. T. SANDERS: THE LAW FOR NO CHRISTIAN

J. T. Sanders negates any claim that the Jewish law has value for
Luke. Sanders admits to the significant positive portrayals of observant Jews in Luke-Acts. He can nevertheless maintain his negative
position on the law because he reads the positive portrayals as part of
the literary pattern which we have above called the disjunctive paradigm. In both the gospel and Acts, things begin Jewish. Yet, by the
end of each book, a break has occurred.

Sanders, therefore, disagrees with Wilson that the gospel and
Acts hold different attitudes toward the law. Both begin with scenes
of devout Jewish piety, yet significant portions of the law are set aside

by Jesus in the gospel and by the apostles in Acts 15.[36] The legal requirements which are taught by Jesus and the apostles are not a part of the Jewish law as interpreted by the Pharisees (Christian or otherwise). Rather, the true law is what is decided by the Christian church which is distinct from empirical Israel and its law.

Sanders also disagrees with Wilson's rejection of the connection between the requirements of Acts 15:20 and Leviticus 17–18. He agrees rather with Jervell that the demands of Acts do come from the part of the Torah which applies to sojourners. Yet Sanders reads the significance of imposing this part of the Torah in a very different way from Jervell. Rather than seeing the demands as imposing upon Gentiles the part of the Jewish law which applies to them, Sanders reads them as an apostolic decree determining what the true law should be. In other words, the apostles select from the Torah certain requirements and determine that from now on these are the only parts of the Torah which have validity for anyone. Following the whole Jewish law is thereby rejected. God has included a few laws to be kept by the Gentile church, but only these are valid. By this means, Luke's church—which no longer follows the Mosaic law—can still claim a connection to it. It is, however, a connection to a law whose requirements have been severely reduced by apostolic decree.[37]

Sanders understands that the law as it is obeyed in the teaching of traditional Judaism is invalid even for Jewish Christians.[38] God no longer expects it. Peter states at the council, "Now therefore why are you putting God to the test by placing on the neck of the disciples a yoke that neither our ancestors nor we have been able to bear?" (Acts 15:10). Sanders sees here a recognition that the true Mosaic law is the law that the apostolic council will soon put into effect. M. M. B. Turner agrees with Sanders on this point, noting that when Peter continues, ". . . we believe that we will be saved through the grace of the Lord Jesus, just as they will" (15:11), one can only conclude that "any attempt to make Peter a champion of nomism (even for Jewish Christians) reduces the whole argument to a non sequitur."[39]

In Sanders' view it is only these few laws which apply to Gentile Christians which are meaningful to Luke. This is because, far from claiming any necessary connection to Israel (as Jervell would hold), Sanders sees God's full will residing in the Gentile church which now carries a reduced portion of the Torah forward as the only valid law. Sanders pushes this point so far as to argue that Jews can only be valid Christians to the extent that they admit that real Christianity has left

Judaism and its understanding of the law behind. For Jewish Christians to continue to observe the traditional Jewish law would be purely a matter of personal preference. Any attempt, however, to push such observance on others (as the Christian Pharisees attempt in Acts 15:1) would render such efforts opposed to the clear intention of God.

> Luke is at pains to show how the early church, like the early Jesus, sought a home of piety and devotion in Judaism, but it would not. And so Jesus and the church turned from Judaism and the Jews to the Gentiles, and Christianity became a Gentile religion, and all the Jewish laws in the Torah were rendered null and void, and Torah observant Jewish Christians became hypocrites.[40]

OTHER DISJUNCTIVE APPROACHES TO THE LAW

Sanders is not alone in his disjunctive approach to the law. The interpretation that the traditional Jewish understanding of Torah has been set aside for both Jewish and Gentile Christians is also held by C. L. Blomberg and M. A. Seifrid. Blomberg criticizes Wilson for analyzing Luke without due attention to his method of historical presentation. According to Blomberg, Luke is showing the manner in which the Torah *lost* its relevance for Christians. Those who follow the law in the gospel do so in a period before the events which inaugurated the new covenant. Those who continue to observe the law in the early chapters of Acts do so because the implications of the new covenant dawn on them only over the course of time. Blomberg concludes:

> . . . after the events of Acts 10 and 15, it is hard to imagine his [Luke's] audience reading these volumes from start to finish in sequence without finding "freedom from the law" the more dominant theme, and that with respect to both Jewish and Gentile Christians.[41]

Seifrid agrees with Wilson that the requirements of Acts 15:20 should not be interpreted as an imposition of even part of the Torah on Gentiles. Seifrid, however, goes further than Wilson who continues to hold a basically positive attitude to the law as practiced by

Jewish Christians. Seifrid would argue that the decision of the council is that preaching of the gospel should consist of Jesus alone, not Jesus and Moses. The requirements of Acts 15:20 make some practical concession to Jewish sensibilities, but the messianic reign of Jesus puts Jew and Gentile on equal footing and undermines the law.

> The basic considerations which determined the decision regarding the Gentiles in Acts 15, apply to Jewish believers as well, since there is no distinction between them and the Gentiles (15:11).[42]

Sanders, Turner, Blomberg, and Seifrid would all conclude that by the end of Acts Luke sees no significance to the law for either Jewish or Gentile Christians. Sanders would make the opposition to the law more explicit than the other authors by connecting it to the charge of hypocrisy. Nevertheless, all of these authors would disagree radically with Jervell. Far from seeing the law as a sign to identify the restored people of God, the Mosaic law is identified with a former time. Its relevance is past.

We have examined three overall interpretations of the law in Luke-Acts as represented by Jervell, Wilson, and Sanders. All three of these understandings have attempted to establish their positions by reading the patterns, emphases, and dramatic turns of Luke-Acts as a whole. However, to establish the precise manner in which subordinating polemic might be present in Luke-Acts, claims of the text toward specific issues of the Jewish law and institutions must be examined. Therefore, we will now discuss the claims of Luke regarding the sabbath and the dietary laws.

The sabbath in Luke-Acts

The issue of the sabbath and appropriate sabbath practice is not a major theme of Luke-Acts. Although throughout Luke-Acts customary observance of the sabbath is recounted on the part of Jesus (Luke 4:16, 31; 6:6; 13:10) and Jesus' disciples (Luke 23:54, 56; Acts 1:12; 13:14; 16:13), it is only in four disputes over the sabbath law found in the gospel that the issue of the sabbath rises to an explicit focus.

AN EXAMINATION OF LUKE'S FOUR SABBATH CONTROVERSIES

In four scenes of Luke the sabbath is specifically a matter of dispute. The conflict story about picking grain on the sabbath (Luke 6:1–5) and the curing of the man with a withered hand on the sabbath (Luke 6:6–11) are shared with Mark and Matthew. The cure of a crippled woman on the sabbath (Luke 13:10–17) and the healing of the man with dropsy on the sabbath (Luke 14:1–6) are unique to Luke.

In none of these scenes does Jesus attack the sabbath directly or announce some abrogation of its importance. What Jesus does do consistently is argue with the Jewish leaders (the Pharisees or a leader of the synagogue) over how the sabbath should be observed. In other words, these sabbath debates are scenes of controversy over the meaning of the sabbath. The arguments are not about the holiness of the sabbath, but the way in which one must keep the sabbath holy.[43] The fact that the sabbath itself is not attacked leads Jervell to claim that "there is no conflict with the law in Jesus' attitude as described in the many disputes about the sabbath."[44] Yet Jervell must maintain such a claim in very strange circumstances. For the implicit thrust of all four sabbath controversies is that Jesus is superior to the sabbath.

The first scene (Luke 6:1–5) lays out the basic emphasis for the other three scenes which follow. Luke's account follows Mark rather closely with one important difference. Mark ends his scene with two assertions of Jesus. Luke omits the first one ("The sabbath was made for humankind, not humankind for the sabbath"—Mark 2:27), and retains the second ("The Son of Man is Lord of the sabbath"—Luke 6:5; Mark 2:28). This most likely is an effort by Luke to let the authority of Jesus as the Son of man stand out in higher relief. As Wilson argues, the point of this first sabbath controversy is found in this christological assertion: Jesus as Lord of the sabbath stands above the law and implicitly claims the right to define it. Practically, this means that "both Jesus and his disciples were free to act in opposition to the current interpretation of Sabbath law."[45]

The emphasis upon the authority of Jesus carries through the other three sabbath controversies. Tyson believes that this can be seen from the way Jesus argues in these debates. Even though the debate is over how the sabbath should be observed, Jesus never appeals directly to the Torah to support his position. In Luke 6:6–11 Jesus appeals to general humane considerations—"Is it lawful to do good or to do harm on the sabbath, to save life or destroy it?" (6:9). In Luke 13:10–17 Jesus appeals to the common practice for the care of animals—"Does not each of you on the sabbath untie your ox or your donkey from the manger, and lead it away to give it water?" (13:15). In Luke 14:1–6 there is another appeal to common practice—"If one of you has a child or an ox that has fallen into a well, will you not immediately pull it out on the sabbath day?" (14:5). Tyson asserts that this avoidance of scriptural argumentation indicates that Luke believes that there are considerations which do override the sabbath and that these considerations need not be determined on the basis of Torah.[46]

SUMMARY: WANTING IT BOTH WAYS

Although Luke does not push the point, the implication of all four of these sabbath controversies is that Jesus is superior to the Torah and that traditional sabbath practice is no longer normative. The focus of the debates is christological, with the issue of the sabbath serving as a backdrop. Yet what is implied in that background is significant. Wilson concludes his discussion by describing Luke's position in a manner which identifies it with a quiet yet consistent subordinating polemic.

> . . . the sabbath institution as such is subordinated to its lord, the Son of Man. Taken to its logical conclusion this christological claim mounts a fundamental challenge to the sabbath and ultimately to the law itself. That a radical conclusion such as this can be drawn, even though Luke shows no inclination to do so, remains significant.[47]

The position of Jervell that Jesus never attacks the law in his sabbath disputes seems altogether too one-sided. Indeed, the law is not made the object of critique. Luke wants the law in his corner. Yet it is not to the law that Luke appeals when he justifies Jesus' position, nor is Jesus' position one which most Jews would recognize as flowing from the law. Tyson's summary is to the point.

> . . . Luke has no interest in drawing attention to the connection between scripture, Torah, and Sabbath observance. By deemphasizing this connection, he could affirm the au-

thority of Torah and scripture but qualify some of its basic content.[48]

In other words, Luke claims the continuity with the Torah at the very time he asserts a new and largely discontinuous relationship with it. "Wanting it both ways" seems to characterize Luke's approach to the sabbath. This double claim for both continuity and discontinuity should be remembered. We will have reason to recall it again before our examination of Luke-Acts is completed. For now let us only note that "wanting it both ways" is a peculiar trait of Luke's subordinating polemic against traditional sabbath practice.

Dietary requirements in Luke-Acts

At first glance it may appear that Luke's position on the validity of the Jewish dietary regulations is more positive than Mark's. The scene which we cited as the clearest indication of Mark's disregard for dietary restrictions (Mark 7:1-23) is missing from Luke's gospel. With this omission the Markan critique against following what is only "human tradition" (Mark 7:8) is lacking in Luke. Jervell cites this omission as an indication that Luke recognizes the "customs of the ancestors" as harmonious with God's law. Therefore, the omission is consistent with Luke's picture of Jerusalem Christians as observant Jews in the first few chapters of Acts.[49]

The picture, however, is not so simple. The omission of Mark 7:1-23 may not result from any conscious motivation on Luke's part, because these verses were part of a much larger block of Markan material (Mark 6:45-8:27) which is missing from Luke. Moreover, although the omission eliminates from Luke's gospel the Markan claim—"Thus he declared all foods clean" (Mark 7:19b)—Luke seems to include a very similar assertion in a saying unique to his gospel. During Luke's diatribe against the Pharisees, he moralizes the meaning of cleanliness away from any ritual concern (Luke 11:39-41):[50]

(39) Now you Pharisees cleanse the outside of the cup and of the dish, but inside you are full of greed and wickedness. (40) You fools! Did not the one who made the outside make the inside also? (41) So give for alms those things which are within; and see, *everything will be clean for you.*

This saying may well be a subtle indication that Luke believes that inner intentions and actions of charity may invalidate ritual concerns.

Yet even if the testimony of the gospel is ambiguous on dietary concerns, the assertions of Acts are not. What is less than clear in the gospel becomes obvious in the Cornelius scenes of Acts 10:1–11:18. The intent of Peter's vision seems quite evident (Acts 10:11–15):

(11) He [Peter] saw the heaven opened, and something like a large sheet coming down, being lowered to the ground by its four corners. (12) In it were all kinds of four-footed creatures and reptiles and birds of the air. (13) Then he heard a voice saying, "Get up Peter; kill and eat." (14) But Peter said, "By no means, Lord; for I have never eaten anything that is profane or unclean." (15) And the voice said to him again, a second time, "What God has made clean, you must not call profane."

The import of this scene for Jewish dietary restrictions is significant. One might adopt the words of the narrator of Mark 7:19b to summarize its meaning: "Thus he declared all foods clean." Moreover, it is difficult to understand this abrogation of the dietary laws only as a freedom for Gentiles. Peter, after all, was a Jewish Christian and Peter would later claim that "God shows no partiality" (Acts 10:34). Therefore, the thrust of the passage indicates that the dietary laws have no further validity even for Jewish Christians, or at least for those working in the mission to the Gentiles. Levitical food laws are overturned.[51]

SUMMARY: WANTING IT BOTH WAYS

A peculiarity of Luke's presentation of the Cornelius scenes can take our examination somewhat further. One of the problems of this account is that even though the vision of Peter in 10:9–16 eliminates dietary restrictions, the interpretation of the vision by Peter himself reaches the much larger conclusion that the distinction between clean and unclean people has been abolished (10:28). In other words, Luke does not have Peter enunciate the obvious fact that the dietary laws have been revoked. Wilson explains the tension by supposing that Luke uses the vision "primarily as a sort of parable about the problem of eating and mixing with unclean people."[52]

While this seems to be compatible with Luke's intention, Tyson ties the significance of Luke's treatment to a theme we have recognized before. As in his treatment of the sabbath issue, Tyson finds in Acts 10:11–15 a reticence to speak out too clearly against the law. Luke seems to know that the elimination of the dietary regulations would seriously alter the law, yet he does not want to emphasize the point.[53] This is because Luke wishes to present the Christian movement as flowing from Judaism and respectful of its Jewish origin.

In a manner similar to Tyson's interpretation of the sabbath controversies, Luke "wants to have it both ways." Luke proclaims such an abrogation of the dietary restrictions on God's authority, knowing that he can find no justification in the law for eliminating them. Nevertheless, at the same time he tries to cover his tracks. Luke would want us to see continuity with the law even as he breaks with the common understanding of the law. Again we encounter a double claim for continuity and discontinuity as part of Luke's subordinating polemic.

Summary: subordinating polemic in Luke-Acts

Drawing together the various threads we have been tracing through Luke-Acts, we may now ask whether major symbols and institutions of Judaism have been subordinated to another value. The answer is affirmative. Luke is not belligerent in his valuation of the sabbath, dietary restrictions, and circumcision. However, by the end of his two-volume work, their value is clearly subordinated to faith in Jesus. Jesus is "Lord of the Sabbath"; all food is "what God has made clean"; circumcision is a yoke which even Jews have never "been able to bear."

Jervell would have us believe that these reinterpretations of Jewish values would apply only to Gentile converts and that it would be important for Jewish Christians to maintain traditional Jewish practices so that the church could be God's people. No interpreter whom we have surveyed would hold that Jewish Christians should be forbidden to follow these practices if they wished. That, however, leads us to the crucial question. Does Luke, in fact, ascribe any essential value to such practices? I think not. For Luke, such practices would be strictly optional. Jervell's claim that they are required for Christian Jews is drawn from implications founded on his overall paradigm. That paradigm claims that empirical Israel is essential for Luke and places a strong emphasis upon those portions of Luke-Acts which portray Jewish practices in a relatively positive light. Yet the text can be interpreted, to my mind more convincingly, in the other direction.

When one remembers that Luke's narrative is an historical presentation, the direction of the historical flow is crucial. That flow is decidedly *away* from the importance of such practices as circumcision, dietary requirements, and traditional sabbath observance. In discussing Luke's view on both circumcision and the dietary requirements as well as the law in general, what was absent or nebulous in the gospel was clarified in Acts—and clarified in a way that was negative toward the law.

Moreover, as one notices the interpretations which key speakers in Acts place upon these legal decisions, the emphasis is not upon the importance of traditional practices which mark Jewish distinctiveness but rather upon the reduction of differences between Jewish and Gentile Christians. Peter interprets the freedom from dietary restrictions as God showing "no partiality" (Acts 10:34), and in the discussion over circumcision he asserts that God, in cleansing their hearts by faith, has "made no distinction between us and them" (15:9). What counts for Luke is not Jewish practices which mark Jewish identity, but the common faith in Jesus which eliminates distinctions. As Peter says, ". . . we believe that we [Jews] will be saved through the grace of the Lord Jesus, just as they [Gentiles] will" (15:11). Luke's stress, then, is not on the importance of such requirements, but upon the freedom from them, and that freedom applies to Jewish Christians as well.

The significant respect which Luke shows to Jewish practices, especially when compared to his sources, should not then be read as an assertion of their abiding value but rather as part of an effort to connect the present Christian church (which is free of such practices) to its Jewish roots. In his approach to the sabbath and the dietary requirements, Luke wants to "have it both ways," claiming connection with these traditional practices even as he overrides them.

The sabbath, circumcision, and the dietary laws have all been subordinated to the new value of faith in Jesus. This alone counts as essential to Luke. If Jewish Christians continue to follow such practices, there is nothing in Luke-Acts which would prevent them from doing so. Yet to give such practices importance either for Gentile or Jewish Christians would be misguided, for it would fail to recognize the flow of Luke-Acts which moves away from any traditional understanding of such practices.

I am aware that to read Luke-Acts as containing such a strong subordinating polemic demonstrates my own preference for interpreting the entire work along the lines of the disjunctive paradigm. Such a decision is inseparable from the stance that one takes upon Luke's attitude towards the role of Israel as a whole. Thus, the reader will find further support for the stance I have taken regarding subordinating polemic as we now discuss the presence of abrogating anti-Judaism in Luke-Acts.

ABROGATING ANTI-JUDAISM IN LUKE-ACTS

The basic groundwork has already been laid for determining the evaluation of Luke-Acts regarding the Jewish people as a whole. The two paradigms which were outlined at the beginning of this evaluative section include two basic stances toward Israel. The continuous paradigm argues that redefined Israel forms the essential foundation of God's people. Thus, those who adopt this paradigm will deny the abrogation of Israel as a whole. Only a portion of the Jews are rejected. A reconstituted or restored Israel continues as the essential foundation of the Christian church. The disjunctive paradigm takes an opposed perspective. It reads Luke-Acts in a way in which the refusal of Israel as a whole to accept the gospel is the cause for its own abrogation. As we shall see, not all who hold to the rejection of Israel will maintain that the rejection is final. With more or less confidence, some interpreters who believe in Israel's present rejection still maintain a hope for its restoration. Still, all the interpretations we shall consider as part of the disjunctive paradigm share with one another two central convictions: that Israel has rejected the gospel and that this rejection occasions a break in salvation history which initiates the replacement of Israel by the Christian church.

We shall now examine the continuous and the disjunctive paradigms in more detail, drawing out the manner in which they attempt to balance the positive and negative assertions within the text and examining how they argue for or against abrogating anti-Judaism in Luke-Acts. The ending of the book of Acts will serve as a focus for our examination, for it is primarily in reference to these closing verses of Luke-Acts that interpreters most clearly express their views on Luke's evaluation of Israel.

The disjunctive paradigm: Israel is rejected

The disjunctive paradigm argues that Israel as a whole has rejected the gospel and that its place has been taken by the Christian church in which Jews have no special status. Rather, Jewish Christians share with Gentile Christians a common standing which is based on faith in Jesus. The claims which we have identified as subordinating polemic have redefined God's people on a new footing, and it is only the community which accepts this new foundation which has validity. Positive representations of Jews and Judaism are not incompatible with this paradigm and do, in fact, serve the important purpose of establishing the connection of the present people of God with their Jewish roots. Yet within the disjunctive paradigm the time for Israel is past and its status has been abrogated by a new entity.

The disjunctive paradigm deals with positive Jewish images and responses by reading them as part of a literary pattern of Luke-Acts. The pattern is one of initial acceptance followed by opposition and rejection. As we have already seen, the first clue to this acceptance-rejection pattern is often located in the sudden reversal of the Nazareth episode (Luke 4:16–30) which begins Jesus' ministry. Initially favorable to Jesus' preaching, the Jews of Nazareth suddenly turn and attempt to kill him. Sanders argues that even in this early scene the connection of salvation with the Gentiles is implied. The twin examples Jesus gives of feeding the Sidonian widow rather than an Israelite widow and healing the Syrian leper rather than an Israelite leper (4:25–27) both suggest that, even in the days of the prophets, God's salvation was for the Gentiles not the Jews.[54]

The sudden shift from acceptance to rejection is then repeated in the shift of the allegiance of the people at the trial before Pilate (Luke 23:13–25) and at the death of Stephen (Acts 7:54–60) which marks the end of the "Jerusalem springtime" in which the Jews had responded positively to the gospel.[55] Again, within the missionary activity of Paul, the same acceptance-rejection pattern is evident. Tyson discerns a consistent pattern of Paul's preaching in the synagogues, acceptance of the gospel by some Jews and Gentiles, and opposition from the Jews. This pattern continues until Paul's last visit to Jerusalem in which the Jewish mob turns against him and seeks his death (Acts 22:22; 25:24). At this point Paul stands with the Jewish people against him, just as Jesus did at his trial.[56]

Although the disjunctive paradigm would recognize that some Jews did indeed accept the gospel, it would argue that—in terms of the pattern—such acceptance was not important. Luke's emphasis is elsewhere. The final note of Luke-Acts is a note of rejection. Crucial to this argument are three programmatic statements made by Paul in Acts. In these statements Paul announces that he is giving up on the Jews and turning his efforts to the Gentiles. The key verses are as follows:

In Pisidian Antioch (Acts 13:46):

Since you reject it [the word of God] and judge yourselves to be unworthy of eternal life, we are now turning to the Gentiles.

In Corinth (Acts 18:5b–6):

Paul was occupied with proclaiming the word, testifying to the Jews that the Messiah was Jesus. When they opposed and reviled him, in protest he shook the dust from his clothes and said to them, "Your blood be upon your own heads! I am innocent. From now on I will go to the Gentiles."

In Rome (Acts 28:25–28):

Paul . . . made one further statement: "The Holy Spirit was right in saying to your ancestors through the prophet Isaiah, 'Go to this people and say, You will indeed listen but never understand, and you will indeed look but never perceive. . . .' Let it be known to you then that this salvation of God has been sent to the Gentiles; they will listen."

These three statements have been widely interpreted as signaling the basic thrust of the disjunctive paradigm: Israel is rejected; the future is with the Gentiles.[57] The three assertions build to the last which, with the exception of two summary verses, closes Luke-Acts. The fact that the last scene of Luke-Acts contains the third of these seeming rejections gives tremendous importance to this final announcement by Paul.

NUANCES WITHIN THE DISJUNCTIVE PARADIGM

Among authors following the disjunctive paradigm, a number of nuances can be discerned in the interpretations proposed for the ending of Acts. Sanders stands at one end of the spectrum arguing that the book ends with a total rejection of all Jews who are not already within the Christian church. Basing his argument on the use of the word "persuade" (*peithō*) rather than Luke's usual expression for conversion which is "believe," Sanders proposes that the statement of Acts 28:24 that "some were persuaded" should not be understood as referring to a conversion to the gospel. Thus Sanders can argue that at the end of Acts there is no actual belief on the part of the Jews, and they are rejected in favor of the Gentiles. "For the author of Luke-Acts, there is no longer, after the time of Acts 28:28, any salvation for any Jews."[58]

Tyson's interpretation of the end of Acts is not as absolute as that of Sanders. Tyson can recognize that even until the end of Acts there are some Jews who continue to accept the gospel, thus causing a division within Israel. Yet even though there is some acceptance, Tyson reads Luke's final word as one of rejection. He notes a small shift in Paul's address to the Jews at Rome. When Paul addresses the Roman Jews originally, he speaks of "the customs of *our* ancestors" (28:17), but by the time he reaches his final address against them, he speaks of "*your* ancestors" (28:25). To Tyson this shift is an indication of a subtle distancing of Paul from the Jews who have rejected his preaching.[59] Founding his argument upon the pattern of acceptance-rejection and the triple turning from the Jews at Pisidian Antioch, Corinth, and Rome, Tyson concludes that for Luke the mission to the Jewish people has failed and now it is terminated.

> Here we see the tension between his [Luke's] condemnation of Jewish rejection and his description of Jewish acceptance. In the final analysis it appears that Jewish acceptance is less important to him than Jewish rejection. Or, to put it differently, he can speak of only a partial Jewish acceptance— and that is not enough. Thus, even the part finally becomes irrelevant.[60]

For Tyson, salvation history is fractured, and Israel is rejected.

Gaston and Wilson read the ending of Acts in fundamentally the same way. Even though the response of the Jews was favorable in earlier passages, it was partial and ultimately incomplete. The final word of Luke-Acts terminates the connection with the Jewish people and leaves them without hope.

> Unremitting efforts had been made to convert the Jews, but after an initial success, they met with increasing opposition. At the end, in Rome, Paul gives a final summary of the Church's Jewish mission of the past and, by implication, points to the hopelessness of continuing this mission in the future: the Jews will no longer hear the gospel, but the Gentiles will. . . . the decision by and about the Jews has been irrevocably made.[61]

Robert Tannehill: Israel as an open question

Robert Tannehill is not to be included in the disjunctive paradigm, because he holds that the final rejection of Israel is not yet certain. The ending of Acts leaves the question of Israel's status open. Nevertheless, Tannehill is not far from the disjunctive paradigm. Although not yet finalized, Tannehill's view of Israel in Luke-Acts is fundamentally pessimistic.

Tannehill reads the end of Acts in connection with the promises made to Israel in the infancy narratives of the gospel. There Simeon promises that the child will be "light" for the Gentiles and "glory" for Israel (Luke 2:29–32). Yet Tannehill admits that after the death of Stephen in Acts this expectation is largely *not* fulfilled, and this lack of fulfillment persists until the end of Acts. This gives Luke-Acts a tragic character. The rejection of the Jews is implied but is neither finalized nor welcomed. Tannehill believes that the refusal of Jews to accept the gospel, which is presented at the end of Acts, "cannot represent a satisfying ending for the author of Luke-Acts."[62] Rather, Luke continues to hope that the rejection of Jesus by Jews will be temporary. Tannehill believes that a mission to Jews remains a possibility. The last two verses present Paul as a model for all future evangelists: Paul "welcomed all who came to him" (Acts 28:30). For Tannehill, the "all" in this verse should not be taken as an idle remark. Jews could continue to approach the gospel.

Yet even with this positive hope Tannehill admits that the final scene is small on promise, and therefore basically tragic.

> Nothing prevents us from understanding the announcement in 28:28 as applying to Rome, leaving open the possibility of preaching to Jews elsewhere. Yet such an announcement at the end of a narrative carries extra weight. Just because the narrative ends, the narrator grants the final situation a certain permanence.[63]

For Tannehill, the final word on Israel is not yet spoken. The tragic nature of Luke-Acts, however, has given it an expected direction. Israel is not yet abrogated, but it seems that shortly this is exactly what will come to pass.

The continuous paradigm: the importance of Israel

A very different picture of the end of Luke-Acts and thus the entire work emerges from the continuous paradigm. Jervell's claim that Israel has been divided over the issue of the gospel (which has been accepted even by members of the disjunctive paradigm) allows interpreters of the continuous paradigm to limit the polemic and rejection of Luke-Acts only to a part of Israel: unrepentant Israel. Thus, even in a text which contains many claims for Jewish rejection, a position which holds the continuing importance of repentant Israel can be maintained. Jervell himself believes that the judgment of Paul at the end of Acts marks the end of the Jewish mission and the rejection of unrepentant Israel. Yet it is crucial for the continuous plan of God that *some* of the Jews did believe and became repentant.

> The unbelieving portion of the people is rejected for all times, and to those who have been converted the promises have been fulfilled. They are the cornerstone of the true Israel into which the Gentiles have now been incorporated.[64]

CONTINUITY IN CHRISTIAN EYES ALONE

Here we encounter one of the anomalies in Jervell's version of the continuous paradigm. The basic claim of Jervell is that salvation history is unbroken because of the continuing presence of restored Israel. However, this restored Israel has in fact been broken away from non-

Christian Israel. In other words, Israel has been redefined in terms of faith in Jesus, and it is *this* Israel which now claims continuity. Therefore, both the continuity and continuing validity of Israel are provided in terms which non-Christian Jews would not recognize. An Israel continues, but it is an Israel only in the eyes of those who accept its essential redefinition around the person of Jesus. Thus, at least according to Jervell's position, there is not much hope for non-Christian Israel. If we classify the evaluative claims of a work in light of the beliefs it holds regarding non-Christian Jews, Jervell's understanding of Luke-Acts would involve abrogating anti-Judaism. Only a Judaism which is Christianized continues with any validity.

Remarkably, from this perspective, Jervell's claim for continuity with Israel is rather close to the position of Sanders who argues for the abrogation of Israel. The difference lies in the importance which Jervell gives to the segment of Israel which does accept the gospel. By emphasizing this segment as an essential point of continuity, Jervell reads Luke-Acts as positive toward Israel, even though the Israel he has in mind would be considered valid and restored only from a Christian perspective. Continuity, then, only appears continuous through Christian eyes.

THE CONTINUOUS PARADIGM AS POSITIVE TO NON-CHRISTIAN ISRAEL

Other authors who can be included within the continuous paradigm, however, have used Jervell's schema of a divided Israel in order to argue for a positive evaluative claim even toward non-Christian Israel.

An inverted sign. D. L. Tiede agrees with Tannehill that the final chapter of Acts must be read in light of the first two chapters of the gospel. Tiede does not, however, read the development between the beginning and end of Luke-Acts as a tragedy. Rather he sees in the oracle of Simeon (Luke 2:34b–35) an inverted sign. The sequence of the words is significant for Tiede. Simeon does not talk about the "rise and fall" of many in Israel but of the "fall and rise" of many in Israel.[65] Thus "many" in Israel will fall *before* they rise.

When the end of Acts is read in light of this inverted oracle, the foreboding ending of Acts can actually be seen as a sign of hope. Tiede argues that Paul's final speech in Acts fulfills the first part of Simeon's oracle (the fall). Acts, however, ends before the second part (the rise) can be accomplished. Therefore, by ending as it does, Acts leads us to the very threshold of Israel's rise and concludes on a note of hope even for unrepentant Israel. Israel is divided, but there is hope even for the unrepentant part.

> God is never done with Israel. . . . Simeon's dire oracle concerning the falling of many in Israel and a sign spoken against has already been amply fulfilled within the narrative and at its end (Acts 28) and probably in Luke's world. But the restoration, the consolation, the redemption, the repentance, forgiveness and the reign of God which Simeon and all those other worthies in Israel expected has only begun to be inaugurated in the present time of Luke's story.[66]

A peaceful ending. R. L. Brawley presents the most extensive argument for a positive attitude toward Israel in Luke-Acts, confronting the disjunctive paradigm at almost every step. Those who reject Jesus in the Nazareth scene do not stand for Israel but only for "that segment of Israel which refuses to believe," and the three rejections of Acts are not meant to be a repudiation of Jews but merely an explanation of why Paul turned to the Gentiles.[67]

Brawley applies this positive view of Judaism in a special way to the final scene of Acts. There the refusal of some Jews to believe leads to Paul's insulting application of the quotation from Isaiah 6:9–10, but Paul does not pronounce any explicit rejection of them. Here as in other passages *some* Jews reject the gospel, but there is no counter-rejection and the mission to reach out to "all" continues (Acts 28:30). In fact, Brawley argues that the last two verses of Luke-Acts end on a peaceful note in which Paul continues preaching in Rome without any further Jewish opposition. This allows Brawley to conclude that "neither Luke's Gospel or Acts ends on a final note of Jewish rejection."[68] Working with Jervell's schema of a divided Israel, even as Acts ends, Brawley finds hope for a continuing positive response from the Jews.

An ironic approach. A final and distinctive interpretation congenial to the continuous paradigm can be found in the work of D. F. Moessner. If Tannehill reads the end of Acts as tragic, Moessner sees it as ironic. Along with Jervell, Moessner holds that a portion of Israel does continue to respond to the gospel throughout Acts. Israel is thus divided over the issue of the gospel.[69] Yet, unlike Tiede, Moessner does not find a positive fulfillment of the promises of the infancy narratives at the end of Acts. Rather, he argues that the end of Acts is a statement that the promises to Israel have *not* been fulfilled and that Israel has instead rejected the gospel.

Moessner, however, inserts this rejection into another pattern which allows him to derive a positive and continuous result. Moessner discerns a Deuteronomistic pattern of "disobedience—destruction—repentance—vindication" throughout Luke-Acts. He would argue that even at the end of Acts Paul's final rejection of the Jews is a part of this same pattern. Disobedience can thus lead to vindication. The rejection of Israel is real, yet, on a level that Israel does not realize, there is also hope. Thus the irony. The very dividing of Israel through hostility and suffering is the accomplishment of God's will and ultimately Israel's glory. Precisely because Israel has proven hostile and has been rejected, there is still room for repentance and hope. "The tension between promise and fulfillment is fundamentally ironic: Israel's rejection actually engenders Israel's glory."[70]

Thus Moessner is able to find the continuity of God's plan in a way that accepts Israel's rejection of the gospel. In light of the Deuteronomistic pattern, however, Israel is not abrogated. God remains open to accept repentance and grant vindication. Rather than taking the gloomy speech which ends Acts as ultimate doom for Israel as a whole, Moessner believes that—following the Deuteronomistic pattern—the promises of God to Israel will finally prevail.

ABROGATING ANTI-JUDAISM IN LUKE-ACTS

At the beginning of this chapter it was noted that Luke-Acts exhibits a complex admixture of polemic and sophistication. By now it should be clear that many possible readings can be deduced from such an ambivalent composition. The positions we have surveyed on Luke's ultimate view of Judaism bear out the truth of this perception. How does a reader begin to choose from the wide variety of suggestions which attempt to present Luke-Acts' evaluative claim? The two paradigms we have examined clearly demonstrate how the same data can be diversely interpreted. Is there any hope of adequately deciding between them? Certainly, no irrefutable stance can be taken. Yet three overall factors from among those we have reviewed persuade me to conclude that the disjunctive paradigm is the stronger alternative, and that in the end Luke's view of Israel is not positive but negative.

The importance of historical progression

First, I return to the literary structure of Luke-Acts with which we began. The literary form of a gospel *with* a history of the early church announces to the reader a bias in favor of historical progression. Thus, the argument of Luke-Acts moves through time. Methods which respect this historical flow are therefore especially apt for interpreting the work. Conversely, it seems to me less persuasive to accentuate positive and isolated images toward Jews and Judaism without connecting them to some temporal pattern. Therefore, the literary patterns espoused by Sanders and Tyson emerge for me as a particularly appropriate method for reading Luke-Acts. Founded upon an appreciation for the importance of the historical flow of the text, they grow in authority, particularly in their interpretation of the ending of Acts.

As we have already noted, Sanders bases his patterns upon the importance of *historical progression.*[71] Despite the rosy beginnings, the growing sense of rejection that builds primarily through the three programmatic statements of Acts prepares for the most important statement of all. Tyson agrees: "The final words are likely to be a distillation of the author's controlling concept."[72] Although (as many have noted) there are possibilities of hope at the end of Acts, it is difficult to imagine that a work which develops over two volumes to reach a conclusion and wishes to say something positive about Judaism would end in the way that Luke-Acts ends. The historical progression of Luke-Acts argues that it is the negative ending rather than the positive beginning that counts.

THE SIGNIFICANCE OF "THE JEWS"

Second, we return to a distinctive feature of Luke-Acts: the use of the term, "the Jews." This expression, used in the negative sense which we have discussed above, argues against limiting Luke's polemic to only a portion of Israel. Jervell's schema of a divided Israel can go a long way to disperse evaluative claims against Israel as a whole, but the repeated use of "the Jews" seems particularly inappropriate to such a reading.

Again, as we have seen, arguments can be made to suggest that in context "the Jews" does not mean "all the Jews." However, the literal scope of the phrase and its increasing usage in the final chapters of Acts seem to argue for a more pessimistic explanation. With a text which can be read so easily one way or the other, arguments mounted against the literal sense that words convey are particularly suspect. One can't help but wonder that if Luke really meant to address rejection to only part of the Jews, why didn't he say so?

JEWISH ACCEPTANCE AS ONLY A SECONDARY CONCERN

Third, I believe that the respect that Luke-Acts demonstrates in various places toward Jews and Judaism is more easily explained as a secondary concern rather than its primary one. Based upon the importance of historical progression in Luke-Acts, we have claimed that the emphasis of the work falls upon the rejection presented in the final scene. The many scenes of devout Jews and deference toward Jewish institutions assume a secondary purpose within this rejection.

I find the argument of M. J. Cook particularly persuasive in this respect. While basically accepting the acceptance-rejection pattern which Tyson and Sanders identify in Luke-Acts, Cook has asked why Luke would have been interested in the "acceptance" part to begin with. Rather than reading the acceptance as a sign of Israel's continuing validity, Cook argues that through these positive beginnings Luke can claim that Christianity is the authentic bearer of God's favor which was once carried by the Judaism of the past.

We have already recognized that the subordinating polemic of Luke-Acts claims continuity even as it redefines what in fact the sabbath or food laws will require. Cook sees this same discontinuity-continuity within Luke's evaluation of Israel. Luke wants to claim that Christianity embodies true Judaism, but he also wants to claim that the Judaism of the past has been rejected and replaced. This explains why Luke begins positively and ends negatively. Both are part of his argument. Cook uses the analogy of a rope in which some strands which begin the rope are replaced by others somewhere before its end.

> Paradoxically as it may sound, as much as Luke needed the presence of Jewish strands in the beginning of the Christian rope, he actually required their absence by the end.[73]

The historical flow of Luke-Acts leads us to conclude that the important issue for Luke is where the rope ends. The presence of initial Jewish acceptance should not be understood in tension with the negative ending but, in a strange way, a support to it. Positive images of Judaism are part of the rope in order to support the claim that the Christian church was Jewish at inception and connected to the best of that tradition. Both positive and negative images actually work together within Luke-Acts in order to achieve one complex effect. What is crucial for interpretation is determining which should predominate. To place primary emphasis upon the positive images would be—shifting to an image of Wilson—to get hold of the wrong end of the stick.[74]

In the end, then, I am persuaded that Luke-Acts presents a disjunctive picture of salvation history wherein the Jews have been rejected at the same time as the Christian church claims Jewish roots. Luke-Acts argues that it is this Christian church—accessible to both Jews and Gentiles on equal terms—which alone possesses access to God in Christ. Those Jews who do not enter this community on its own terms are rejected. Even though Luke-Acts asserts this rejection amidst images positive to Jews and Judaism, those images are not primary and serve another purpose, namely to demonstrate continuity with roots which have been left in the past.

Luke is a sophisticated author. He does not beat the drum of Jewish rejection with the fury of a heavy-metal band. Instead, he orchestrates his competing themes with symphonic phrasing, alternating from major to minor keys according to a predetermined pattern. The subordinating polemic is found interwoven with other, more cheerful, strains. Therefore, it is only when Luke-Acts builds to the final coda that the listener recognizes that the last chord sounds the rejection of Israel. It is no wonder that the complexity and subtlety of Luke's score has led to such a diversity of interpretation. Yet, at least to my ears, the melody which Luke-Acts offers includes no victory march for Israel. Rather, with subordinating polemic sounding in its lower registers, it builds into an ominous dirge of abrogating anti-Judaism.

4
THE GOSPEL OF JOHN: ABROGATING ANTI-JUDAISM THAT CUTS BOTH WAYS

The gospel of John has been notoriously associated with anti-Jewish polemic. The dramatic claims of this gospel together with its distinctive mode of expression conspire to give the impression of a straightforward attack upon the Jewish people as a whole. In John, Jesus does not struggle only with the religious leaders or even with the crowds. His opponents are routinely identified as "the Jews." Moreover, what is said about "the Jews" is neither equivocal nor timid. The gospel claims that "the Jews" seek to kill Jesus (John 5:18; 7:1; 8:37; 11:8; 19:7, 15) and are not Jesus' sheep (10:26) but offspring of the devil (8:44). At the turn of the century Kaufmann Kohler could call John "a gospel of Christian love and Jew hatred."[1]

There are, of course, factors which can be seen to reduce the impact of John's rhetoric. When the gospel is taken at face value, however—as it is today by most Christians who read it—the result can be disastrous. As Eldon Epp has observed,

> ... the Fourth Gospel, more than any other book in the canonical body of Christian writings, is responsible for the frequent anti-Semitic expressions by Christians during the last eighteen or nineteen centuries and particularly for the unfortunate and still existent characterization of the Jewish people by some Christians as "Christ killers."[2]

134

With such stakes set in the popular understanding, grappling with the polemic of the Fourth Gospel cannot be undertaken lightly. Understanding the polemic of John, however, is no simple endeavor. As we have already seen in the discussion of the other gospels, a deeper analysis of the text often compounds interpretive possibilities even as it attempts to clarify them. Nevertheless, the unity of John's theology and a rather widespread consensus among scholars on a number of aspects of the Fourth Gospel do at least reduce the number of issues which must be entertained.

This chapter will unfold in three steps. First, we shall enumerate some common presuppositions which will be adopted in our treatment of the Fourth Gospel. Second, we shall briefly compare John's account to those of the synoptic gospels in respect to possible anti-Jewish presentations. Third, we shall attempt to determine the evaluative claims of the gospel.

COMMON PRESUPPOSITIONS IN UNDERSTANDING THE GOSPEL OF JOHN

Throughout this chapter a number of widely-held opinions on the gospel of John will be presumed. John is the latest of the gospels, reaching its final form probably in the 90s of the first century. Both the stories that John tells and the way in which they are arranged vary markedly from those of the synoptic gospels. This seems to result from John's use of traditional materials which were not available to the other gospel writers. Moreover, John's manner of elaborating the tradition is directed by a clear and consistent theological thrust which gives to the Fourth Gospel its own peculiar voice.

CHRISTOLOGY AND DUALISM

The center of John's theological interest is the person of Jesus and the necessity of faith in him. As the gospel itself says, "these [signs] are written so that you may come to believe that Jesus is the Messiah, the Son of God, and that through believing you may have life in his name" (John 20:31). Although it is true that the synoptic gospels also center on the person of Jesus, none of them focuses upon him with the same brilliant light that is found in the Fourth Gospel. Particular ethical teachings, legal discussions, and even the "content"

of faith itself are all radically simplified by John into the acceptance
of faith in Jesus.[3]

Jesus is everything in the Fourth Gospel. The famous "I AM"
(*egō eimi*) sayings only state explicitly what is everywhere implied.
Jesus is the bread of life (6:35); the light of the world (8:12); the
sheepgate and the shepherd (10:7, 11); the resurrection and the life
(11:25); the way, the truth, and the life (14:6); and the real vine
(15:1). Throughout the gospel there is one fundamental question
posed to all characters and underlying all their decisions: "Are you for
or against Jesus, the one God has sent?" In the words of Robert
Kysar, "It belabors the obvious to say that the Gospel [of John] re-
volves on an axis of Christology."[4]

This two-way choice, for or against Jesus, is connected with a
pervasive dualistic view of reality which divides the world of the gospel into a variety of paired opposites. The language of the gospel
functions in terms of light/darkness, life/death, God/Satan, above/
below, heaven/earth, spirit/flesh, truth/falsehood. All of these pairs
directly correspond to the opposites of belief/unbelief in the person of
Jesus. This dualism in John's thought and expression leaves little
room for indecision or compromise. There is no gray area in which to
hide. As we shall see, this either-or approach of the gospel not only
provides the foundation for a strong and universal assertion of faith in
Jesus but also a basis for an equally strong and universal rejection of
those who fail to accept such belief.

THE TWO LEVELS OF JOHN'S NARRATION

Another presupposition in our discussion of John relates to the
history of the Johannine community. We have already seen in our
examination of the synoptic gospels that issues and beliefs of the community which writes the gospel are regularly read back into the narrative of Jesus' life and ministry. A growing number of scholars are
persuaded that the gospel of John reflects this common tendency in
an amplified and distinctive manner. J. L. Martyn and R. E. Brown
have argued that the text of John can be read on two levels: one which
describes the events of Jesus' life and another which relates the experiences of the Johannine community through various stages of its
life.[5]

When the man who was born blind is thrown out from the synagogue (9:34), Martyn believes that the exclusion tells us that, at one

point in its history, the community of John was excluded from the synagogue and that the importance of that event was still so remembered within the community that it became a part of the gospel.

> ... the literary history behind the Fourth Gospel reflects to a large degree the history of a single community which maintained over a period of some duration its particular and rather peculiar identity. It obviously follows that we may hope to draw from the *Gospel's literary history* certain conclusions about the *community's social and theological history.*[6]

Some of the more specific details by which Martyn attempts to fill out the picture of the Johannine community have been challenged, but the contention that the history of the Johannine community can be discovered within the gospel narrative has been widely accepted.[7] We will be standing within a strong scholarly consensus when we presume that the narration of the gospel takes place on two levels and that part of the history of the Johannine community included an expulsion from the synagogue.

In summary, the gospel of John is characterized by an overriding christology, a dualistic worldview, and a narrative approach which functions on two levels. With these few fundamental presuppositions stated, we may proceed to compare John's gospel with the synoptics and ask what similarities and differences can be located in its polemic toward Jews and Judaism.

A COMPARISON BETWEEN JOHN AND THE SYNOPTICS IN THE PRESENTATION OF JEWS AND JUDAISM

There is no consensus among scholars regarding John's relationship to the synoptic gospels. Similarities between John and the first three canonical gospels can be explained either by some literary interdependence among them or by the use of a common tradition. It is not our purpose here to delve into these matters of source criticism. We shall, however, briefly examine some key differences between John and the synoptics.

John is similar to the synoptics in presenting a large part of the opposition to Jesus originating from the Jewish religious leadership. Yet John has its own nuances. The chief priests and the Pharisees are Jesus' primary adversaries. The "authorities" seem open to faith but afraid to express it, and the crowd entertains the possibility of faith but refuses to believe.[8]

John also seems to introduce "the Pharisees" into the narrative in a problematic manner. In John 11:47 the Pharisees are said to convoke the Sanhedrin together with the chief priests. However, according to our best historical understanding of the period in which Jesus lived, the Pharisees had no authority to convene the Sanhedrin. The three estates of the Sanhedrin were the chief priests, the elders, and the scribes. Therefore, the joint decision of the chief priests and Pharisees in John 11:47 seems to be the result of John's editorial activity. Without claiming any direct literary dependence, compare the Johannine passage in question with a similar passage in Matthew.

Matt 26:3–4   (3) Then *the chief priests and the elders of the people* gathered in the palace of the high priest, who was called Caiaphas, (4) and they conspired to arrest Jesus by stealth and kill him.

John 11:47–53   (47) So *the chief priests and the Pharisees* called a meeting of the council, . . . (49) But one of them, Caiaphas, who was high priest that year, said to them, . . . (53) So from that day on they planned to put him to death.

It seems likely that John has replaced a more traditional group associated with Jesus' death with the Pharisees.

This tendency to introduce the Pharisees is even clearer in John's garden scene when Jesus is arrested. Compare Mark and John.

Mark 14:43   And immediately, while he was still speaking, Judas, one of the twelve, arrived; and with him there was a crowd with swords and clubs, *from the chief priests, the scribes, and the elders.*

John 18:3   So Judas brought a detachment of soldiers together with police *from the chief priests and the Pharisees,* and they came there with lanterns and torches and weapons.

Again it seems that John has introduced a reference to the Pharisees into his narrative.[9] This is confirmed when we realize that the Pharisees are normally absent from the passion accounts in all four gospels. In fact, verse 18:3 in John is the only place in any gospel in which the Pharisees are connected with the major events of the passion.[10]

John's increased use of the Pharisees and their unlikely linkage with the chief priests is best explained as a result of the gospel's reading of its own history back into the events of Jesus' ministry and death. In other words, in the two-level drama that John presents, the prominence of the Pharisees is more connected to the history of the Johannine community than to the ministry of Jesus.

Writing after the destruction of the temple when the successors to the Pharisees were the leading Jewish group, John seems less interested in being precise about other Jewish groups which existed in earlier times. He therefore retains only two of the religious groups found in the synoptics as opponents of Jesus: the chief priests and the Pharisees, giving wider play to both groups within the gospel and feeling free to join them together in opposition to Jesus.[11]

When we compare John's passion narrative to those of the synoptic gospels, John seems in many ways more favorable to Jews than the synoptic accounts. There is no official meeting of the Sanhedrin.[12] There is significantly less abuse of Jesus by Jews during the passion.[13] Roman involvement is heightened in both the arrest of Jesus and the prominence given to the trial before Pilate.[14] Finally, two weak but kindly Jewish disciples close the passion by providing Jesus with a burial according to Jewish burial customs.[15]

Yet, what John gives with one hand, he takes away with the other. John leaves the impression with the reader that Jesus was turned over by Pilate into Jewish hands for crucifixion.[16] Most importantly, the use of John's term, "the Jews," tends to erase the distinctions between the various agents of the passion and inclines the reader to identify Jesus' opponents and those who push for his death with the widest common denominator which the term will allow.[17]

We shall soon see that many suggestions have been made to limit the extension of "the Jews." From our present perspective, however, John's use of "the Jews" within the passion account seems ominously problematic. Despite several differences from the synoptics which ameliorate John's presentation of the Jews within the passion narrative, it is his use of "the Jews" more than any other factor which has made John a prime candidate for the most overtly anti-Jewish account in the gospels.

THE EVALUATIVE CLAIMS OF JOHN
REGARDING JEWS AND JUDAISM

Now that we have drawn a number of comparisons between John and the synoptic gospels in their treatment of Jews and Judaism, we begin an attempt to examine and classify the evaluative stance of the Fourth Gospel itself. Employing the same system of classification which we have used in the analysis of the synoptics, we shall first review key passages of John which will determine the presence of subordinating polemic and then take up the question of whether John's gospel manifests abrogating anti-Judaism.

SUBORDINATING POLEMIC IN JOHN

Does the Fourth Gospel subordinate central symbols of Jewish belief to another principle? On one level the answer to this question is immediate and clear. On another level it becomes clouded and open to debate. On the level of christology there can be no doubt. On the level of communal practice there is room to surmise. We have already noted at the beginning of this chapter that the Fourth Gospel so centers on the person of Jesus that other concerns and issues often go untouched. On the level of christology all is subordinated to Jesus' person. What is less clear is to what extent this overriding christology has actually led John to adopt alterations in specific religious practice. We may be able to determine that Jesus is superior to the law, but it is more difficult to establish whether certain parts of the law have been altered or remain in effect.

As we have already stated, every Jewish group had its own explanation of the law, and there was a certain toleration among Jewish groups over differing interpretations. However, when an interpretation led to an alteration of a basic Jewish symbol, this challenge took direct aim at the self-identity of Judaism. We have decided to classify such efforts to alter central Jewish symbols as subordinating polemic. Yet the ability to determine such concrete alterations in Jewish practice is particularly problematic in John. This is precisely because the gospel's real concern is its christology rather than any practical ramifications which might flow from it. Sabbath practice, temple worship, circumcision, and the issue of ritual purification may be mentioned within the text, but these references are so subservient to the christological discussion that they never become an object of discourse in their own right. There is, in other words, a christological whiteout in John. Issues of concrete religious practice must be reconstructed from the indistinct forms barely discernible behind the blinding light of Jesus' person.

In discussing the possibility of subordinating polemic in John, therefore, we shall begin with what is most clear and work toward that which is less so. We shall first examine the christological relationship between Jesus and the law. Using that relationship as an interpretive key, we will then attempt to establish John's more specific stance on the sabbath, Jewish feasts, and the temple.

Christ and the law in John

There is no detailed discussion of Jewish legal matters in the Fourth Gospel. This does not mean, however, that the Jewish law is absent from John. In a number of discourses throughout the gospel (5:16–47; 7:14–35; 8:12–59; 10:22–39) Jesus argues with his opponents over his actions and his person. In those arguments, the place of the law occurs frequently among the claims and counter-claims. Specific commandments of the law, however, are never discussed. In fact, the only commandment (*entolē*) which is given any content in John is the commandment to love (13:34). Although Jesus does insist on the keeping of "his commandments" (*entolai*—14:15, 21; 15:10), what these commandments specifically prescribe is never expressed.[18] What sense can be made of this disembodied presence of the law in John?

SEVERINO PANCARO: CHRIST REPLACES THE LAW

The most complete and valuable treatment of the law in John has been provided by Severino Pancaro. After examining in depth the use of the law, especially in the arguments between Jesus and his opponents, Pancaro states:

> The Law for John could only be said to contain "truth" and "life" in an improper sense: in so far as it leads to Jesus, who is the truth and the life. With the coming of Christ (and John is concerned only with this), "life" is possible for man

only if he accepts the teaching of Jesus, the "truth" he proclaims (viz., the "truth" he is). . . . . it is of no avail to search the Scriptures (viz., the Law) in the hope of finding truth in them, it is to be found only in Jesus.[19]

For Pancaro the law in the Fourth Gospel is totally subordinated to the centrality of Jesus' person and revelation. This is the basic assertion which Pancaro believes the gospel makes concerning the law. The reason John does not enter into any debates over the validity or the interpretation of specific Jewish laws is that he does not make the law the ground for his argumentation. For Jesus, seeking the authority of the law is unnecessary. Jesus' opponents attempt to found their arguments upon the authority of the law. John, however, does not permit Jesus to engage them on that level, but swiftly moves the interchange to center on Jesus himself.

Jesus takes to himself the attributes which the Jewish tradition applied to the Torah. In the Jewish tradition the Torah was called "bread," "water," "light," and the source of "life." In John, not the Torah, but Jesus is life (5:39–40), the bread of life (6:25–59), the living water (4:10–15), and the light of life (8:12).[20] Rather than adopting a strategy whereby Jesus presents an interpretation of Pentateuchal law which is superior to that of his opponents, the entire legal foundation is replaced with another foundation: the unique revelation of Jesus' person. Unlike Matthew who presents a specifically Christian approach to the Jewish law, John's authority is elsewhere. As a result, the practical issues of the law and the specific objections of Jesus' opponents fall into the background. John refuses to discuss them on the opponents' ground. As Sean Fryne states, "The silence is deafening; it is as though there is a conscious attempt to destroy the opponents' world by refusing to take it seriously."[21]

What the law can provide and what Jesus can provide are two different realities. The opening prologue proclaims the contrast: "The law indeed was given through Moses; grace and truth came through Jesus Christ" (1:17). Pancaro will not even accept the revelation of Jesus as a "new Torah" or a "new Law." Such an understanding would imply too much continuity between Jesus and the law. Jesus' revelation is not a development from nor strictly even a fulfillment of the law. This is why it is even possible for Jesus to speak to his opponents about "your law" (8:17; 10:34) and "their law" (15:25).[22] By such expressions John does not deny Jesus' Jewishness, but recognizes that Jesus has replaced what was central to Jewish self-identity.

The law, the ancestors, the entire Jewish tradition witness to Jesus. This testimony, according to Pancaro, is the law's one positive function. Those who really accept the law should become disciples of Jesus. If they refuse to do so, John would claim they could not be called disciples of Moses nor followers of the law. Both Moses and the law would testify against them.[23]

Non-Christian Jews, of course, would not accept this understanding of the law. From their perspective, John has turned the entire tradition upside down. Yet the overwhelming centrality of John's christology brushes such objections aside. Christ is superior to all that has come before him. The law is not evil nor opposed to Jesus. In fact, Moses and the law witness to Jesus. Nevertheless, with the coming of Christ, who is superior to all the ancestors, the law has ended its function. Christ has replaced the law.

RODNEY A. WHITACRE: CONTINUITY WITH THE TORAH

A challenge to Pancaro's understanding of the law in John has been offered by Rodney A. Whitacre. Whitacre agrees with most of Pancaro's significant assertions: Jesus is superior to the Torah; the scriptures witness to Jesus; and those who reject Jesus do not understand either Moses or the law.[24] Where Whitacre differs from Pancaro is in the degree of continuity that he would see between Jesus and the law. Drawing upon the lack of specific anti-law polemic in John (which as we have seen Pancaro himself recognizes), Whitacre argues that the Torah has for John "a continuing, permanent value."[25] This value is more than its prophetic character which Pancaro himself would accept.

According to Whitacre, the Jewish tradition also provides the older, imperfect, and yet true knowledge out of which the fuller knowledge of Christ can flow. Even though Jesus surpasses the Torah, Whitacre argues that John does not intend to imply a break with the Torah. The break is with the opponents of Jesus (and John) who would interpret the law differently than the Johannine perspective. This claim leads to Whitacre's understanding that the use of "your law" and "their law" in John is not a disparagement of the law but rather a disparagement of the Jewish opponents' use of it.[26]

By placing a different emphasis upon the positive aspect of the law in John, Whitacre argues that the law and the respect for it is a common factor shared by both John and John's opponents. It is not that the law has been replaced; it has been fulfilled. It is not that its value has ended; but that it has not been correctly interpreted by those who do not accept Jesus. Whitacre claims that both John and his opponents stand in a common tradition (emphasis added):

> He [John] attempts to uncover their [his opponents'] error by appealing to the traditions he holds in common with them. In *his loyalty to these traditions* he seeks to demonstrate how he is in continuity with the traditions and how they are not. This continuity in tradition is the key working principle of his polemic in both documents [the gospel and the first letter of John].[27]

According to Whitacre, John is "loyal" to the traditions of Israel. In fact he can claim that it is "the essential continuity between Jesus and Torah which provides the ground for Jesus' superiority over Torah."[28] In other words, Whitacre claims that John stands *within* the tradition and attempts to persuade others of his unique christological interpretation of it.

Pancaro asserts a more definite break. Jesus is a new beginning. The law witnesses to him and in that is its value. It is, however, a value from the outside. Though expressed in Jewish categories, according to Pancaro, Jesus' teaching is no development from Jewish teaching. His is a new teaching not found in the law.[29]

SUMMARY: SUBORDINATING POLEMIC AND JOHN'S VIEW OF THE LAW

Whitacre's understanding of Johannine polemic would draw it closer to the position which we have suggested for Matthew's gospel — the exclusive claim for one interpretation of the tradition over other interpretations competing within a common tradition. Pancaro's understanding will not permit the basis of a shared authoritative tradition. The only authority in John comes from the new revelation in Christ. The Torah can point to it, but it is not a part of it. Precisely because John's emphasis is so much upon Christ and so little upon the law, it is difficult to decide between these two understandings. The law in John serves basically as a foil to Jesus, or more precisely as a weapon to attack those who would refuse to accept Jesus.

The difference between Pancaro and Whitacre does not, however, bear great significance in terms of determining the presence of subordinating polemic in John. Both authors would clearly assert the superiority of Christ to the Torah. Both would recognize that the christology of the gospel will permit only one way of salvation. For Pancaro there is a break and total replacement; for Whitacre the law is still a value but it is totally subservient to Christ. Regardless of the degree of continuity with the past, Christ now is superior to the past. Christ does not stand under the Torah, but the Torah under Christ.

The centrality of Jesus within the gospel has made one conclusion inescapable: Christ is a higher principle than the law. There is a clear subordinating polemic in John against any effort of the law to be placed on a level equal to Christ. This subordinating polemic does not, however, necessarily demand that concrete practices of the law be eliminated. If Whitacre's position is accepted, there is, in fact, a way in which specific practices of worship and ritual practice could retain value as long as they were subordinated to the superior value of Christ.

Subordinating polemic and central Jewish symbols

Does the Fourth Gospel betray any signs of either retaining or eliminating central Jewish symbols? We have already noted how the christological whiteout of the gospel provides us with very little data on which to base such judgments. Concrete religious practices only enter the discussion in relation to John's christology. Nevertheless, it is possible to examine those places within the gospel where such issues emerge, if only in a secondary manner.

In terms of sabbath practice, John says very little. The sabbath is not attacked, but neither is it fostered. Christ is clearly superior to the sabbath, but whether John expects some sabbath norm to be observed is not stated. The conflict within the gospel centers on the person of Jesus, and John does not tip his hand in terms of sabbath observance.[30]

Unlike the synoptic gospels which narrate only one journey of Jesus to Jerusalem at the end of his ministry, John recounts several visits of Jesus to Jerusalem usually connected with the celebration of Jewish festivals. The mention of these Jewish feasts does not lead to any attempt by John to attack them. In fact, Jesus' association with these celebrations imparts to them a neutral if not positive coloration. Nevertheless, John seems to draw specific comparisons between the religious import of these festivals and the person of Jesus, and—as we would expect—the Jewish feasts are found lacking.

Chapters five through ten of John's gospel can be structured around principal feasts of the Jews. Chapter five is associated with the sabbath and Jesus' superiority to it. In chapter six we are told that the multiplication of loaves took place when "the Passover, the festival of the Jews, was near" (6:4). Chapters seven through nine are associated with the feast of Tabernacles (7:2, 14, 37). In chapter ten Jesus is in the temple area while the feast of the Dedication was taking place (10:22).

On the occasion of each one of these feasts, there is a quality of Jesus which is shown to be superior to a dimension of the Jewish tradition. During the Passover celebration Jesus declares himself the bread of life, the true bread superior to the manna given by Moses in the Passover-Exodus story (6:32–35). During the feast of Tabernacles when Israel remembered the gift of water and light, Jesus proclaims himself to be the source of living water (7:37–38) and the light of the world (8:12). During the feast of the Dedication when Israel remembered the reconsecration of the temple and its altar by Judas Maccabeus, Jesus claims that he is the one whom the Father has consecrated and sent into the world (10:36).

This superiority of Jesus to the temple is confirmed when, after the cleansing of the temple, the reliable narrator associates the temple in Jerusalem with the temple of Jesus' body (2:21–22). The same point of superiority is made when Jesus assures the woman of Samaria that soon true worship will replace worship both in Jerusalem and Samaria (4:21–23). The resurrected Jesus *is* the temple in the Johannine perspective. As Kysar says, "the presence of God in the world is no longer to be identified with a *place* but now with a *person*."[31]

Summary: subordinating polemic in John

How shall we summarize this series of observations regarding subordinating polemic in John? There can be no doubt that the gospel would claim the subordination of the law and all Jewish feasts and customs to the person of Christ. The overwhelming christology of the Fourth Gospel leads invariably to this conclusion. As we have already concluded, there is clearly subordinating polemic in the Fourth Gospel.

When we began to explore the nature of the subordinating polemic, however, two possibilities presented themselves. On one hand, John could be promoting a subordination which takes place within a common shared tradition, wherein a certain—though radically reinterpreted—connection to Jewish law and customs is maintained.[32] On the other hand, John could also be advocating a subordination which stands outside the Jewish tradition and understands the superiority of Christ as a replacement of laws and practices which would retain no continuing value.[33] Precisely because the emphasis in John is so christological and the christological superiority is assured in both understandings, determining a choice between the two subordinating possibilities proves problematic. The critique of Jewish law and customs is indirect and symbolic. This leaves the interpreter uncertain whether John says so little about these Jewish concerns because he is convinced of their worthlessness, or simply because his real interest is elsewhere. In effect, the question is how to read John's silence.

In this discussion regarding the type of subordinating polemic in John, I am inclined to interpret the silence as a disregard for Jewish law and customs, flowing from the conviction that the earlier Jewish revelation has been replaced by that of Jesus. I would, in other words, side with what I believe is the majority opinion of scholars who would stress discontinuity rather than a reinterpretation within a common tradition.

If John were really attempting to offer his own exclusive interpretation of the law within a common tradition, I would expect more legal argumentation involving the tradition. John would, in other words, take on more of the characteristics associated with Matthew, providing his own interpretations on specific tenets of the law. Such attention to the law, however, is lacking in John. The overall impression is that the law only emerges when John wishes to deflate his opponents' confidence in it. The only value the law seems to have in John is that it points to the Johannine view of Christ. The gospel does not seem to take the law seriously in itself. In a similar manner, were John really interested in reinterpreting the meaning of Jewish feasts and customs rather than replacing them, it would seem that they should emerge with more contours than they do. Their present status in the text seems to be primarily as a foil to Christ's superiority.

One can of course argue that the continuing (though reinterpreted) value of both the law and feasts is simply presumed by John. Yet it seems more probable that the lack of specific polemic against them should be interpreted as a sign of their irrelevancy rather than of their importance. Although the centrality of John's christology makes our distinctions between types of subordinating polemic far from secure, I would argue that the subordination of all to Christ in John leans more toward replacement than fulfillment. John does not mention the law or Jewish feasts because he wishes to reinterpret them as abiding values, but only because they serve as a basis of comparison with Christ, who in his person renders them ultimately irrelevant.

THE QUESTION OF ABROGATING
ANTI-JUDAISM IN JOHN

If one is inclined to accept the conclusion of the last section that John espouses a replacement theology rather than a fulfillment theology, it could be credibly maintained that an abrogating anti-Judaism has already been established within the Fourth Gospel. Does not the replacement of law, feasts, and worship automatically imply an abrogation of Israel? This observation carries a significant amount of weight. Nevertheless, two cautions should be observed before rushing too hastily to such a conclusion. First, as we have seen, because of John's silence on specific Jewish practices, the preference of replacement over fulfillment was a very difficult choice to determine. Second, the replacement of numerous Jewish symbols and institutions need not imply in itself the rejection of the entire tradition, however much it may incline us in that direction.

Positive elements in John's presentation of Jews and Judaism

We may add to these cautions the not-infrequent statements within the gospel which seem to ascribe positive value to Judaism. We have already mentioned at least some limited value to the law's ability to witness to Christ. To this we may add the following positive elements. The gospel of John is willing to identify Jesus himself as a Jew (4:9). In his response to the Samaritan woman, Jesus seems to ascribe to the Jewish people some positive role in God's salvific plan: "You worship what you do not know; we worship what we know, for salvation is from the Jews" (4:22).[34]

Moreover, the gospel seems to provide a place for a continuing Jewish presence within God's salvific plan. In John 11:49–52, Caiaphas argues for Jesus' death. However, from the comments of the narrator which follow, it becomes clear that John understands Caiaphas' words in a deeper sense than was intended by their speaker.

> (49) But one of them, Caiaphas, who was high priest that year said to them, "You know nothing at all! (50) You do not understand that it is better for you to have one man die for the people than to have the whole nation destroyed." (51) He did not say this on his own, but being high priest that year he prophesied that Jesus was about to die for the nation, (52) and not for the nation only, but to gather into one the dispersed children of God.

According to the narrator, Jesus will give his life both for the nation (Israel) and for the dispersed children of God (the Gentiles). Thus, although it does not say that all of the Jewish nation will be included in salvation, the Jewish people are not excluded as a group.[35]

A final positive element toward Jews and Judaism in John is provided by the gospel's use of the term "Israel" or "Israelite." There are five occurrences of this term in John, and it is always used with a favorable bias. John the Baptist announces that his mission is so directed that Jesus "might be revealed to Israel" (1:31). Jesus honors Nathanael by calling him "truly an Israelite, in whom there is no deceit" (1:47). Jesus calls Nicodemus "a teacher of Israel" (3:10) with an ironic twist which makes it clear that the true teacher of Israel is Jesus himself. On two occasions Jesus is called "the King of Israel," once by Nathanael (1:49) and once by the crowd welcoming him to Jerusalem (12:13).[36]

The symbolic function of "Israel" can only be determined when it is related to other terms and aspects of John's theology. We shall see that it plays a particular role within the gospel as a contrast to John's use of "the Jews." At present, however, it should be clear that "Israel" carries for John a positive sense.

These positive strains within John's gospel remind us that John's view of Jews and Judaism is complex. Even if Jesus is shown to be superior to several Jewish symbols and institutions, one need not automatically conclude that the position of the Jewish people is abrogated. In order to reach such a judgment, one would need to find some clearer indication within the gospel that the Jewish people as a whole have been rejected. This, according to our system of classification of polemic, would establish the presence of abrogating anti-Judaism in John. In order to determine whether such anti-Judaism is present within the gospel, we must examine two key terms within the Fourth Gospel that express rejection for John: "the world" and "the Jews."

Rejection in John: "the world"

As has already been noted at the beginning of this chapter, the combination of christology and dualism within the Fourth Gospel leaves no room for indecision or compromise. Every person and group within the gospel is judged upon the basis of two stark opposites: belief or unbelief in Jesus. Therefore, the gospel rejects any person or group which will not accept the identity and significance of the Johannine Jesus. Rejection of Jesus implies the gospel's rejection of the rejecters. When lack of belief is connected with individuals or specific groups, those whom the gospel rejects is clear. There is no doubt, for example, that John rejects Pilate, Caiaphas, Judas, the chief priests, and the Pharisees. They stand on the wrong side of John's dualism and choose darkness rather than the light.

John, however, also uses collective terms which seem to show some flexibility in their reference and whose meaning is more difficult to determine. Both John's use of "the world" (*kosmos*) and "the Jews" (*hoi Ioudaioi*) fall within this category.

"The world" (*kosmos*) is a significant term for John. It occurs seventy-eight times within the Fourth Gospel, compared to three times in Mark and Luke and eight times in Matthew. The term refers to the created universe, but in a particular way to that part of creation which is capable of a response to God.[37] Thus in most cases "the world" can be understood as humanity precisely in its potential to believe or not to believe in Jesus.

Furthermore, "the world" can be used by John in either a neutral or negative sense. In its neutral sense "the world" is often used to describe humankind as the object of God's love and salvific purpose. God loved the world (3:16) and sent the Son to save the world (3:17). Jesus is the savior of the world (4:42) who takes away the sin of the world (1:29), who has come into the world to witness to the truth (18:37) and give life to the world (6:33) as the world's light (8:12; 9:5).

However, despite this characterization of "the world" as the object of God's love and salvation, the overall usage of the term carries a negative thrust. This is because "the world" in John is used most prominently as the term to describe the negative response of humankind to Jesus. The world does not know Jesus (1:10) and hates Jesus and his followers (7:7; 15:19). There is therefore a division between those who love Jesus and those who belong to the world (16:20; 17:14). Jesus' kingship is not of this world (18:36). Unlike those who love Jesus, the world will never receive the Paraclete (14:17) and never see Jesus again (14:22).[38] Jesus' very coming is a judgment against the world (9:39) and Jesus' death and resurrection is victory over the world (12:31; 16:33).

"THE WORLD" AND JOHANNINE SECTARIANISM

The use of such an extensive term as "the world" to indicate a negative response to Jesus seems to result in a rather pessimistic view of humanity. To equate the rejection of Jesus with "the world" implies that John believes that most of humanity will not respond and that love of and true belief in Jesus are limited to a small group of believers. This pessimistic dimension of John is most commonly explained by recourse to the two-level structure of the gospel. The strong rejection of all those who do not accept the Johannine Jesus is read as a reflection of the Johannine community which rejects and opposes the beliefs of those outside its community boundaries. Thus the opposition to all who do not accept Jesus within the gospel is, on another level, the opposition of the Johannine community against non-members. This understanding would paint the Johannine community as a sectarian or quasi-sectarian group which rejects larger society and even other Christian groups. Sociologically, the Johannine community would literally see itself as "us against the world."

Although such attempts to describe the community which produced the gospel are always hypothetical, understanding John's opposition to "the world" in terms of the Johannine community's own social condition has become an established tenet of Johannine research.[39] "The world" is against Jesus in the gospel because the Johannine community sees itself against "the world." "The world" does not believe in Jesus in the gospel because those outside of the Johannine community do not accept its understanding of Jesus. "The world" is rejecting and rejected in the gospel because the vast number of John's contemporaries are both rejecting of and rejected by the Johannine community.

The scope of our topic does not force us to accept or to reject the sectarian nature of the Johannine community as the explanation for the negative use of "the world" in the Fourth Gospel. It is clear, however, that the dualism of the gospel presents us with an either-or choice for Jesus, and that a significant number of potential believers seem to have chosen not to believe. Those who do not believe are designated as "the world." They are judged and rejected by the gospel. In John's perspective, no life or salvation is possible without the acceptance of the Johannine Jesus. Therefore, those who stand in unbelief are clearly abrogated by the gospel. What remains to be determined is to what extent does that abrogation apply to "the Jews."

Rejection in John: "the Jews"

The second collective term which possesses a particular usage in the Fourth Gospel is "the Jews" (*hoi Ioudaioi*). This term occurs 195 times in the New Testament. Outside of the four gospels, it occurs 80 times in the book of Acts and only 28 times in the rest of the New Testament canon. This leaves a remainder of 87 occurrences within the four gospels, and the distribution of the term among them is instructive. Only 16 times does the term occur in the synoptic gospels (Matthew, 5; Mark, 6; Luke, 5—all in the plural). John has 71 instances—67 in the plural.[40] Thus John uses the term almost twelve times as frequently as any other gospel writer. This usage is even more dramatic when it is noted that 8 of the 16 synoptic uses consist of passages paralleled by another synoptic gospel, leaving only 11 different instances of "the Jews" within Mark, Matthew, and Luke, compared to 67 plural occurrences in John.[41]

This concrete vocabulary comparison amply demonstrates John's inclination to use the term. Our examination of the significance of his usage, however, will require many distinctions and nuances. In a way very similar to the use of "the world" in John, the significance of "the Jews" seems to fluctuate between a neutral and a polemical sense. Although our primary interest in this book is the polemical usage, we will begin by exploring those instances in which "the Jews" carries a neutral sense.

THE NEUTRAL SENSE OF "THE JEWS"

Whether a particular instance of "the Jews" in John is a neutral or polemical example is, of course, a matter of dispute. There is, however, a rather wide consensus about the majority of the instances of the neutral use. Rather than attempting to relate here the varying arguments of scholars over particular verses, I will adopt the analysis of Urban C. von Wahlde who has examined the occurrences of "the Jews" most extensively. Any reader anxious to review the debate over specific instances can consult von Wahlde who presents the opinions of other scholars as well as his own.[42]

Von Wahlde surveys the work of ten other scholars and concludes that there is a consensus among them over the division between the neutral and polemical senses. In 27 instances, most of the ten authors agree on a neutral sense. In 31 instances, there is unanimous agreement on the polemical sense.[43] This leaves only 13 instances which are open to significant dispute. Thus, the argument over which verses are or are not examples of John's polemical use is a rather limited one. For his own part, von Wahlde considers 38 of the instances of "the Jews" polemical and 33 of the instances neutral.[44]

The neutral uses of "the Jews" are varied.[45] They include references to religious and national customs and feasts, such as "the burial custom of the Jews" (19:40) and "the Passover of the Jews" (11:55). In one instance, the term is used to refer to the land of Judea (3:22). Persons are identified by the term when they hold a special role within Judaism, such as "Nicodemus, a leader of the Jews" (3:1). The neutral sense is present when Jews are contrasted with non-Jews, such as the Samaritan woman's comment to Jesus ("How is it that you, a Jew, ask a drink of me, a woman of Samaria?"—4:9) or Pilate's comment ("I am not a Jew, am I?"—18:35).

There are also a number of references to "Jews" who clearly do not exhibit the hostility which is typical of John's polemical sense. Thus there are Jews who come to Martha and Mary to console them (11:19), Jews who come to see Jesus and Lazarus (12:9), Jews who see what Jesus does and believe in him (11:45; 12:11), and Jews who read the inscription on the cross (19:20). Finally there are six references to the stereotyped phrase "the King of the Jews," a usage that John shares with the synoptics and which carries in itself no negative implications.

The neutral use and stages of literary development. The observant reader has already noted that many of the positive descriptions of Jews and Judaism which we have previously examined can be located within these neutral uses. It is here that John can assert that Jesus is a Jew (4:9) and can be buried as a Jew (19:40) and that salvation is from the Jews (4:22). In order to explain the existence of such positive uses together with the polemical ones, scholars often appeal to the theory of successive stages of formation of the gospel. If the gospel was written over a span of time and through various reformulations and editings, then attitudes from various stages of the community's life have been preserved in the final text. Thus, more positive attitudes to Jews and Judaism may have been retained from earlier phases, when the community still regarded itself connected to other Jewish groups. Correspondingly, more negative and polemical attitudes may derive from later phases, after the community was separated from the synagogue and was defining itself against the growing influence of Yavneh.[46]

It is valuable to accept a model of successive stages of literary development in order to explain the origin of the present text. Such a model can explain the tensions between neutral and polemical uses of "the Jews" within the same work. Models describing the origin of the text do not, however, provide us with an immediate conclusion regarding the evaluative stance of the gospel in its final form. Although more favorable presentations of Jews and Judaism may remain in the text, the presence of polemical and derogatory images can easily nullify them. The neutral uses of "the Jews" in John can therefore be accepted and cited as a positive strain within the gospel. The polemical usage, however, must be examined and clearly understood, because it is our final judgment upon this negative usage that will ultimately determine the classification of John's evaluative stance.

THE POLEMICAL OR JOHANNINE USE OF "THE JEWS"

In 31 instances most authors would agree that John is using "the Jews" in a sense particular to his gospel. This polemical sense is frequently called "the Johannine use" of the term. This Johannine usage can be identified by the presence of hostility and the ability of "the Jews" to replace other characters in the gospel.

Hostility and "the Jews." The most important characteristic of the Johannine use of "the Jews" is the hostility which this usage carries towards Jesus. "The Jews" in the Johannine sense try to kill, attack, and slander Jesus. There are also examples of the usage which are less intense. Sometimes the negative attitude is one of mere skepticism and unbelief (1:19; 2:18, 22).[47] However, the Johannine use of "the Jews" never places them in a positive light. They are clearly the opponents of Jesus.

The ability to replace the Pharisees. A second characteristic of the Johannine usage is its ability to suddenly emerge as a replacement for another more familiar term. A clear example of this occurs in chapter 9, in the story of the man born blind. After the healing takes place, we are told that the man was brought "to the Pharisees" (9:13, 15, 16). But a few verses later the narrator suddenly begins talking about "the Jews" (9:18, 22). By 9:40 the narrator again refers to "some of the Pharisees," but not before we realize that the same group within the story has been designated by two different terms. Without a blink or explanation the Pharisees become the Jews and then revert to the Pharisees again. A similar sudden substitution occurs in chapter 8. In 8:12–13 Jesus' opponents are clearly "the Pharisees," yet by 8:21–22 they have become "the Jews."

We have already noted how the Pharisees are used in John as a replacement for other Jewish leaders, namely the elders and scribes. In John "the chief priests, elders, and scribes" can become "the chief priests and the Pharisees." Now it should also be clear that the Pharisees themselves can be replaced with another term. They can become "the Jews." The presence of this substitution can be confirmed from another perspective. The debates over the sabbath, which in the synoptics take place between Jesus and the Pharisees (Mark 2:23–3:6; Matt 12:1–14; Luke 6:1–11), take place in John between Jesus and "the Jews" (5:10, 15, 16).[48]

The ability to replace the chief priests, elders, and scribes. The Pharisees are not, however, the only religious leadership group which can be replaced by "the Jews." In 18:14 the narrator identifies Caiaphas as "the one who had advised the Jews that it was better to have one person die for the people." The reader can clearly remember the scene in 11:45–53 where Caiaphas gave that advice before the Sanhedrin. In this case, then, "the Jews" are made to stand for that religious body. In the Fourth Gospel, "the Jews" can assume roles which are played out in the synoptics by the Sanhedrin authorities, namely, the chief priests, elders, and scribes. In John it is "the police of the Jews" who are involved in Jesus' arrest (18:12). It is "the Jews" who argue with Pilate (18:31, 38) and into whose hands Jesus says he is being handed over (18:36). It is "the Jews" who call for Jesus' death (19:7, 12, 14).

Furthermore, some of the arguments Jesus has with "the Jews" before the passion mirror the arguments with the Sanhedrin officials in the synoptic gospels. In John it is "the Jews" who demand a sign from Jesus after the cleansing of the temple (John 2:18, 20) instead of "the chief priests, elders, and scribes" who do so in the synoptics (Mark 11:27; Matt 21:23; Luke 20:1). Moreover, Jesus' response to "the Jews" concerning the destruction of the temple (John 2:19–22) mirrors the debate about the destruction of the temple which Mark (14:58) and Matthew (26:31) locate within the night trial before the Sanhedrin.

The other question which arises in the synoptic passion accounts during the official inquiry before the Jewish officials is the question of Jesus' identity (Mark 14:61; Matt 26:63; Luke 22:67). In John a very similar argument occurs in chapter 10, but there Jesus' interrogators are not the chief priests, elders, and scribes nor the high priest but rather "the Jews" (John 10:24–25).[49] Note the strong similarity in wording between the Lukan and Johannine versions:

Luke 22:66–67   (66) When day came, the assembly of *the elders of the people, both chief priests and scribes*, gathered together, and they brought him to their council. (67) They said, "If you are the Messiah, tell us." He replied, "If I tell you, you will not believe."

John 10:24–25   (24) So *the Jews* gathered around him and said to him, "How long will you keep us in suspense? If you are the Messiah, tell us plainly." (25) Jesus answered, "I have told you and you do not believe."

Similar to the manner in which "the Jews" in John can stand for the Pharisees, "the Jews" can also represent at times the activity of the chief priests, elders, and the scribes.

The ability to replace the crowd. "The Jews" can also suddenly assume the position of the crowd. In chapter 6 of John it is "the crowd" (6:22, 24) which begins to question Jesus. It is not long into the debate, however, that Jesus finds himself arguing with "the Jews" (6:41, 52).

Throughout the gospel, therefore, "the Jews" in the Johannine sense possess the remarkable ability to replace other groups which demonstrate hostility to Jesus. John seems free to introduce this term as a new designation for opposition groups which are identified by other more specific terminology within the synoptics and even within John's own narrative. This phenomenon raises a major problem when one attempts to specify a particular identity for "the Jews" within John's gospel. The scope of the term simply shows too much flexibility. As M. J. Cook has remarked,

> . . . the variety of contexts in John wherein "the Jews" appears does create confusion. For the *scope* of the group referred to does seem inconsistent—contracting and expanding, shrinking down to only a representative subgroup of the Jewish people active in the story line, or enlarging to the point of encompassing not only the whole of the Jewish people but seemingly the world at large.[50]

A number of commentators have attempted to save John from the charge of anti-Judaism by insisting that the reference of the Johannine use of "the Jews" should be understood in a restricted sense. It should be obvious, however, how difficult it is to evaluate these suggestions when the term shows as much flexibility as it does. Even the effort to survey the suggestions is a daunting one. Nevertheless, we must now undertake such an effort because our final judgment on John's polemic is closely tied to our understanding of "the Jews" in the Johannine sense.

SENSE AND REFERENCE IN A LITERARY WORK

John Ashton has introduced an important distinction into the discussion of the Johannine use of "the Jews." As in any work of literature, the character of "the Jews" in John can be identified by its referent and by its sense.[51]

By referent, Ashton means the identity of a particular entity to which a word points. For example, *Hamlet* has as its referent a character who can be identified as the nephew to Claudius, King of Denmark, or as the son of Gertrude, Queen of Denmark. To establish such a referent, however, does not automatically determine the sense or meaning of *Hamlet*. In order to really understand Hamlet as a character, he must be seen in action, in the flow of the narrative. It is only when we see him acting and interacting within the story that we appreciate that it is his anger, fear, and indecisiveness which really determine the sense of the character.

Reference and sense are, therefore, distinct. One can be sure of the referent of a term without gaining any certainty of its sense within the narrative. Conversely, one can be uncertain of the exact referent of a term and yet find that its sense is clear.

Reference and sense: an example. A simplistic example might prove helpful in drawing out the implications in the distinction between reference and sense. Consider the following parable:

> One of the saints arose to a new day. The sky was blue; the wind was calm; he was at peace. All in the city knew him to be a holy person. They sought his blessing. They asked for his prayers. They begged for even a small thread from his brown habit or for but one hair from his tonsured crown. Any relic would be valuable from such a holy person. After a simple breakfast, the saint went out to his daily work. He passed those without food and he consciously let his shadow fall on them so that they would feel God's presence. He smiled as he passed the sick stretched out on their pallets. A smile from him would allow them to think of higher things than their own sickness. He saw two bullies attacking a small child but could not stop because he was off to preach to the birds and build Christmas creches. The saint was the last to know his own worthlessness and hypocrisy.

The central character in this little story is "one of the saints." The sense that this character carries within the story is rather clear. The saint is a worthless hypocrite who is satisfied with his own holiness and really does nothing to help others. The story clearly intends to take a polemical stance against the saint and what the saint stands for.

When we ask the question of who "the saint" stands for, however, the answer is more difficult to determine. "The saint" is open to receive a number of possible referents. In its widest scope, "the saint" could refer to all holy people, and this parable would then be an attack upon any religious attitude or claim. In this way the parable would function as an attack upon religion itself and "the saint" would refer to any person who espoused a faith stance.

A narrower referent for "the saint" might be those among religious people who are popularly recognized as holy persons. The request for relics within the story and the widespread popular recognition might be used to limit the referent of the term to "canonized saints" or "saints acclaimed by popular devotion." With this referent, the polemic would not be an attack on all religious people but only upon those who stand out as holy in the popular imagination or by official pronouncements.

Finally, a much more limited referent could be argued from the details in the story. The brown habit, tonsure, preaching to birds, and Christmas crèches could be used to argue that "the saint" here refers to "St. Francis of Assisi." In this case, the polemic would be an attack upon the particular status of this one individual or the tradition he began.

Although the sense of the polemic within the parable is clear, the precise referents are varied. There exist a number of increasingly specific referents to which "the saint" could refer. Diagram A presents these various possibilities in visual form.

DIAGRAM A:
Sense and Possible Referents for "the Saint"

SENSE   *POSSIBLE REFERENTS*

worthless
hypocrite(s)

all religious people
canonized or popularly acclaimed saints
St. Francis of Assisi

The value of this simple schema regarding the use of "the saint" is that it can be used to illustrate the much more complex issue of the Johannine use of "the Jews."

THE SENSE OF "THE JEWS" IN JOHN'S GOSPEL

Within the scholarly literature there is really no debate over the *sense* of the Johannine use of "the Jews." Although authors will speak of "what they symbolize" or "how the term functions," John's particular use of "the Jews" is always understood to represent those who do not believe in Jesus and who actively oppose him.[52] Rudolph Bultmann's description of the portrayal of the Jews within the gospel is frequently cited.

> The term *hoi Ioudaioi*, characteristic of the Evangelist, gives an overall portrayal of the Jews, viewed from the standpoint of Christian faith, as the representatives of unbelief (and thereby, as will appear, of the unbelieving "world" in general). The Jews are spoken of as an alien people, not merely from the point of view of Greek readers, but also, and indeed only properly, from the stand-point of faith; for Jesus himself speaks to them as a stranger and correspondingly, those in whom the stirrings of faith or of the search for Jesus are to be found are distinguished from the "Jews," even if they are themselves Jews. In this connection therefore even the Baptist does not appear to belong to the "Jews." This usage leads to the recession or to the complete disappearance of the distinctions made in the Synoptics between different elements of the Jewish people; Jesus stands over against the Jews.[53]

Therefore, the *sense* of the Johannine use of "the Jews" is those who do not believe. They align themselves with the unbelieving "world" which is opposed to Jesus, and therefore stand on the wrong side of the overall dualism of the gospel.

Sense in a two-level drama. When we accept the two-level nature of the gospel, a further dimension to the Johannine sense of "the Jews" can be identified. "The Jews" may be said to represent not only the opponents of Jesus but also the opponents of the Johannine community. Since the Fourth Gospel weaves its own history into its version of the story of Jesus, "the Jews" may be seen to represent those who oppose and refuse to believe in the teaching of the Johannine community. From this perspective, the sense of the Jews for the original readers would have a double focus: those who reject Jesus and those who reject the Johannine community.

In a refinement of this understanding, R. Brown has suggested that the use of "the Jews" reflects an earlier stage of the Johannine community's history when the community was rejected by fellow Jews. Brown goes on to argue that the use of "the world" reflects a later stage when the community began to realize that unbelief could come from non-Jews as well.[54] Whether we accept Brown's suggestion or not, "the Jews" together with "the world" symbolize opposition and unbelief on two levels: toward Jesus and toward the community of the Fourth Gospel.

THE REFERENT OF "THE JEWS" IN JOHN'S GOSPEL

If it is clear what the symbolic sense of "the Jews" is within the gospel, the referent or identity of "the Jews" within the narrative of the gospel remains in dispute. Several different groups have been suggested as possible identifications for "the Jews." That is to say, the referent of "the Jews" is debated, even though the sense of "the Jews" is clear. We found this same phenomenon in the parable about "the saint." Although the sense of "the saint" was clearly one of a worthless hypocrite, the referent of "the saint" could be any one of a number of choices.

In the scholarly discussion regarding the referents for the Johannine use of "the Jews," a number of possibilities have been suggested with an increasing range of specificity. "The Jews" have been said to refer to "the Jewish people as a whole" which would at first seem to be the literal reference of the term. Another argument attempts to limit the reference of the term only to "the Judeans," those who inhabit a particular territory of Palestine. Finally, by means of a contextual argument, the term has been read as a technical term within the gospel referring only to "the Jewish authorities." Diagram B illustrates the manner in which the sense and possible references of the Johannine Jews can be understood.

DIAGRAM B:
Sense and Possible Referents for the Johannine "Jews"

SENSE   *POSSIBLE REFERENTS*

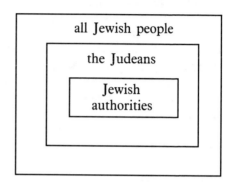

unbelievers and
opponents of Jesus
(opponents of the
Johannine community)

In order to evaluate the significance of the possible referents and their relationship to the sense of the term, it is important to understand the reasons why different referents have been suggested. We shall therefore examine the arguments for the three referents illustrated above before we attempt how best to understand the Johannine usage of "the Jews."

The referent as "all Jewish people." The most expected and seemingly obvious referent of *hoi Ioudaioi* is "all Jewish people"—the common understanding conveyed by the English translation "the Jews." To use *hoi Ioudaioi* to refer to "all Jewish people" was not unusual in ancient writings. The term was used by non-Jews to identify both individual Jews and the Jewish people as a whole. Although Jews in Palestine would usually use the term "Israel" when they spoke of themselves, *hoi Ioudaioi* could be used in works by Palestinian Jews when Gentiles were speaking of them. This seems to be the case in the first book of Maccabees. For Jews of the Diaspora, it was acceptable to use *hoi Ioudaioi* even when they spoke of themselves. This use can be attested in 2 and 3 Maccabees and in Philo and Josephus.[55]

We can therefore assume that the referent of "all Jewish people" or "the whole Jewish people" was a commonly understood referent at the time of the Fourth Gospel. Although it would not in itself carry any pejorative connotation, John could certainly employ the term within the gospel to carry the negative sense of the unbelievers and opponents of Jesus. In fact, for the referent of *hoi Ioudaioi* to be somehow less than "all the Jews," one would have to establish some reason to reduce the extension of the term. We will now examine two attempts to achieve such a limitation on the scope of "the Jews."

The referent as "the Judeans." An effort to reduce the extension of *hoi Ioudaioi* from "all Jewish people" has been forcibly argued by Malcolm Lowe.[56] Lowe bases his argument upon the fact that there is no verbal distinction in Greek between "the Jews" and "the Judeans." The term *hoi Ioudaioi* can be translated into English in either way, and Lowe believes that *hoi Ioudaioi* should be consistently translated as "the Judeans" within the Fourth Gospel.

Lowe begins his argument by enumerating three basic ways to understand *hoi Ioudaioi*. First, as referring to members of the tribe of Judah as opposed to other tribes. Second, as referring to "Judeans" as opposed to people living in (or originating from) other areas, such as Galileans or Samaritans. Third, as referring to "Jews" as opposed to members of other religions, such as Samaritans, Romans, or Greeks.[57] Lowe then argues that the primary meaning of the term within the New Testament period was the second—the geographical—usage and that this is the usage which is employed in the Fourth Gospel.[58]

To accept Lowe's conclusion might at first appear strange and unlikely, for it would lead to such translations as "the feast of the Judeans" in John 5:1; 6:4; 7:1 and "the Passover of the Judeans" in 2:13; 11:55. Moreover, the common phrase "the King of the Jews" would become, according to Lowe, "the King of the Judeans." This manner of speaking seems strange because it is clear that *hoi Ioudaioi* can refer within the gospel to persons obviously living outside of the territory of Judea. However, identifying a person or custom by a specific geographical territory is a phenomenon of the English language as well as of the Greek. In English, one can speak of a "Polish religious custom" even if it is taking place in Texas. One can say "Fred is German" even if Fred is an American citizen living in Cleveland. The name of the country in which the custom originated or in which the person's ancestry is rooted can be applied to customs and persons wherever they are found. In the same way in the Greco-Roman world, persons and customs were associated with the regions and nations from which they originated, and Judaism was primarily the religion of Judea.[59] As Wayne Meeks has stated,

... ancient authors in the age of syncretism tend to identify a cultic community either by its principal deity (the worshippers of Isis, the servant of the God of Heaven) or by its place of origin (the Phrygian cult, the Syrian goddess). When pagan authors speak of *Ioudaioi*, as they do when referring to the people we call the Jews, the term denotes the visible, recognizable group with their more or less well-known customs, who have their origin in Judea but preserve what we would call their "ethnic identity" in the diaspora.[60]

From this perspective, to translate "the feast of the Judeans" and "the King of the Judeans" would mirror in translation the very practice of the ancient world: identifying a feast or a people by the region from which it originated.

This matter, however, has yet another twist. Even though the use of "Judeans" would mirror the verbal expression of the ancient world, it would carry in English a connotation which was not contained in the original Greek. In Greek, the same term (*hoi Ioudaioi*) could be used in a strict connotation to refer to *only* those who live in the actual territory of Judea and in a wider connotation to include all those people and customs which originate from that territory. English, however, has a separate word for each possibility. "The Judeans" would stand for the strict rendering of *hoi Ioudaioi*, whereas "the Jews" would stand for the wider extension of the term. If, therefore, we wish to translate *hoi Ioudaioi* as "the Judeans" we must establish a reason to argue that the Fourth Gospel wishes to use the term in only that strict connotation.

This is precisely what Lowe attempts to argue. He insists that the specifically Johannine use of the term should always be understood in the strict connotation. He points out that the Johannine use of *hoi Ioudaioi* takes place in contexts in which it refers either to the crowd before Jesus or the Jerusalem leaders who oppose Jesus. Lowe argues that these references are meant to refer to *Judean* crowds and *Judean* leaders in a strict connotation. His argument is strongest in two instances where the text actually seems to mention the territory of Judea.[61] I present these two instances below. Where *hoi Ioudaioi* occurs I have provided the option for either "the Judeans" or "the Jews." Note how easily "the Judeans" fits the context.

John 7:1	After this Jesus went about in Galilee. He did not wish to go about in Judea because the (Judeans/ Jews) were looking for an opportunity to kill him.
John 11:7–8	Then after this he said to the disciples, "Let us go to Judea again." The disciples said to him, "Rabbi, the (Judeans/Jews) were just now trying to stone you, and you are going there again?"

As convincing as these two examples might be for the strict rendering ("Judeans") rather than the wider rendering ("Jews"), the remainder of the instances of *hoi Ioudaioi* are far less clear.

As just mentioned, *hoi Ioudaioi* seems to refer either to the leaders or the crowds. Lowe considers each of these possibilities in turn. However, his attempt to argue for the strict connotation of "the Judeans" in all cases diminishes in force as he moves away from the two passages cited above. In arguing for the translation of "Judean leaders" rather than "Jewish leaders," Lowe can only point to the obvious fact that the events of the passion take place in Judea and that the power of the Sanhedrin leaders extended only to the area governed by Pilate, rather than to the whole of Palestine. Therefore, Lowe believes that *hoi Ioudaioi* within the passion should be understood strictly and be translated as the "(native) Judean authorities."[62]

When Lowe discusses instances in which the term seems to apply to the crowds, he admits that in almost every case one could understand the term in either the strict or the wider connotation. Lowe does, however, attempt to locate "clues" within the text which he believes make "the Judeans" the more likely choice. Most of these clues have to do with the geography of the gospel. Lowe claims that 36 occurrences of the term are in a Judean context, whereas only two (6:41, 52) are in a Galilean context.[63] On the basis of this geographical location, he argues for the translation, "the Judeans."

However, arguments founded upon geographical regions are problematic in the Fourth Gospel. R. T. Fortna, for example, has argued that in John, Galilee is to be understood as a land of acceptance and refuge for Jesus, whereas Judea is a place of rejection and danger.[64] The linkage of John's theology to his geography, however, can be seriously questioned. The theme of Galilean acceptance versus Judean rejection is very limited within the gospel, occurring explicitly only in 4:43–45 and 7:47–52. The bulk of the gospel has a Judean setting, and the fact that many occurrences of rejection and hostility occur there, cannot be simply presumed to have special significance. Moreover, there are a number of references to Jesus' popularity in Judea (3:22, 26; 4:1; 7:3; 9:35–39), and—most importantly—a major rejection of Jesus occurs in chapter 6 which seems to take place in Galilee.[65] The argument from geographical location does not, therefore, seem to lend much support to Lowe's claims for the strict connotation.

Overall what Lowe's theory lacks is some substantial reason to suppose that the Fourth Gospel always intends that *hoi Ioudaioi* be read in its strict connotation. To use the words of Ashton, Lowe's theory proves unconvincing as it stands because "it fails to explain *why* the evangelist should have such hostility to the inhabitants of the tiny province of Judea."[66]

Therefore, although one could argue quite credibly that *hoi Ioudaioi* refers primarily to Judeans but includes as well all those who trace their origins and customs to that territory, the proper English word to translate that understanding would be "the Jews." To argue for the translation to be "the Judeans" one would have to show that John intends to limit his use *only* to those who live in the territory of Judea, and this is what we have found is most difficult to establish.

The referent as "the religious leaders." Whereas Lowe's effort to limit the extension of *hoi Ioudaioi* is based on the double connotations of the Greek word itself, a second attempt to limit the referent bases its argumentation on the contexts in which the term is employed. A case can be made that the contexts of the Johannine use of *hoi Ioudaioi* limit its referent to "the religious authorities." Leaving aside the neutral uses and a special strata of material in chapters 11–12, Brown asserts that "the Fourth Gospel uses 'the Jews' as almost a technical title for *the religious authorities, particularly those who are hostile to Jesus.*"[67] Brown bases his argument upon the way that the gospel can interchange "the Jews" with the chief priests and the Pharisees as well as the way "the Jews" can replace the titles for religious leaders that are found in the synoptics.

Von Wahlde mounts the most extensive argument for the use of "the Jews" as a title for the authorities alone. Von Wahlde does not consider the possibility of "the Judeans" but reduces the referents to only two possibilities: "the people"—by which he understands the common Jewish people—or "the authorities." On only two occasions does von Wahlde admit that the polemical use of *hoi Ioudaioi* refers to the common people. These are in 6:41, 52, and they are dismissed as coming from the hand of a later redactor.[68] After enumerating many instances in which *hoi Ioudaioi* is clearly linked with the religious authorities by context, von Wahlde faces 14 occurrences in which the context provides no clear linkage to the authorities.

These occurrences are, of course, the most dangerous precisely because the lack of association with the authorities does make it seem that "the Jews" is here referring to "the Jewish people." Note how von Wahlde argues against this implication.

> There is no evidence to indicate that the people are the common people. Given the problematic nature of only two texts in the gospel which seem to refer clearly to the Jews as common people, and taking into account the nature of language which would not attempt to identify all instances of such usage woodenly, it seems best to treat these texts too as referring to authorities.[69]

The argument is an argument from silence. It does, however, carry some weight, precisely because of the number of instances within the gospel in which *hoi Ioudaioi* is closely connected to the authorities by context.[70]

Nevertheless, some real questions remain. If the gospel intends the referent of *hoi Ioudaioi* to be limited only to the religious authorities, why is such an expansive term used in the first place? There were, after all, very specific terms which could be used for the religious authorities, if the aim was actually to narrow the scope of the referent to such a subgroup. In fact, the interchangeability of *hoi Ioudaioi* and specific terms for the religious authorities, which is often used to argue the identity between them, can also be used to argue that the gospel wishes to move beyond a reference to the authorities alone. If the gospel replaces a more specific term such as "the Pharisees" with *hoi Ioudaioi*, can we not argue that something wider than simply the religious authorities is intended? This must be taken as a real possibility. I believe, however, that this wider reality is not to be found primarily in the category of "referent" but in that of "sense." It is, therefore, to the relationship between the sense and the referent of "the Jews" that we must now return.

THE DOMINANCE OF "SENSE" IN JOHN'S USE OF "THE JEWS"

Among those scholars who argue that the referent of *hoi Ioudaioi*
should be limited to either "the Judeans" or "the religious authorities" there is a certain presumption that, by so limiting the referent,
the anti-Jewish potential of the gospel is reduced or even eliminated.
A. S. Geyser, who accepts Lowe's analysis of "the Jews" as Judeans,
concludes, "Anti-Judean the fourth Gospel is, but not anti-Jewish."[71]
D. M. Smith, who holds that "the Jews" refers in John to religious
leaders, can state:

> It is these authorities, not the Jewish people generally, who
> are portrayed as hostile to Jesus throughout *John* and make
> that gospel appear anti-Jewish. This being the case, it is
> reasonable—and probably correct—to contend that the anti-
> Jewish aura of the Fourth Gospel is a misreading of the text
> and, presumably, of the intention of its author(s).[72]

Such proclamations that the polemic of the gospel can be successfully
limited to a subgroup of Jews are somewhat premature. The argument
breaks down in two distinct ways.

The slippage of the limited referents. The first problem can be derived from our survey of the efforts to reduce the extension of *hoi
Ioudaioi* within the gospel. We are able to discern a certain slippage
that occurs in the arguments for the more limited referents. We have
seen that it is difficult to establish that John wishes to limit the referent of "the Jews" simply to territorial Judeans, even though the
term in itself could be used in that way. We have seen that if it was
his intention to limit the reference only to the authorities, it is difficult to explain why John would replace specific terms referring to
religious authorities with a term with a wider possible reference.
Therefore, arguments which intend to limit the referent of "the Jews"
invariably tend to slip into an ever-widening extension until the reference approximates all Jewish people.

A sense which overwhelms the referent. The second way in which
limited referents for *hoi Ioudaioi* fail to reduce the term to a subgroup
of Jews is tied to the relationship of referent to sense. Even if one
were able to limit the *referent* of "the Jews" to only the Judeans or
religious authorities, when this term begins to function within the
gospel itself, it clearly carries a wider *sense*. As *hoi Ioudaioi* in its

Johannine usage is situated within the context of John's gospel, it consistently aligns itself with the negative side of the gospel's dualism and relates directly to the negative sense of "the world." Drawing upon the pattern illustrated in Diagram B, whatever referent "the Jews" may identify in the Johannine narrative, that referent is meant to carry the sense of all those who do not believe and all those who oppose Jesus and the Johannine community. The sense of the gospel usage, therefore, is to place on the side of darkness all those who do not believe in Jesus and accept the teaching of the Johannine community. Clearly included among these are all Jewish people who do not believe in Jesus.

This is, in fact, the most likely reason why the gospel can so easily replace terms for specific Jewish leadership groups with the more extensive term "the Jews." Even though within the story line the *referent* might well be "the Pharisees," the *sense* of John's usage makes such an identity representative of "all Jews who do not believe." To place this in other terms, the *sense* of "the Jews" overwhelms the *reference* of "the Jews" within the narrative, even leading to a disregard for referential precision. Concerns larger than the consistency of the characters within the narrative (such as John's dualistic theology or historical argument with the non-Christian Jews of his own day) dominate the story and impose the sense of rejection on a wider group than the story itself would normally permit.

Confirmations of the dominance of sense. This dominance of the *sense* of "the Jews" has been recognized even by authors who would argue for a limited referent. R. T. Fortna, who argues that *hoi Ioudaioi* does refer specifically to those who inhabit the territory of Judea as opposed to the territories of Galilee and Samaria, nevertheless feels that the translation of *hoi Ioudaioi* is more correctly rendered "the Jews."

> John's point is not that the Jews are representative of Judea, thought of in a concrete geographical way, but rather that Judea is the place of "the Jews" and symbolizes the mentality, the response to God's truth, which they represent. In other words, a case can be made . . . for consistently translating *Ioudaia* not as "Judea" but as "Jewry." That topography in John's handling is obvious, and so it ceases to be mere topography and becomes instead a symbol of human

attitude. . . . It is finally not Judea but the Jews who stand for the negative human response.[73]

Fortna's assertion is that the theological sense overwhelms the terminological reference.

H. Thyen makes a similar assertion on historical grounds. Noting that at the time of John's writing the community was standing in opposition to the growing strength of the rabbis at Yavneh, Thyen understands the historical sense of *hoi Ioudaioi* as those Jews outside of and opposed to the Johannine community. These historical non-Christian Jews are therefore the sense which the *hoi Ioudaioi* carrys. Thyen argues that even if the reference of the term on linguistic grounds were "the Judeans," to translate *hoi Ioudaioi* as "the Jews" would be correct, because the term is used to indicate the group which is vying with John's community. Against Lowe who would insist that "the Judeans" is the only correct reference, Thyen would argue that when the historical dimension is factored in, "the 'incorrect' translation of 'the Jews' is in the end the only right one."[74]

R. E. Brown reaches a similar conclusion, even though he considers the referent of "the Jews" to be "the religious authorities." As we have seen, Brown holds that "the Jews" refers to the Jewish authorities of Jesus' time. Yet Brown also holds that "the Jews" refers to the hostile inhabitants of the synagogue of John's time. When Brown admits that "this makes John guilty of offensive and dangerous generalizing," it is tantamount in our terminology to recognizing that the specific reference of "the Jews" within the story is expanded to carry a larger sense.[75]

Whether one attempts to limit the reference of "the Jews" to only "the Judeans" or to only "the religious authorities," the functioning of the term within the gospel widens it to a more extensive sense. The Johannine "Jews" invariably take their place on the negative side of John's dualism and by means of that dualism are intended to express the rejection of all those who do not believe in Jesus. This certainly and specifically includes all non-Christian Jews. As Pancaro and others have noted, any Jews who have accepted Jesus are no longer included within the Johannine "Jews" but become part of "Israel," which as we have seen has a thoroughly positive sense within the gospel.[76] Those who refuse to believe, however, are numbered among "the Jews" who are both judged and excluded from life.

Summary: Anti-Judaism in John

Having allotted extensive discussion to the issue of "the Jews" within the gospel, it is now possible to conclude by relating the term to John's overall evaluative stance on Jews and Judaism. What we have found is that the *sense* of the term associates it with the rejection that flows from John's dualism and exclusive christology. At the same time the Jewishness of the possible referents—whatever their extension—imparts to the rejection a specifically Jewish dimension.

Regarding the particular referent of the term, I am inclined to adopt the contextual argument of von Wahlde and understand "the Jews" to refer to "the Jewish religious leaders." Yet the adoption of this referent cannot be said to limit the extension of the term to the religious leaders alone. When "the Jews" is used by the gospel to symbolize a much wider reality, the referent is enlarged in relation to the wider sense. In other words, it is impossible to limit the sense of the term to the confines of a limited reference and thus claim that the gospel is only opposed to religious authorities. As the sense of the term projects the referent on an expanding and even cosmic screen, the polemic of the referent is also enlarged. In this manner the inherent Jewishness of the referent (the Jewish religious authorities—or even the Judeans) is expanded along with the larger sense. A limited anti-Jewish polemic grows into a universal one.

THE FAILURE OF THE SYMBOLIC ARGUMENT

This understanding of the relationship of reference to sense undercuts attempts to dismiss the anti-Jewish polemic of the gospel as being "only symbolic." Such attempts argue that "the Jews" are meant to represent "the sinful people of God of all time" or " 'the world' in all its moral ambiguity," and therefore try to conclude the term contains no specific anti-Jewish thrust. These arguments, however, betray a rather simplistic understanding of symbolic discourse.[77] The referent which is used in the symbolic function is hardly indifferent. "The Jews" is not simply a neutral equivalent for "the world." Although the Johannine use of "the Jews" is related to the negative use of "the world," the use of "the Jews" is more specific than that of "the world." That specificity is of immense importance. "The Jews" focuses the unbelief of "the world" onto a specific subgroup, and that subgroup is decidedly Jewish. Therefore, even though "the Jews" is used symbolically and is related to the larger polemic against "the world," the symbolic use does not disarm the anti-Jewish polemic. As Townsend has noted,

> Using "the Jews" to denote, not only the Jewish opponents of Jesus, but the whole sinful world is scarcely pro-Jewish. In such a case "the Jews" have become the epitome for what is evil![78]

The failure of Jews to believe is not left to be counted anonymously as part of the unbelieving world but is specifically cited within the Fourth Gospel by the Johannine use of "the Jews." Even if the referent of the term should be understood as "the Jewish religious leaders," it is this specifically Jewish subgroup which is used as a primary symbol of unbelief and rejection. The symbolic use of "the Jews" does not eliminate its anti-Jewish character.

A POLEMIC WHICH CUTS BOTH WAYS

From another perspective, however, the symbolic use does at least partially lessen the anti-Jewish character of the term. The Jewish non-believers are not alone. "The world" includes all who fail to believe. The fundamental polemic of John is to attack all who do not accept the Johannine Jesus regardless of their heritage or origins. "The Jews" are notorious for being one specific group among these.

In other words, the symbolic nature of the gospel and the resultant relationship between "the world" and "the Jews" cuts both ways. As D. Granskou has succinctly stated:

> It [the relationship between "the world" and "the Jews"] could spread the hostility toward Jesus out beyond the Jews, thereby diluting the gospel's anti-Judaism. Or it could heighten the anti-Judaism by suggesting that the quintessence of the world's unbelief can be seen in Judaism.[79]

The nature of John's writing does, in fact, accomplish both of these possibilities. From one perspective, the symbolic relationship lessens the anti-Jewish thrust by making the Jewish element only an example of a larger cosmic rejection of Jesus. From the other point of view, the frequency of the use of the Johannine Jews and the hostile contexts in which the gospel places them give to "the Jews" and their rejection of Jesus a focus and a cosmic sweep which is not accorded any other unbelieving group.

However we gauge its intensity, the presence of anti-Jewish polemic cannot be eliminated from the Fourth Gospel. Moreover, the exclusive christology of the gospel gives to the polemic an abrogating character. Much like Matthew's gospel, John's exclusive stance will not tolerate other positions on the importance of Jesus. Unlike Matthew, however, it is difficult to find indications that such an abrogating polemic is taking place within a serious discussion of Jewish issues. John's thoroughgoing replacement theme gives little attention to questions of Jewish law or practice. John's use of "the Jews" with its referential slippage and symbolic sense indicates a comfort with portraying a specifically Jewish element as the paradigm of unbelief. John's exclusive christology obliterates all that does not acquiesce to its demands. The laws, customs, and persons of Judaism stand as shadows in the blinding light of the Johannine Jesus. They simply lose their importance. As J. E. Leibig has stated:

> The witness of the Johannine community to Jesus as the Messiah became so overwhelming, so absolute, so final that no room was left for Judaism as a valid response to God.[80]

Whether we judge that John's anti-Jewish polemic is lessened by its cosmic sweep or intensified by its Jewish referents, it is clear that there is no way to God left in John's cosmos other than the way of the Johannine Christ. It cannot be doubted that non-believing Jews and non-Christianized Judaism are rejected. Attempts to limit the referent of "the Jews" are overwhelmed by the christological sense which divides all into a dualism apportioning life to those who believe and rejection to those who do not. The either-or dualism of the gospel will allow no other place to stand. Although the gospel of John looks with sectarian eyes beyond "the Jews" to the greater darkness of the unbelieving "world," unbelieving Jews cannot be said to stand in the light. They stand with those who are rejected and condemned and testify to the abrogating anti-Judaism of the Fourth Gospel.

CONCLUSION: PAST POLEMIC
AND PRESENT GOSPEL

After reading the kind of survey which this book offers, it should be obvious that the canonical gospels contain a great amount of polemic against Jews and Judaism. It should also be clear, however, how exceedingly difficult it is to understand and classify that polemic. Almost every section of the gospels which we have discussed is open to divergent interpretations, and frequently the interpretive options are radically opposed to each other in their evaluations of the Jewish people. Therefore, when the time comes to summarize our conclusions, it would be foolhardy to wrap them in an air of security. I am content to summarize the positions which I have taken in this book, consciously aware that other credible positions can be adopted in the classification of anti-Jewish polemic.

I have argued that the gospel of Mark contains an evaluative stance which should be classified as subordinating polemic, but that it should not be interpreted as asserting the abrogation of Israel. I am convinced that a stronger polemic can be located in Luke-Acts and the gospel of John. Both of these writings, to my mind, assert the rejection of the Jewish people as such and are most properly classified as examples of an abrogating anti-Judaism. It is true, as we have seen, that both Luke and John express their evaluative claims in ways which somewhat soften the impact of the polemic. Luke's approach is both sophisticated and intricate, balancing positive and negative evaluations against each other in an elaborate literary pattern. John asserts his exclusive claim for Christ in a symbolic manner, using Jewish agents as a specific reflection of a larger evil. Nevertheless, I am persuaded that neither Luke-Acts nor the gospel of John would accept the continuing validity of Israel, unless by Israel one understands a Christianized Israel.

The gospel of Matthew must be classified in a special category. Although this gospel contains some of the most violent attacks on Jews in the entire New Testament, I have argued that it would be misleading to conclude that Matthew promotes an abrogating anti-Judaism. Matthew's high investment in the law and in several key Jewish ritual practices argues that the gospel's polemic is a means to assert control over the direction of Judaism. From Matthew's point of view, therefore, the gospel does not attack Judaism but proclaims a Judaism which has been redefined in light of Jesus.

Indeed, the sectarian nature of Matthew's community leads the gospel to assert its claims exclusively, and other Jews whose Judaism would be rejected by Matthew's exclusive stance would see the gospel as an abrogating attack upon them. Nevertheless, from Matthew's point of view, the polemic of the gospel would not be anti-Judaic. Attempting to capture the intra-Jewish nature of Matthew's polemic as well as its exclusive claims, I have suggested that the classification of "abrogating polemic" be used to describe the nature of Matthew's attacks upon other Jews. This classification reminds us that Matthew would understand his polemic as an argument between Jews rather than an attack upon Judaism itself.

However, even if the gospel was originally written from this point of view, an anti-Jewish potential still remains within Matthew. For whenever Matthew's gospel is read by those who see themselves as distinct from Judaism, the significance of the gospel's polemic changes. A reader who sees Jews and Judaism as foreign realities is likely to understand Matthew's attacks upon other Jews as attacks upon the Jewish people as a whole. This is exactly what happened as Matthew's gospel was taken up and read by Gentile Christian communities. Polemic which was a part of a family dispute was interpreted as polemic against all Jews and things Jewish. The violent rejection which Matthew hurled against his Jewish opponents then seemed to support the violent rejection of Judaism itself.

By means of this shift in context, a gospel which treasured its Jewish identity became one of the chief supports for the denigration of Judaism. To this day, when read through Gentile eyes, Matthew's forceful attacks against other Jews can all too easily shift into arguments for the rejection of Israel. Thus, in the popular understanding,

the gospel of Matthew joins its polemic with that of Luke and John
in asserting an abrogating anti-Judaism.

THE TENSION BETWEEN PAST POLEMIC
AND PRESENT GOSPEL

If this book has succeeded in heightening the awareness of anti-
Jewish polemic in the canonical gospels, many Christian believers
may find themselves introduced into a new and disturbing tension. I
have argued that in several sections of our Christian scriptures the
Jewish people are held responsible for the death of Jesus, and the
biblical authors have asserted the abrogation of non-Christian Israel.
Yet it is these very scriptural evaluations which are being disavowed
by the majority of contemporary Christian churches.

The declaration, *Nostra Aetate*, of the Second Vatican Council
began in 1965 a new direction in the relationship between Roman
Catholics and Jews. That document stated that Jesus' death "cannot
be charged against all Jews, without distinction, then alive, nor
against the Jews of today." It also directed that in Catholic teaching
and preaching "the Jews should not be presented as rejected or ac-
cursed by God, as if this followed from the Holy Scriptures."[1]

In 1968 the Faith and Order Commission of the World Council
of Churches accepted a report which outlined guidelines to direct the
dialogue between Christians and Jews. That report took a definite
stand on the role of the Jewish people in Jesus' death:

> Modern scholarship has generally come to the conclusion
> that it is historically wrong to hold the Jewish people of
> Jesus' time responsible as a whole for his death. . . . More-
> over, it is impossible to hold the Jews of today responsible
> for what a few of their forefathers may have participated in
> nearly twenty centuries ago. . . . Those passages of the New
> Testament which charge Jews with the Crucifixion of Jesus
> must be read within the wider biblical understanding of Is-
> rael as representative of all men.[2]

In a manner similar to the assertions of *Nostra Aetate*, the report was
also able to assert God's faithfulness to the Jewish people:

... it also seems to us that by their very existence in spite of all attempts to destroy them, they [the Jewish people] make it manifest that God has not abandoned them. In this way they are a living and visible sign of God's faithfulness to men, an indication that he also upholds those who do not find it possible to recognize him in his Son.[3]

These beliefs have continued to be supported and further developed in subsequent official statements of Christian church bodies.[4]

Contemporary Christian churches are aware of the grave injustices that have been leveled against Jews throughout history and are rightly committed to disavow any understanding which promotes anti-Semitism or claims that the Jews are rejected by God. It is unlikely, however, that Christians can make such disavowals without taking exception to some of the assertions made by the original authors of the scriptures. As I would read the text, both Luke-Acts and the gospel of John would hold the abrogation of Israel. Moreover, we have documented a bias throughout all the gospels which attempts to shift the responsibility for Jesus' death into Jewish hands. All of these factors place us in a tension between certain evaluations of the New Testament and the valid efforts of our contemporary Christian churches to respect the value of the Jewish religion and to eliminate any further basis for anti-Semitism.

In my opinion, it is best to face this tension head on. Rather than attempting to deny the polemical claims of the scriptures, it seems more honest to admit the presence of such negative strains within the New Testament. Certainly there are many qualifications which are possible and necessary. Not every attack within the scriptures against Jews should be taken as an assault upon the Jewish people as a whole, and much of the violence may be a part of an intra-Jewish debate. Matthew's gospel is a probable example of this, as we have seen. Nevertheless, even though we may disagree upon the exact passages which make the most devastating claims, it is likely that the Christian scriptures do in several instances place the responsibility for Jesus' death at the feet of the Jewish people and announce the abrogation of Israel. How do we deal with this tension?

A CALL FOR THE REPUDIATION OF POLEMIC

The Christian churches certainly have the right and duty to interpret the New Testament under the guidance of the Holy Spirit. Even though Christians hold in faith that their scriptures are the inspired Word of God, this need not imply that the writings of the New Testament are free from the limitations and prejudices of their human authors. Therefore, contemporary Christians are free to recognize that certain attitudes and beliefs contained within the scriptures are harmful to persons in our own day and are the result of the imperfect human condition in which we all stand.

Once this is admitted, the way is open for our churches to assert that such polemics of the past are not part of the Christian gospel we are called to proclaim today. As believers in Christ we may indeed decide that attitudes and claims which can prove damaging to persons within or without the Christian community are properly repudiated by those who seek to promote the peace and justice of God's reign. The word "repudiate" is chosen consciously.[5] To repudiate the abrogating anti-Judaism of the New Testament does not mean to deny its presence in our tradition. It means that Christian churches choose to disown such anti-Jewish polemic and refuse to accept such beliefs as part of the gospel which we proclaim or as determinative for church life and practice. Such repudiation can find support in the directives of *Nostra Aetate* which state that Catholics should not conclude that the rejection of Jews "follow[s] from the Holy Scriptures."

It is, in other words, the duty of the churches to determine in every age what in the scriptures is gospel and what is to be understood as conditioned by the circumstances and prejudices of the original authors. Making such determinations within the scriptures should not be seen as a new phenomenon for Christians. We have in the past repudiated the practice of human slavery which the New Testament accepts. Also, many church bodies are presently engaged in the repudiation of those parts of the scripture which flow from the patriarchy of the biblical cultures and support the oppression of women. The repudiation of anti-Jewish polemic should be seen as part of this larger effort to clarify the liberating message of salvation within our scriptures.

Of course, the repudiation of certain claims of the scriptures should not be made casually or impetuously. Nevertheless, when the stakes involve the devaluation of other human beings, those who wish to proclaim the gospel of Jesus must not shrink from separating the gospel from polemic and prejudice.

THE MEANS OF REPUDIATION

Yet even if it is agreed that certain evaluations in the scriptures should be repudiated, it is not automatically evident what means should be taken to achieve that end. No one would dispute the need for the further education of our church memberships, informing them of the insights of modern biblical study and the duty of the churches to read the scriptures in a manner that is both accurate and just. Education is essential. Moreover, there are no theological obstacles that complicate the efforts to raise issues of anti-Jewish polemic in preaching, catechesis, and spiritual direction. Every effort should be expended in making Christian believers aware of the polemic which exists in our scriptures and of our responsibility to repudiate those claims which can cause damage to others. I fully support efforts of education, and this book has been an attempt to advance them.

More problematic issues emerge, however, when we begin to ask whether the task of repudiation should involve alterations in the scriptural text itself. It has been suggested that those specific portions of the scripture which most clearly express sentiments of anti-Judaism be excised from the canonical text. This suggestion is a radical one. Christians hold the canonical text of the New Testament in high regard and are justly wary of allowing the concerns of any particular age, however well-motivated, from tampering with it. Moreover, the elimination of offensive passages within the New Testament opens the possibility that the polemical nature of the early Christian movement and the subsequent injustices against Jews will be denied rather than repudiated. We have a responsibility to accept the truth of our past even when we disagree with it.

I do not believe it would be responsible to eliminate sections of our scriptures which we find offensive as a means of repudiating anti-Jewish claims. I believe we should continue to maintain the complete Greek text of the New Testament, including those passages which may justly embarrass us.

By taking this stance, however, I do not mean to suggest that all attempts to adapt the biblical text should be avoided. Most Christians read the New Testament in translation, and it is on this level that I believe we can take some responsible action to check the impact of

anti-Jewish statements. There are options in both interpretation and
in translation as we have frequently seen in the preceding pages. I
believe that the ways in which we choose to translate certain scriptural
passages can serve the repudiation of anti-Jewish claims. Where there
exists an honest disagreement between responsible scholarly opinions
regarding the translation or interpretation of a text, the translator
should be encouraged to adopt the understanding which most forcibly
repudiates the anti-Jewish claims of the text. Those charged with
translation should exercise a preferential option for the translation
which least fosters the text's anti-Jewish stance.

This is especially important in the translations which will be used
in liturgy. In the classroom and in private use, anti-Jewish evaluations
within the scripture can be disarmed through the use of biblical in-
troductions and explanatory footnotes. Such contextualizations are
not viable in liturgy. Moreover, the presence of anti-Jewish statements, which are always offensive, are rendered even more inappropriate when the church gathers for prayer and strives both to proclaim
and receive the scriptures as God's word of salvation.

It is important, therefore, to employ every responsible means of
repudiation in approaching texts destined for liturgical use. This specific need was partially recognized in the "Guidelines and Suggestions
for Implementing the Conciliar Declaration *Nostra Aetate (n. 4)*"
which was issued by the Vatican Commission for Religious Relations
with the Jews in January, 1975. Although the Guidelines espouse no
repudiation of any biblical text, they give encouragement to the flexible translation of those passages of the scriptures which might mislead those who hear them. The Vatican Commission states that in
preparing translations of the scripture destined for liturgical use,

> . . . there should be an overriding preoccupation to bring
> out explicitly the meaning of a text, while taking scriptural
> studies into account. (Thus the formula "the Jews," in St.
> John, sometimes according to the context means "the lead-
> ers of the Jews," or "the adversaries of Jesus," terms which
> express better the thought of the Evangelist and avoid ap-
> pearing to arraign the Jewish people as such. Another ex-
> ample is the use of the words "Pharisee" and "Pharisaism"
> which have taken on a largely pejorative meaning.)[6]

The examples given by the Guidelines, if adopted, could assist greatly in the task of repudiating the anti-Judaism of the New Testament. The scholarly basis for such suggestions should be understandable to someone who has followed the arguments presented in this book. We discussed at length the problem of "the Jews" in John's gospel, and determined that even a limited referent such as "the religious leaders" could not absolve the gospel from carrying a sense which conveyed an abrogating anti-Judaism. Nevertheless, if a liturgical translation opted to translate "the Jews" as "the religious leaders," it would be exercising a valid translative option and the impact of the anti-Judaism would be significantly lessened. This would be especially true in liturgical settings where only a small portion of John would be read at one time. In that context the symbolic manner in which the entire gospel employs the Jewish referent would not be obvious.

Similarly, one might choose in several cases within the gospels to translate "the Pharisees" by "the opponents of Jesus." As we have seen, the Pharisees may well have been inserted into the gospel texts as a replacement for Jewish opposition groups due to the polemic of later church disputes. This insight from biblical research can be employed to justify a translation in which the specificity of "the Pharisees" is eliminated from the text. We need not continue to proclaim the opposition to Jesus as Pharisaic opposition, as if this were a reflection of historical fact or of salvific significance.

Of course, such translative options will not work with all types of polemic. In certain sections of the scriptures the anti-Jewish claims are so tightly woven into the narratives that to attempt to remove them might well distort the narratives beyond recognition. The passion narratives can be seen as examples of this type of polemic. When proclaiming such passages at liturgy, special care should be taken by those charged with pastoral care. In a way which does not destroy the flow or the impact of the liturgical action, pastors should discover means to remind the assembly of the dangerous mix of gospel and polemic which the text contains.

ENCOURAGEMENT FOR THE TASK AHEAD

The task of repudiating the anti-Jewish polemic of the New Testament is a daunting one. The need is both serious and personally troublesome. It can be a deep shock for many of us to discover such polemical statements within the inspired texts which we cherish. This distress can be compounded by our personal experiences. Some of us know full well the goodness and value of Jewish persons with whom we live and work. The abiding value of their religious tradition which continues to support and ennoble them is undeniable. Caught as we are in the tension between past polemic and present gospel, the way to a responsible resolution is not always clear. Our efforts to disavow the polemical stances of the canonical gospels are complicated by our inability to agree as to which scriptural texts are the most troublesome and what means should be taken to deal with them.

Nevertheless, there is still sufficient reason to make the final word of this book a word of encouragement. Many Christian churches have begun to insist that it is incompatible with the gospel to hold that the Jewish people are rejected by God or responsible for the death of Jesus. Dialogue between Christians and Jews is flourishing, and, even if we are far from agreement on many issues, we seem to be more comfortable with each other's presence than we have been for centuries.

It is in such times as these that we Christians might find it possible to look at our scriptures with new eyes, eyes which can see our Jewish roots as well as our distinctive belief in Jesus as the Christ. It is in such times as these that we may, with God's help, find ways to repudiate those parts of our scriptures which demean or insult our Jewish brothers and sisters. It is in such times as these that we may discover that such repudiation will not diminish our scriptures but allow them to emerge more liberated and liberating. However difficult this repudiation might be, the task is set before us. It is a task at which we must not demur. For to take it up would give clear notice that we are children of the God whom both Jews and Christians adore—the God of Abraham, Isaac, and Jacob, of whose Jewish lineage Jesus of Nazareth was born.

NOTES

INTRODUCTION

1. See the discussion of this in N. A. Beck, *Mature Christianity: The Recognition and Repudiation of the Anti-Jewish Polemic of the New Testament* (Selinsgrove: Susquehanna University, 1985) 21–30.

2. R. R. Ruether, *Faith and Fratricide: The Theological Roots of Anti-Semitism* (Minneapolis: Seabury, 1974). For an important series of essays discussing the merits of Ruether's theses, see A. Davies (ed.), *Anti-Semitism and the Foundations of Christianity* (New York: Paulist, 1979).

3. W. Klassen, "Anti-Judaism in Early Christianity: The State of the Question," *Anti-Judaism in Early Christianity: Volume One: Paul and the Gospels* (ed. P. Richardson; Waterloo, Ontario: Wilfrid Laurier University, 1986) 1–19, esp. p. 9.

4. E. H. Flannery, "Anti-Judaism—Anti-Semitism: A Necessary Distinction," *JES* 10 (1973) 581–88, quotation p. 582.

5. R. Ruether, "Theological Anti-Semitism in the New Testament," *Christian Century* 85 (1968) 191–96; J. E. Leibig, "John and 'the Jews': Theological Anti-Semitism in the Fourth Gospel," *JES* 20 (1983) 209–34; E. J. Epp, "Anti-Semitism and the Popularity of the Fourth Gospel," *CCAR Journal* 22 (1975) 35–43, 45–52.

6. Leibig (223–27) argues for the use of "theological anti-Semitism."

7. D. Hare, "The Rejection of the Jews in the Synoptic Gospels and Acts," *Anti-Semitism and the Foundations of Christianity* (ed. A. Davies; New York: Paulist, 1979) 27–47, esp. pp. 28–32.

8. Luke T. Johnson, "The New Testament's Anti-Jewish Slander and the Conventions of Ancient Polemic," *JBL* 108 (1989) 419–41, quotation p. 427.

9. J. G. Gager, *The Origins of Anti-Semitism* (New York: Oxford University, 1985) 9.

10. W. D. Davies, *Paul and Rabbinic Judaism* (London: SPCK, third ed., 1970) x.

11. Johnson, 425.

12. R. E. Brown, "Not Jewish Christianity and Gentile Christianity, but Types of Jewish/Gentile Christianity," *CBQ* 45 (1983) 74–79.

1. THE GOSPEL OF MARK: SUBORDINATING POLEMIC AND SILENCE

1. A. E. Harvey, *Jesus and the Constraints of History* (Philadelphia: Westminster, 1982) 1.

2. M. J. Cook, "Anti-Judaism in the New Testament," *USQR* 38 (1983) 125–38, esp. p. 131.

3. M. J. Cook, *Mark's Treatment of the Jewish Leaders* (Leiden: E. J. Brill, 1978) 29–31; for an earlier yet still helpful study see J. C. Weber, "Jesus' Opponents in the Gospel of Mark," *JBR* (July 1966) 214–22.

4. Cook, *Leaders*, 29–51, 61–67.

5. *ibid.*, 1 (the emphasis is Cook's).

6. Weber, 218; P. Winter, *On the Trial of Jesus* (Berlin: Walter de Gruyter, 1974) 158–89.

7. M. J. Cook, "Jesus and the Pharisees: The Problem as It Stands Today," *JES* (Summer 1978) 441–60, quotation 451 (the emphasis is Cook's).

8. Winter, 162–63 (the emphasis is Winter's); see also Cook, *Leaders*, 52–58.

9. E. P. Sanders, *Jesus and Judaism* (Philadelphia: Fortress, 1985) 264; Cook, "Jesus and the Pharisees," 453.

10. Sanders, *Jesus and Judaism*, 245–340; E. Rivkin, *What Crucified Jesus?* (Nashville: Abingdon, 1984); for an excellent survey of recent efforts see J. T. Pawlikowski, "The Trial and Death of Jesus: Reflections in Light of a New Understanding of Judaism," *Chicago Studies* 25 (1986) 79–94.

11. Sanders, *Jesus and Judaism*, 294–318; Harvey, 11–35.

12. D. Juel, *Messiah and Temple* (Missoula: Scholars Press, 1977) 1–5, also 59–63, 85–94.

13. R. P. Booth, *Jesus and the Laws of Purity* (Sheffield: JSOT, 1986) 221; H. Räisänen, "Jesus and the Food Laws: Reflections of Mark 7:15," *JSNT* (1982) 79–100, esp. 82; M. FitzPatrick, "From Ritual Observance to Ethics: The Argument of Mark 7:1–23," *AusBR* 35 (1987) 22–27, esp. p. 26.

14. M. Lowe, "Real and Imagined Anti-Jewish Elements in the Synoptic Gospels and Acts," *JES* 24 (1987) 267–84, esp. p. 271.

15. Räisänen, "Food Laws," 90.

16. FitzPatrick, 26.

17. T. Callan, *Forgetting the Root: The Emergence of Christianity from Judaism* (New York: Paulist, 1986) 82; Lowe, "Real and Imagined," 280.

18. Hare, "Rejection of the Jews," 34.

19. J. R. Donahue, "Temple, Trial, and Royal Christology," *The Passion in Mark* (ed. W. H. Kelber; Philadelphia: Fortress, 1976) 69.

20. L. Gaston, *No Stone On Another* (Leiden: Brill, 1970) 475.

21. T. A. Burkill, "Blasphemy: St. Mark's Gospel as Damnation History," *Christianity, Judaism, and Other Graeco-Roman Cults: Studies for Morton Smith at Sixty* (ed. J. Neusner; Leiden: Brill, 1975) Volume 1:51–74, esp. pp. 60–61.

22. Hare, "Rejection of the Jews," 33.

23. Juel, *Messiah and Temple*, 131.

24. P. J. Achtemeier, *Mark* (Philadelphia: Fortress, 1975) 24–26.

25. J. R. Donahue, *Are You the Christ: The Trial Narrative in the Gospel of Mark* (Missoula: Society of Biblical Literature, 1973) 104–113.

26. *ibid.*, 114.

27. E. Best, *Following Jesus: Discipleship in the Gospel of Mark* (Sheffield: JSOT, 1981) 218–19.

28. A. A. Milavec, "A Fresh Analysis of the Parable of the Wicked Husbandmen in the Light of Jewish-Christian Dialogue," *Parable and Story in Judaism and Christianity* (ed. C. Thoma and M. Wyschogrod; New York: Paulist, A Stimulus Book, 1989) 103.

29. Hare, "Rejection of the Jews," 33–34; K. Snodgrass, *The Parable of the Wicked Tenants* (Tübingen: Mohr, 1983) 77, 90–92; L. H. Feldman, "Is the New Testament Anti-Semitic?" *Tokyo: International Christian University Publication IV-B, Humanities Christianity and Culture* 21 (1987) 1–14, esp. p. 6.

30. Donahue, *Are You*, 122–27.
31. Best, *Following Jesus*, 219–20.
32. Gaston, *No Stone*, 476; Burkill, "Blasphemy," 61.
33. Juel, *Messiah and Temple*, 213.

2. THE GOSPEL OF MATTHEW: ABROGATING POLEMIC WITH VIOLENCE

1. J. P. Meier, *Law and History in Matthew's Gospel* (AnBib, 71; Rome: Biblical Institute, 1976) 8.

2. W. D. Davies and D. C. Allison, *The Gospel According to Saint Matthew* (ICC; 3 Vols.; Edinburgh: T. & T. Clark, 1988) 26–27.

3. Davies/Allison, 559, 589; E. A. Russell, "The Image of the Jew in Matthew's Gospel," *Studia Evangelica VII*, ed. E. A. Livingstone (1982) 427–42, esp. pp. 433–34.

4. J. P. Meier, *Matthew* (Wilmington, Delaware: Glazier, 1980) 55–63; Russell, "Image," 433–34.

5. Davies/Allison, 29–31.

6. *ibid.*, 27.

7. R. P. Booth, 221–23.

8. M. J. Cook, "The New Testament and Judaism: An Historical Perspective on the Theme," *RevExp* 84 (1987) 183–99, esp. pp. 192–93.

9. *ibid.*, 191; E. Buck, "Anti-Jewish Sentiments in the Passion Narrative According to Matthew," *Anti-Judaism in Early Christianity* (Vol. 1; ed. P. Richardson; Waterloo, Ontario: Wilfrid Laurier, 1986) 165–80, esp. pp. 165–71.

10. D. E. Cook, "The Gospel Portrait of the Pharisees," *RevExp* 84 (1987) 221–33, esp. pp. 224, 230; B. Przybylski, "The Setting of Matthean Anti-Judaism," *Anti-Judaism in Early Christianity* (Vol. 1; ed. P. Richardson; Waterloo, Ontario: Wilfrid Laurier, 1986) 181–200, esp. pp. 191–97; M. J. Cook, "Historical Perspective," 195–96; Buck, 176–78; E. A. Russell, " 'Antisemitism' in the Gospel of Matthew," *IBS* 8 (1986) 183–96, esp. p. 187.

11. D. Flusser, "The Jewish-Christian Schism (Part I)," *Immanuel* 16 (1983) 32–49, esp. pp. 42–44; I. Havener, *Q: The Sayings of Jesus* (Wilmington, Delaware: Glazier, 1987) 102–103; Meier, *Matthew*, 239–49.

12. R. E. Brown, *The Birth of the Messiah* (Garden City, New York: Doubleday, 1977) 183. For additional comments on the polemical nature of the infancy narratives see: Przybylski, 181; Beck, 151–52.

13. Brown, *Birth*, 174–75.

14. *ibid.*, 232.

15. Beck, 159.

16. E. Schweizer, *The Good News According to Matthew* (trans. D. E. Green; Atlanta: John Knox, 1975) 520, 526.

17. *ibid.*, 519.

18. D. E. Cook, 225.

19. *ibid.*, 230.

20. S. Freyne, "Vilifying the Other and Defining the Self: Matthew's and John's Anti-Jewish Polemic in Focus," *"To See Ourselves as Others See Us"—Christians, Jews, "Others" in Late Antiquity* (ed. J. Neusner and E. S. Frerichs; Chico, CA: Scholars Press, 1985) 117–43, esp. pp. 118–19.

21. Johnson, 433.

22. Freyne, 132–34; D. E. Garland, *The Intention of Matthew 23* (NovTSup 52; Leiden: Brill, 1979) 115–17.

23. For a readable introduction to this period, J. Neusner, *First Century Judaism in Crisis: Yohanan ben Zakkai and the Renaissance of the Torah* (Nashville: Abingdon, 1975).

24. Winter, 171–73.

25. Meier, *Law and History*, 125–61.

26. Davies/Allison, 481–571.

27. Meier, *Law and History*, 57–65.

28. Davies/Allison, 494–95.

29. *ibid.*, 481–82.

30. D. T. Smith, "The Matthean Exception Clauses in the Light of Matthew's Theology and Community," *Studia Biblica et Theologica* 17 (1989) 55–82, quotation p. 78.

31. L. Gaston, "The Messiah of Israel as Teacher of the Gentiles," *Int* 29 (1975) 24–40, esp. p. 36.

32. Russell, "Image," 431.

33. Hare, "Rejection of the Jews," 40.

34. Davies/Allison, 506.

35. *ibid.*, 487.

36. This phrase is that of J. Koenig, *Jews and Christians in Dialogue: New Testament Foundations* (Philadelphia: Westminster, 1979) 96.

37. Freyne, 121.

38. B. T. Viviano, "The Pharisees in Matthew 23," *Bible Today* Nov (1989) 342.

39. D. Flusser, "Two Anti-Jewish Montages in Matthew," *Immanuel* 5 (1975) 37–45, esp. p. 43.

40. Meier, *Matthew*, 245; Schweizer, *Matthew*, 414; G. N. Stanton, "The Gospel of Matthew and Judaism," *BJRL* 66 (1983–84) 264–84, esp. pp. 268–69; Lowe, "Real and Imagined," 272–73.

41. Gaston, "Messiah of Israel," 33.

42. These insights by Harrington will soon be published in a new commentary on Matthew. I thank him for allowing me to see and use the section of his manuscript which applies to this parable.

43. Davies/Allison, 24.

44. F. J. Matera, *Passion Narratives and Gospel Theologies* (New York: Paulist, 1986) 109; F. Mussner, *Tractate on the Jews* (trans. L. Swidler; Philadelphia: Fortress, 1984) 195.

45. F. A. Niedner, "Rereading Matthew on Jerusalem and Judaism," *BTB* 19 (1989) 43–47, esp. pp. 44–45.

46. F. J. Matera, "His Blood Be on Us and on Our Children," *Bible Today* Nov (1989) 345–50, quotation p. 348.

47. Hare, "Rejection of the Jews," 38; Mussner, 195–96; Meier, *Matthew*, 342–43.

48. Davies/Allison, 24.

49. Koenig, 95; Feldman, 5.

50. O. L. Cope, *Matthew: A Scribe Trained for the Kingdom of Heaven* (CBQMS 5; Washington: CBA, 1976) 128; Matera, "His Blood," 347–48.

51. Cope, 129.

52. Przybylski, 200.

53. *ibid.*, 199; see also Russell, "Antisemitism," 193.

54. Freyne, 135.

55. Stanton, "Matthew and Judaism," 274.

56. *ibid.*, 269 and 271.

57. *ibid.*, 283.

58. A presentation of Qumran's self-identity as "true Israel" can be found in G. Vermes, "Dead Sea Scrolls," in *IDBSup* 217.

3. LUKE-ACTS: ABROGATING ANTI-JUDAISM WITH SOPHISTICATION

1. H. Conzelmann, *The Theology of St. Luke* (New York: Harper and Row, 1961; German original, 1953); for a summary of Conzelmann's periodization: J. A. Fitzmyer, *The Gospel According to Luke* (Anchor Bible, 28–28a; Garden City, New York: Doubleday, 1981–85) 179–92.

2. J. T. Sanders, *The Jews in Luke-Acts* (Philadelphia: Fortress, 1987) 71; J. T. Sanders, "The Jewish People in Luke-Acts," *Luke-Acts and the Jewish People* (ed. J. B. Tyson; Minneapolis: Augsburg, 1988) 51–75, esp. p. 70.

3. D. Slingerland, " 'The Jews' in the Pauline Portion of Acts," *JAAR* 54 (1986) 305–21, esp. p. 315.

4. L. Gaston, "Anti-Judaism and the Passion Narrative in Luke and Acts," *Anti-Judaism in Early Christianity: Volume One: Paul and the Gospels* (ed. P. Richardson; Waterloo, Ontario: Wilfrid Laurier University, 1986) 127–54, esp. pp. 137–38.

5. J. T. Sanders, "Jewish People," 72.

6. J. B. Tyson, "The Problem with Jewish Rejection in Acts," *Luke-Acts and the Jewish People* (ed. J. B. Tyson; Minneapolis: Augsburg, 1988) 124–37, esp. pp. 131–32.

7. D. L. Tiede, " 'Glory to Thy People Israel!': Luke-Acts and the Jews," *Luke-Acts and the Jewish People* (ed. J. B. Tyson; Minneapolis: Augsburg, 1988) 21–34, esp. p. 29, note 18.

8. M. Lowe, "Who Were the *Ioudaioi*?" *NovT* 18 (1976) 101–30, esp. pp. 127, 129.

9. Lowe, "Real and Imagined," 270–71.

10. M. Salmon, "Insider or Outsider? Luke's Relationship with Judaism," *Luke-Acts and the Jewish People* (ed. J. B. Tyson; Minneapolis: Augsburg, 1988) 76–82, esp. p. 82.

11. Gaston, "Passion," 127.

12. J. Jervell, *Luke and the People of God* (Minneapolis: Augsburg, 1972) 44–49.

13. *ibid.*, 53.

14. *ibid.*, 49–55.

15. *ibid.*, 56–67.

16. Fitzmyer, 55; D. L. Tiede, *Prophecy and History in Luke-Acts* (Philadelphia: Fortress, 1980) 7–11; D. Juel, *Luke-Acts: The Promise of History* (Atlanta: John Knox, 1983) 109–12; R. L. Brawley, *Luke-*

Acts and the Jews: Conflict, Apology, and Conciliation (SBLMS 33; Atlanta: Scholars Press, 1987) 3–4.

17. Juel, *Promise*, 9–24; Tiede, *Prophecy*, 23–33.

18. J. T. Sanders, *Jews in Luke-Acts*, 48.

19. *ibid.*, 50–64, esp. p. 63.

20. J. Kodell, "Luke's Use of *Laos*, 'People,' Especially in the Jerusalem Narrative (Lk 19:28–24:53)," *CBQ* 31 (1969) 327–43; J. B. Tyson, "The Jewish Public in Luke-Acts," *NTS* 30 (1984) 574–83, esp. p. 578; J. T. Sanders, *Jews in Luke-Acts*, 65–69, 225–26; R. C. Tannehill, *The Narrative Unity of Luke-Acts* (2 volumes; Minneapolis: Fortress, 1986–90) 1:164; Matera, *Passion Narratives*, 179; D. P. Moessner, "The 'Leaven of the Pharisees' and 'This Generation': Israel's Rejection of Jesus According to Luke," *JSNT* 34 (1988) 21–46, esp. p. 41; J. E. Via, "According to Luke, Who Put Jesus to Death?" *Political Issues in Luke-Acts* (ed. R. J. Cassidy and P. J. Scharper; Maryknoll, New York: Orbis, 1983) 122–45, esp. p. 132.

21. J. T. Sanders, *Jews in Luke-Acts*, 64–80.

22. *ibid.*, 83.

23. *ibid.*, 81 (the emphasis is Sanders').

24. Tyson, "Problem," 137; S. G. Wilson, *The Gentiles and the Gentile Mission in Luke-Acts* (SNTSMS 23; Cambridge: University Press, 1973) 233.

25. Jervell, *People of God*, 137.

26. *ibid.*, 144.

27. *ibid.*, 143.

28. *ibid.*, 137–40, 163. Salmon (79) and Lowe ("Real and Imagined," 271) also emphasize Luke's positive stance to the law through the treatment of these characters.

29. Juel, *Promise*, 108.

30. Jervell, *People of God*, 143. Juel (*Promise*, 106) and Callan (63) would agree with Jervell's stance on the law.

31. S. G. Wilson, *Luke and the Law* (SNTSMS 50; Cambridge: University Press, 1983) 56–57.

32. *ibid.*, 43–51.

33. *ibid.*, 84–102.

34. *ibid.*, 104–105.

35. *ibid.*, 104.

36. J. T. Sanders, *Jews in Luke-Acts*, 124–28. The Pharisees in Acts are *Christian* Pharisees, and Sanders' interpretation of the overall pat-

tern of Luke-Acts depends in part upon his particular understanding of the Pharisees (see *ibid.*, 84–131, esp. pp. 100–101).

37. *ibid.*, 114–17.

38. *ibid.*, 118.

39. M. M. B. Turner, "The Sabbath, Sunday, and the Law in Luke-Acts," *From Sabbath to Lord's Day* (ed. D. A. Carson; Grand Rapids: Zondervan, 1982) 99–157, esp. p. 119.

40. J. T. Sanders, *Jews in Luke-Acts*, 128.

41. C. L. Blomberg, "The Law in Luke-Acts," *JSNT* 22 (1984) 53–80, esp. p. 70.

42. M. A. Seifrid, "Jesus and the Law in Acts," *JSNT* 30 (1987) 39–57, esp. p. 51.

43. J. T. Sanders, *Jews in Luke-Acts*, 91.

44. Jervell, *People of God*, 140.

45. Wilson, *Law*, 33; also, Blomberg, 59; Turner, 104.

46. J. B. Tyson "Scripture, Torah, and Sabbath in Luke-Acts," *Jesus, the Gospels, and the Church* (ed. E. P. Sanders; Macon GA: Mercer University, 1987) 89–104, esp. pp. 99–104.

47. Wilson, *Law*, 39.

48. Tyson, "Sabbath," 103.

49. Jervell, *People of God*, 139–40.

50. Blomberg, 60; Turner, 111.

51. Wilson, *Law*, 70; Seifrid, "Law," 43; Blomberg, 64.

52. Wilson, *Law*, 69.

53. J. B. Tyson, "The Gentile Mission and the Authority of Scripture in Acts," *NTS* 33 (1987) 619–31, esp. pp. 628–30.

54. J. T. Sanders, *Jews in Luke-Acts*, 167. The importance of the Nazareth scene is also recognized by Tyson ("Public," 578) and Moessner ("Leaven," 24).

55. J. T. Sanders, *Jews in Luke-Acts*, 74; also: Tyson, "Public," 580; Gaston, "Passion," 133; R. C. Tannehill, "Israel in Luke-Acts: A Tragic Story," *JBL* 104 (1985) 69–85, esp. p. 74.

56. Tyson, "Public," 580–81; Tyson, "Problem," 132–33; J. T. Sanders, *Jews in Luke-Acts*, 75–80.

57. Tyson, "Public," 581; Slingerland, 318; M. J. Cook, "The Mission to the Jews in Acts: Unraveling Luke's 'Myth of the Myriads,' " *Luke-Acts and the Jewish People* (ed. J. B. Tyson; Minneapolis: Augsburg, 1988) 102–23, esp. pp. 104–105; R. C. Tannehill, "Rejection by Jews and Turning to Gentiles: The Pattern of Paul's Mis-

sion in Acts," *Luke-Acts and the Jewish People* (ed. J. B. Tyson; Minneapolis: Augsburg, 1988) 83–101; J. T. Sanders, *Jews in Luke-Acts*, 262.

58. J. T. Sanders, "The Salvation of the Jews in Luke-Acts," *Luke-Acts: New Perspectives* (ed. C. H. Talbert; New York: Crossroad, 1984) 104–128, quotation p. 113; also J. T. Sanders, *Jews in Luke-Acts*, 80–81, 259–63, 297–99. Tannehill (*Narrative Unity*, 2:347) agrees that *peithō* does not imply a conversion. Unlike Sanders, however, he would not conclude that it implies rejection. Rather he argues that the Jews were "in the process of being persuaded but had made no lasting decision."

59. Tyson, "Problem," 129.

60. *ibid.*, 137; Tyson, "Public," 581–82.

61. Wilson, *Gentiles*, 247; Gaston, "Passion," 139, 151; Slingerland, 318.

62. Tannehill, "Tragic," 82. Because the situation is not yet resolved, Tannehill does not believe the category of "anti-Jewish" can be applied to Luke-Acts and the persistent missions to the Jews are a sign of Luke's loyalty to Israel (*Narrative Unity*, 2:2–3, 175).

63. Tannehill, "Rejection," 139; Tannehill, *Narrative Unity*, 2:350.

64. Jervell, *People of God*, 64; also Juel, *Promise*, 111–12.

65. Tiede, "Glory," 147.

66. *ibid.*, 151.

67. Brawley, 26, 61–83.

68. *ibid.*, 143–44, 70–78.

69. D. P. Moessner, "The Ironic Fulfillment of Israel's Glory," *Luke-Acts and the Jewish People* (ed. J. B. Tyson; Minneapolis: Augsburg, 1988) 35–50, esp. p. 47.

70. *ibid.*, 48; also D. P. Moessner, "Paul in Acts: Preacher of Eschatological Repentance to Israel," *NTS* 34 (1988) 96–104, esp. pp. 102–103.

71. J. T. Sanders, *Jews in Luke-Acts*, 83.

72. Tyson, "Public," 582; Tannehill, *Narrative Unity*, 2:344.

73. M. J. Cook, "Myriads," 120.

74. Wilson, *Gentiles*, 233.

4. THE GOSPEL OF JOHN: ABROGATING ANTI-JUDAISM THAT CUTS BOTH WAYS

1. K. Kohler, "New Testament," *Jewish Encyclopedia* 9 (1905) 251.

2. Epp, 35.

3. See the excellent discussion of John's theological perspective in R. Schnackenburg, *The Gospel According to John* (3 volumes; New York: Seabury/Crossroad, 1980–82) 1:154–64.

4. R. Kysar, "The Gospel of John in Current Research," *RelSRev* 9:4 (1983) 314–23, quotation, p. 319.

5. J. L. Martyn, *History and Theology in the Fourth Gospel* (2nd edition; Nashville: Abingdon, 1979); R. E. Brown, *The Community of the Beloved Disciple* (New York: Paulist, 1979).

6. J. L. Martyn, "Glimpses into the History of the Johannine Community," *L'Evangile de Jean: Sources, rédaction, théologie* (ed. M. de Jonge; Louvain, 1977) 149–75, quotation, pp. 129–30 (the emphasis is Martyn's).

7. Among the authors who accept the two levels of John's narration are R. E. Brown, *The Gospel According to John* (Anchor Bible 29–29a; Garden City, New York: Doubleday, 1966–70) lxxiv; R. Fuller, "The 'Jews' in the Fourth Gospel," *Dialog* 16 (1977) 31–37, esp. p. 35; J. T. Townsend, "The Gospel of John and the Jews: The Story of a Religious Divorce," *Antisemitism and the Foundations of Christianity* (ed. A. Davies; New York: Paulist, 1979) 72–97, esp. pp. 84–88; F. F. Segovia, "The Love and Hatred of Jesus and Johannine Sectarianism," *CBQ* 43 (1981) 258–72, esp. p. 271; Leibig, 218; R. A. Culpepper, "The Gospel of John and the Jews," *RevExp* 84 (1987) 273–88, esp. p. 81; P. S. Kaufman, "Anti-Semitism in the New Testament: The Witness of the Beloved Disciple," *Worship* 63 (1989) 386–401, esp. p. 391. The authors above tend to follow Martyn (*History and Theology*, 42–62) in his association of the Johannine community's expulsion from the synagogue with the *Birkath ha-Minim* or twelfth benediction which was understood as a curse added to the Jewish worship service to expel heretics, including Christian Jews. More recently, however, any direct linkage between the twelfth benediction and the Fourth Gospel has been questioned even by those who would still maintain the two levels of narration. See W. A. Meeks, "Breaking Away: Three New Testament Pictures of Christianity's Separation from Jewish Communities," *"To See Ourselves as Others*

See Us": Christians, Jews, and "Others" in Late Antiquity (ed. J. Neusner and E. S. Frerichs; Chico, CA: Scholars, 1985) 93–115, esp. pp. 102–103; D. M. Smith, "Judaism and the Gospel of John," *Jews and Christians: Exploring the Past, Present, and Future* (ed. J. H. Charlesworth; New York: Crossroad, 1990) 76–96, esp. pp. 83–88; S. T. Katz, "Issues in the Separation of Judaism and Christianity After 70CE: A Reconsideration," *JBL* 103 (1984) 43–76, esp. pp. 48–53.

8. R. A. Culpepper, *Anatomy of the Fourth Gospel: A Study in Literary Design* (Philadelphia: Fortress, 1983) 132; D. Granskou, "Anti-Judaism in the Passion Accounts of the Fourth Gospel," *Anti-Judaism in Early Christianity: Volume One: Paul and the Gospels* (ed. P. Richardson; Waterloo, Ontario: Wilfrid Laurier University, 1986) 201–16, esp. p. 207.

9. See J. Ashton, "The Identity and Function of the *Ioudaioi* in the Fourth Gospel," *NovT* 27 (1985) 40–75, esp. pp. 63–64.

10. They also occur in Matthew 27:62 in the scene in which the Pharisees together with the chief priests ask Pilate to set a guard at the tomb. This scene, however, occurs only in Matthew and takes place after Jesus' death.

11. Brown, *John*, lxxii, 439; Ashton, 60–62; D. M. Smith, 80–81; and W. Grundmann, "The Decision of the Supreme Court to Put Jesus to Death (Jn. 11:47–57) in Its Context: Tradition and Redaction in the Gospel of John," *Jesus and the Politics of His Day* (ed. E. Bammel; Cambridge: University, 1984) 295–318, esp. pp. 297–98.

12. Granskou, 212; Townsend, 77; Kaufman, 396; E. Haenchen, "History and Interpretation in the Johannine Passion Narrative," *Int* 24 (1970) 198–219, esp. p. 204.

13. Brown, *John*, 832; Granskou, 212, 214; Kaufman, 399–400.

14. Kaufman, 394–95; Granskou, 211.

15. Granskou, 215; Culpepper, *Anatomy*, 136.

16. Granskou, 214.

17. Ashton, 64; Granskou, 213.

18. Freyne, 123–24. The similarity of "keeping the commandments of Jesus" and "doing the will of God," "doing the works of God," and "keeping the word" is examined by S. Pancaro, *The Law in the Fourth Gospel* (NovTSup 42; Leiden: Brill, 1975) 364–451.

19. Pancaro, *Law*, 539.

20. *ibid.*, 452–87.

21. Freyne, 124.

22. Pancaro, *Law*, 542; Brown, *John*, lxxii.

23. Pancaro, *Law*, 130–304, esp. pp. 261, 525–26.

24. R. A. Whitacre, *Johannine Polemic: The Role of Tradition and Theology* (SBLDS 67; Chico, CA: Scholars, 1982) 64–65.

25. *ibid.*, 67.

26. *ibid.*, 66.

27. *ibid.*, 181.

28. *ibid.*, 67.

29. Pancaro, *Law*, 116.

30. D. A. Carson, "Jesus and the Sabbath in the Four Gospels," *From Sabbath to the Lord's Day* (ed. D. A. Carson; Grand Rapids: Zondervan, 1982) 57–97, esp. pp. 81–82; Pancaro, *Law*, 29–30; Freyne, 123; S. Bacchiocchi, *From Sabbath to Sunday* (Rome: Gregorian University, 1977) 47.

31. Kysar, *John*, 51 (the emphasis is Kysar's).

32. Koenig, 125.

33. Brown, *Community*, 48–49. Confer also the additional comments of Brown (*John*, 201–204, 411) and those of M. A. Getty ("The Jews and John's Passion Narrative," *Liturgy* 22 [1977] 6–10, esp. p. 7.)

34. Townsend, 74–75; Feldman, 8; C. J. A. Hickling, "Attitudes to Judaism in the Fourth Gospel," *L'Evangile de Jean: Sources, rédaction, théologie* (ed. M. de Jonge; Louvain, 1977) 347–54, esp. p. 350.

35. Mussner, 186–87; Granskou, 215.

36. Brown, *John*, lxxii–lxxiii; Townsend, 81; S. Pancaro, "The Relationship of the Church to Israel in the Gospel of St. John," *NTS* 21 (1974–75) 396–405, esp. pp. 398–401.

37. Brown, *John*, 508–509; Granskou, 215.

38. Segovia, 269; Brown, *John*, 509.

39. Kysar, "Current Research," 318; see Brown's discussion of John's ecclesiology in reference to outsiders in *Community*, 14–16.

40. A count of 70 is sometimes given for the term (Culpepper, "the Jews," 273; M. H. Shepherd, "The Jews in the Gospel of John: Another Level of Meaning," *ATR* 56 Supplement Series [1974] 95–112, esp. p. 96; Fuller, 31). This is due to the fact that the parenthetical comment in the latter part of 4:9, "(Jews do not share things in common with Samaritans.)" is considered by some experts as a textual gloss.

41. Epp, 40; M. J. Cook, "The Gospel of John and the Jews," *RevExp* 84 (1987) 259–71, esp. p. 262.

42. U. C. von Wahlde, "The Johannine 'Jews': A Critical Survey," *NTS* 28 (1982) 33–60. See especially the chart which von Wahlde provides on pp. 39–40.

43. *ibid.*, 41. The 31 instances are: 1:19; 2:18, 20; 5:10, 15, 16, 18; 6:41, 52; 7:1, 11, 13, 15; 8:22, 48, 52, 57; 9:18, 22a, 22b; 10:24, 31, 33; 13:33; 18:14, 31, 36; 19:7, 31, 38; 20:19 (von Wahlde, 57, note 68).

44. There are seven debated passages of which two (8:31 and 10:19) remain dubious. Von Wahlde (50–51) assigns these two to a redactor but does not specifically say if they are examples of the Johannine use. I have arrived at the number 38 from his chart on pp. 39–40.

45. Von Wahlde, 46; Townsend, 79; Fuller, 32.

46. Townsend, 81–88; Hickling, 345–54.

47. Von Wahlde, 47.

48. Fuller, 33.

49. *ibid.*, 34.

50. M. J. Cook, "the Jews," 264 (the emphasis is Cook's).

51. Ashton, 57–59.

52. ". . . they are part of that division of men who are in dualistic opposition to Jesus and refuse to come to him as the light," (Brown, *John*, lxxii); ". . . the literary function of the Jews is to symbolize or personify *unbelief*," (M. J. Cook, "the Jews," 267 [emphasis is Cook's]); "Through the Jews, John explores the heart and soul of unbelief," (Culpepper, *Anatomy*, 129); "Thus the 'Jews' become for the evangelist the quintessential expression of 'unbelief,' " (Fuller, 36); ". . . representatives of the godless 'world' in general," (Schnackenburg, 1:287); also Leibig, 215; Mussner, 184; Segovia, 270; Getty, 9.

53. From Bultmann's *Gospel of John*, quoted in Ashton, 60.

54. Brown, *Community*, 63–65.

55. M. J. Cook, "the Jews," 263.

56. M. Lowe, "Who Were the *Ioudaioi*?" *NovT* 18 (1976) 101–130.

57. *ibid.*, 102–103.

58. *ibid.*, 106–107.

59. *ibid.*, 107–108; Ashton, 43–48.

60. W. A. Meeks, " 'Am I a Jew?' Johannine Christianity and Judaism," *Christianity, Judaism, and Other Graeco-Roman Cults: Studies for Morton Smith at Sixty* (ed. J. Neusner; Leiden: Brill, 1975) 163–86, quotation p. 182.

61. Lowe, "Who Were," 120.

62. *ibid.*, 123–24.

63. *ibid.*, 121–22.

64. R. T. Fortna, "The Theological Use of Locale in the Fourth Gospel," *ATR* Supplement 56 (1974) 58–95.

65. J. M. Bassler, "The Galileans: A Neglected Factor in Johannine Community Research," *CBQ* 43 (1981) 243–57, esp. pp. 250–51; Brown, *Community*, 39–40; Ashton, 71.

66. Ashton, 70 (the emphasis is Ashton's).

67. Brown, *John*, lxxi (the emphasis is Brown's).

68. Von Wahlde, 42–44.

69. *ibid.*, 48.

70. Other scholars who see the referent as "the authorities" include: D. M. Crossann, "Anti-Semitism and the Gospel," *TS* 26 (1965) 189–214, esp. p. 199; Mussner, 184; D. M. Smith, 82.

71. A. S. Geyser, "Israel in the Fourth Gospel," *Neot* 20 (1986) 13–20, quotation, p. 15.

72. D. M. Smith, 82.

73. Fortna, 93.

74. As quoted in Ashton, 42. Lowe himself ("Who Were," 110) recognizes that a further sense may be involved: ". . . there is no need to see in John's Gospel some fantastic allegorical meaning of the word (though its author may have intended to convey an allegorical message too.)"

75. Brown, *Community*, 41, note 65.

76. Pancaro, "Church to Israel," 402.

77. Attempts to dismiss anti-Judaic charges by recourse to "symbolism" can be seen in G. A. F. Knight, "Antisemitism in the Fourth Gospel," *Reform Theological Review* 27 (1968): 81–88, esp. p. 85; J. R. Michaels, "Alleged Anti-Semitism in the Fourth Gospel," *Gordon Review* 11 (1968) 12–24, esp. p. 18. For a criticism of this approach to symbol, see Leibig, 225.

78. Townsend, 79.

79. Granskou, 204–205.

80. Leibig, 221.

CONCLUSION: PAST POLEMIC AND PRESENT GOSPEL

1. Quoted from H. Croner, ed., *Stepping Stones to Further Jewish-Christian Relations: An Unabridged Collection of Christian Documents* (London: Stimulus Books, 1977) 2.

2. *ibid.*, 83–84.
3. *ibid.*, 78.
4. See H. Croner, ed., *More Stepping Stones to Jewish-Christian Relations: An Unabridged Collection of Christian Documents 1975–1983* (New York: Paulist, A Stimulus Book, 1985).
5. The suggestion for "repudiation" is that of N. Beck, 34–35 and 37, note 9.
6. Croner, *Stepping Stones*, 13.

BIBLIOGRAPHY

Achtemeier, P. J. *Mark*. Philadelphia: Fortress, 1975.

Ashton, J. "The Identity and Function of the *Ioudaioi* in the Fourth Gospel." *NovT* 27 (1985) 40–75.

Bacchiocchi, S. *From Sabbath to Sunday*. Rome: Gregorian University, 1977.

Bassler, J. M. "The Galileans: A Neglected Factor in Johannine Community Research." *CBQ* 43 (1981) 243–57.

Beck, N. A. *Mature Christianity: The Recognition and Repudiation of the Anti-Jewish Polemic of the New Testament*. Selinsgrove: Susquehanna University, 1985.

Best, E. *Following Jesus: Discipleship in the Gospel of Mark*. Sheffield: JSOT, 1981.

Blomberg, C. L. "The Law in Luke-Acts." *JSNT* 22 (1984) 53–80.

Booth, R. P. *Jesus and the Laws of Purity*. Sheffield: JSOT, 1986.

Brawley, R. L. *Luke-Acts and the Jews: Conflict, Apology, and Conciliation*. SBLMS 33. Atlanta: Scholars Press, 1987.

Brown, R. E. *The Gospel According to John*. Anchor Bible 29–29a. Garden City, New York: Doubleday, 1966–70.

_____. *The Birth of the Messiah*. Garden City, New York: Doubleday, 1977.

_____. *The Community of the Beloved Disciple*. New York: Paulist, 1979.

_____. "Not Jewish Christianity and Gentile Christianity, but Types of Jewish/Gentile Christianity." *CBQ* 45 (1983) 74–79.

Buck, E. "Anti-Jewish Sentiments in the Passion Narrative According to Matthew." In *Anti-Judaism in Early Christianity*, Vol. 1, pp.

165–80. Edited by P. Richardson. Waterloo, Ontario: Wilfrid Laurier, 1986.

Burkill, T. A. "Blasphemy: St. Mark's Gospel as Damnation History." In *Christianity, Judaism, and Other Graeco-Roman Cults: Studies for Morton Smith at Sixty*, Volume one, pp. 51–74. Edited by J. Neusner. Leiden: Brill, 1975.

Callan, T. *Forgetting the Root: The Emergence of Christianity from Judaism*. New York: Paulist, 1986.

Carson, D. A. "Jesus and the Sabbath in the Four Gospels." In *From Sabbath to the Lord's Day*, pp. 57–97. Edited by D. A. Carson. Grand Rapids: Zondervan, 1982.

Cook, D. E. "The Gospel Portrait of the Pharisees." *RevExp* 84 (1987) 221–33.

Cook, M. J. "Jesus and the Pharisees: The Problem as It Stands Today." *JES* (Summer 1978) 441–60.

_____. *Mark's Treatment of the Jewish Leaders*. Leiden: E. J. Brill, 1978.

_____. "Anti-Judaism in the New Testament." *USQR* 38 (1983) 125–38.

_____. "The Gospel of John and the Jews." *RevExp* 84 (1987) 259–71.

_____. "The New Testament and Judaism: An Historical Perspective on the Theme." *RevExp* 84 (1987) 183–99.

_____. "The Mission to the Jews in Acts: Unraveling Luke's 'Myth of the Myriads.' " In *Luke-Acts and the Jewish People*, pp. 102–123. Edited by J. B. Tyson. Minneapolis: Augsburg, 1988.

Conzelmann, H. *The Theology of St. Luke*. New York: Harper and Row, 1961. German original, 1953.

Cope, O. L. *Matthew: A Scribe Trained for the Kingdom of Heaven*. CBQMS 5. Washington: CBA, 1976.

Croner, H., ed. *Stepping Stones to Further Jewish-Christian Relations: An Unabridged Collection of Christian Documents*. London: Stimulus Books, 1977.

_____, ed. *More Stepping Stones to Jewish-Christian Relations: An Unabridged Collection of Christian Documents 1975–1983*. New York: Paulist, 1985.

Crossan, D. M. "Anti-Semitism and the Gospel." *TS* 26 (1965) 189–214.

Culpepper, R. A. *Anatomy of the Fourth Gospel: A Study in Literary Design*. Philadelphia: Fortress, 1983.

_____. "The Gospel of John and the Jews." *RevExp* 84 (1987) 273–88.

Davies, A., ed. *Anti-Semitism and the Foundations of Christianity.* New York: Paulist, 1979.

Davies, W. D. *Paul and Rabbinic Judaism.* Third edition. London: SPCK, 1970.

_____., and Allison, D. C. *The Gospel According to Saint Matthew.* ICC; 3 Vols. Edinburgh: T. & T. Clark, 1988.

Donahue, J. R. *Are You the Christ: The Trial Narrative in the Gospel of Mark.* Missoula: Society of Biblical Literature, 1973.

_____. "Temple, Trial, and Royal Christology." In *The Passion in Mark*, pp. 61–79. Edited by W. H. Kelber. Philadelphia: Fortress, 1976.

Epp, E. J. "Anti-Semitism and the Popularity of the Fourth Gospel." *CCAR Journal* 22 (1975) 35–57.

Feldman, L. H. "Is the New Testament Anti-Semitic?" *Tokyo: International Christian University Publication IV-B, Humanities Christianity and Culture* 21 (1987) 1–14.

Fitzmyer, J. A. *The Gospel According to Luke.* Anchor Bible, 28–28a. Garden City, New York: Doubleday, 1981–85.

FitzPatrick, M. "From Ritual Observance to Ethics: The Argument of Mark 7:1–23." *AusBR* 35 (1987) 22–27.

Flannery, E. H. "Anti-Judaism—Anti-Semitism: A Necessary Distinction." *JES* 10 (1973) 581–88.

Flusser, D. "Two Anti-Jewish Montages in Matthew." *Immanuel* 5 (1975) 37–45.

_____. "The Jewish-Christian Schism (Part I)." *Immanuel* 16 (1983) 32–49.

Fortna, R. T. "The Theological Use of Locale in the Fourth Gospel." *ATR* Supplement 56 (1974) 58–95.

Freyne, S. "Vilifying the Other and Defining the Self: Matthew's and John's Anti-Jewish Polemic in Focus." In *"To See Ourselves as Others See Us"—Christians, Jews, "Others" in Late Antiquity*, pp. 117–43. Edited by J. Neusner and E. S. Frerichs. Chico, CA: Scholars Press, 1985.

Fuller, R. "The 'Jews' in the Fourth Gospel." *Dialog* 16 (1977) 31–37.

Gager, J. G. *The Origins of Anti-Semitism.* New York: Oxford University Press, 1985.

Garland, D. E. *The Intention of Matthew 23.* NovTSup 52. Leiden: Brill, 1979.

Gaston, L. *No Stone On Another.* Leiden: Brill, 1970.

_____. "The Messiah of Israel as Teacher of the Gentiles." *Int* 29 (1975) 24–40.

_____. "Anti-Judaism and the Passion Narrative in Luke and Acts." In *Anti-Judaism in Early Christianity: Volume One: Paul and the Gospels*, pp. 127–54. Edited by P. Richardson. Waterloo, Ontario: Wilfrid Laurier University, 1986.

Getty, M. A. "The Jews and John's Passion Narrative." *Liturgy* 22 (1977) 6–10.

Geyser, A. S. "Israel in the Fourth Gospel." *Neot* 20 (1986) 13–20.

Granskou, D. "Anti-Judaism in the Passion Accounts of the Fourth Gospel." In *Anti-Judaism in Early Christianity: Volume One: Paul and the Gospels*, pp. 201–216. Edited by P. Richardson. Waterloo, Ontario: Wilfrid Laurier University, 1986.

Grundmann, W. "The Decision of the Supreme Court to Put Jesus to Death (Jn. 11:47–57) in Its Context: Tradition and Redaction in the Gospel of John." In *Jesus and the Politics of His Day*, pp. 295–318. Edited by E. Bammel. Cambridge: University, 1984.

Haenchen, E. "History and Interpretation in the Johannine Passion Narrative." *Int* 24 (1970) 198–219.

Hare, D. "The Rejection of the Jews in the Synoptic Gospels and Acts." In *Anti-Semitism and the Foundations of Christianity*, pp. 27–47. Edited by A. Davies. New York: Paulist, 1979.

Harvey, A. E. *Jesus and the Constraints of History.* Philadelphia: Westminster, 1982.

Havener, I. *Q: The Sayings of Jesus.* Wilmington, Delaware: Glazier, 1987.

Hickling, J. A. "Attitudes to Judaism in the Fourth Gospel." In *L'Evangile de Jean: Sources, rédaction, théologie*, pp. 347–54. Edited by M. de Jonge. Louvain, 1977.

Jervell, J. *Luke and the People of God.* Minneapolis: Augsburg, 1972.

Johnson, L. T. "The New Testament's Anti-Jewish Slander and the Conventions of Ancient Polemic." *JBL* 108 (1989) 419–441.

Juel, D. *Messiah and Temple.* Missoula: Scholars Press, 1977.

_____. *Luke-Acts: The Promise of History.* Atlanta: John Knox, 1983.

Katz, S. T. "Issues in the Separation of Judaism and Christianity After 70CE: A Reconsideration." *JBL* 103 (1984) 43–76.

Kaufman, P. S. "Anti-Semitism in the New Testament: The Witness of the Beloved Disciple." *Worship* 63 (1989) 386–401.

Klassen, W. "Anti-Judaism in Early Christianity: The State of the Question." In *Anti-Judaism in Early Christianity: Volume One: Paul and the Gospels*, pp. 1–19. Edited by P. Richardson. Waterloo, Ontario: Wilfrid Laurier University, 1986.

Knight, G. A. F. "Antisemitism in the Fourth Gospel." *Reform Theological Review* 27 (1968) 81–88.

Kodell, J. "Luke's Use of *Laos*, 'People,' Especially in the Jerusalem Narrative (Lk 19:28–24:53)." *CBQ* 31 (1969) 327–43.

Koenig, J. *Jews and Christians in Dialogue: New Testament Foundations*. Philadelphia: Westminster, 1979.

Kysar, R. "The Gospel of John in Current Research." *RelSRev* 9:4 (1983) 314–23.

Leibig, J. E. "John and 'the Jews': Theological Anti-Semitism in the Fourth Gospel." *JES* 20 (1983) 209–234.

Lowe, M. "Who Were the *Ioudaioi*?" *NovT* 18 (1976) 101–130.

_____. "Real and Imagined Anti-Jewish Elements in the Synoptic Gospels and Acts." *JES* 24 (1987) 267–84.

Martyn, J. L. "Glimpses into the History of the Johannine Community." In *L'Evangile de Jean: Sources, rédaction, théologie*, pp. 149–79. Edited by M. de Jonge. Louvain, 1977.

_____. *History and Theology in the Fourth Gospel*. 2nd edition. Nashville: Abingdon, 1979.

Matera, F. J. *Passion Narratives and Gospel Theologies*. New York: Paulist, 1986.

_____. "His Blood Be on Us and on Our Children." *Bible Today* Nov (1989) 345–50.

Meeks, W. A. " 'Am I a Jew?' Johannine Christianity and Judaism." In *Christianity, Judaism, and Other Graeco-Roman Cults: Studies for Morton Smith at Sixty*, pp. 163–86. Edited by J. Neusner. Leiden: Brill, 1975.

_____. "Breaking Away: Three New Testament Pictures of Christianity's Separation from Jewish Communities." In *"To See Ourselves as Others See Us": Christians, Jews, and "Others" in Late Antiquity*, pp. 93–115. Edited by J. Neusner and E. S. Frerichs. Chico, CA: Scholars, 1985.

Meier, J. P. *Law and History in Matthew's Gospel*. AnBib, 71. Rome: Biblical Institute, 1976.

_____. *Matthew*. Wilmington, Delaware: Glazier, 1980.

Michaels, J. R. "Alleged Anti-Semitism in the Fourth Gospel." *Gordon Review* 11 (1968) 12–24.

Milavec, A. A. "A Fresh Analysis of the Parable of the Wicked Husbandmen in the Light of Jewish-Christian Dialogue." In *Parable and Story in Judaism and Christianity*, pp. 81–117. Edited by C. Thoma and M. Wyschogrod. New York: Paulist, 1989.

Moessner, D. P. "The Ironic Fulfillment of Israel's Glory." In *Luke-Acts and the Jewish People*, pp. 35–50. Edited by J. B. Tyson. Minneapolis: Augsburg, 1988.

_____. "The 'Leaven of the Pharisees' and 'This Generation': Israel's Rejection of Jesus According to Luke." *JSNT* 34 (1988) 21–46.

_____. "Paul in Acts: Preacher of Eschatological Repentance to Israel." *NTS* 34 (1988) 96–104.

Mussner, F. *Tractate on the Jews*. Translated by L. Swidler. Philadelphia: Fortress, 1984.

Neusner, J. *First Century Judaism in Crisis: Yohanan ben Zakkai and the Renaissance of the Torah*. Nashville: Abingdon, 1975.

Niedner, F. A. "Rereading Matthew on Jerusalem and Judaism." *BTB* 19 (1989) 43–47.

Pancaro, S. "The Relationship of the Church to Israel in the Gospel of St. John." *NTS* 21 (1974–75) 396–405.

_____. *The Law in the Fourth Gospel*. NovTSup 42. Leiden: Brill, 1975.

Pawlikowski, J. T. "The Trial and Death of Jesus: Reflections in Light of a New Understanding of Judaism." *Chicago Studies* 25 (1986) 79–94.

Przybylski, B. "The Setting of Matthean Anti-Judaism." In *Anti-Judaism in Early Christianity*, Vol. 1, pp. 181–200. Edited by P. Richardson. Waterloo, Ontario: Wilfrid Laurier, 1986.

Räisänen, H. "Jesus and the Food Laws: Reflections of Mark 7:15." *JSNT* 16 (1982) 79–100.

Rivkin, E. *What Crucified Jesus?*. Nashville: Abingdon, 1984.

Ruether, R. R. "Theological Anti-Semitism in the New Testament." *Christian Century* 85 (1968) 191–96.

_____. *Faith and Fratricide: The Theological Roots of Anti-Semitism*. Minneapolis: Seabury, 1974.

Russell, E. A. "The Image of the Jew in Matthew's Gospel." *Studia Evangelica VII*. Edited by E. A. Livingstone (1982) 427–42.

_____. " 'Antisemitism' in the Gospel of Matthew." *IBS* 8 (1986) 183–96.

Salmon, M. "Insider or Outsider? Luke's Relationship with Judaism." In *Luke-Acts and the Jewish People*, pp. 76–82. Edited by J. B. Tyson. Minneapolis: Augsburg, 1988.

Sanders, E. P. *Jesus and Judaism*. Philadelphia: Fortress, 1985.

Sanders, J. T. "The Salvation of the Jews in Luke-Acts." In *Luke-Acts: New Perspectives*, pp. 104–128. Edited by C. H. Talbert. New York: Crossroad, 1984.

_____. *The Jews in Luke-Acts*. Philadelphia: Fortress, 1987.

_____. "The Jewish People in Luke-Acts." In *Luke-Acts and the Jewish People*, pp. 51–75. Edited by J. B. Tyson. Minneapolis: Augsburg, 1988.

Schnackenburg, R. *The Gospel According to John*. 3 volumes. New York: Seabury/Crossroad, 1980–82.

Schweizer, E. *The Good News According to Matthew*. Translated by D. E. Green. Atlanta: John Knox, 1975.

Segovia, F. F. "The Love and Hatred of Jesus and Johannine Sectarianism." *CBQ* 43 (1981) 258–72.

Seifrid, M. A. "Jesus and the Law in Acts." *JSNT* 30 (1987) 39–57.

Shepherd, M. H. "The Jews in the Gospel of John: Another Level of Meaning." *ATR* 56 Supplement Series (1974) 95–112.

Slingerland, D. " 'The Jews' in the Pauline Portion of Acts." *JAAR* 54 (1986) 305–321.

Smith, D. M. "Judaism and the Gospel of John." In *Jews and Christians: Exploring the Past, Present, and Future*, pp. 76–96. Edited by J. H. Charlesworth. New York: Crossroad, 1990.

Smith, D. T. "The Matthean Exception Clauses in the Light of Matthew's Theology and Community." *Studia Biblica et Theologica* 17 (1989) 55–82.

Snodgrass, K. *The Parable of the Wicked Tenants*. Tübingen: Mohr, 1983.

Stanton, G. N. "The Gospel of Matthew and Judaism." *BJRL* 66 (1983–84) 264–84.

Tannehill, R. C. "Israel in Luke-Acts: A Tragic Story." *JBL* 104 (1985) 69–85.

_____. *The Narrative Unity of Luke-Acts*. 2 volumes. Minneapolis: Fortress, 1986–90.

_____. "Rejection by Jews and Turning to Gentiles: The Pattern of Paul's Mission in Acts." In *Luke-Acts and the Jewish People*, pp. 83–101. Edited by J. B. Tyson. Minneapolis: Augsburg, 1988.

Tiede, D. L. *Prophecy and History in Luke-Acts*. Philadelphia: Fortress, 1980.

_____. " 'Glory to Thy People Israel!': Luke-Acts and the Jews." In *Luke-Acts and the Jewish People*, pp. 21–34. Edited by J. B. Tyson. Minneapolis: Augsburg, 1988.

Townsend, J. T. "The Gospel of John and the Jews: The Story of a Religious Divorce." In *Antisemitism and the Foundations of Christianity*, pp. 72–97. Edited by A. Davies. New York: Paulist, 1979.

Turner, M. M. B. "The Sabbath, Sunday, and the Law in Luke-Acts." In *From Sabbath to Lord's Day*, pp. 99–157. Edited by D. A. Carson. Grand Rapids: Zondervan, 1982.

Tyson, J. B. "The Jewish Public in Luke-Acts." *NTS* 30 (1984) 574–83.

_____. "The Gentile Mission and the Authority of Scripture in Acts." *NTS* 33 (1987) 619–31.

_____. "Scripture, Torah, and Sabbath in Luke-Acts." In *Jesus, the Gospels, and the Church*, pp. 89–104. Edited by E. P. Sanders. Macon GA: Mercer University, 1987.

_____. "The Problem with Jewish Rejection in Acts." In *Luke-Acts and the Jewish People*, pp. 124–37. Edited by J. B. Tyson. Minneapolis: Augsburg, 1988.

Vermes, G. "Dead Sea Scrolls." In *IDBSup*, pp. 210–19.

Via, J. E. "According to Luke, Who Put Jesus to Death?" In *Political Issues in Luke-Acts*, pp. 122–45. Edited by R. J. Cassidy and P. J. Scharper. Maryknoll, New York: Orbis, 1983.

Viviano, B. T. "The Pharisees in Matthew 23." *Bible Today* Nov (1989) 338–44.

von Wahlde, U. C. "The Johannine 'Jews': A Critical Survey." *NTS* 28 (1982) 33–60.

Weber, J. C. "Jesus' Opponents in the Gospel of Mark." *JBR* (July 1966) 214–22.

Whitacre, R. A. *Johannine Polemic: The Role of Tradition and Theology*. SBLDS 67. Chico, CA: Scholars, 1982.

Wilson, S. G. *The Gentiles and the Gentile Mission in Luke-Acts*. SNTSMS 23. Cambridge: University Press, 1973.

_____. *Luke and the Law*. SNTSMS 50. Cambridge: University Press, 1983.

Winter, P. *On the Trial of Jesus*. Berlin: Walter de Gruyter, 1974.

INDEX

207

Essenes, 67
Ethnos, 83

Faith and Fratricide (Ruether), 7
Faith and Order Commission,
176–77
Fig tree, 41–43
Fitzmyer, J., 105
Food laws, 38–39, 49, 56–57,
99–100, 115–19
Fortna, R. T., 165, 169–70
Freyne, Sean, 63, 80, 142

Gager, John, 15
Gaston, Lloyd, 41–42, 48, 74,
83, 103, 126
Gentiles, 110–12
Geyser, A. S., 168
Granskou, D., 172
"Guidelines and Suggestions for
Implementing the Conciliar
Declaration *Nostra Aetate*,"
180

Haberim, 67
Haenchen, E., 106
Hamlet, 157–58
Hare, Douglas, 12–18, 42, 75
Harrington, Daniel, 84
Harvey, A. E., 28
Hebrew Union College, 4
Hellenism, 16
Herod, 59
Hillel, 16
Holocaust, 6
Hosea, 55

Infancy narratives, 109
Isaiah, 18
Islam, 5

Israel, 21, 80–85, 90–94

Jervell, Jacob, 104–07, 109–21,
127–29
Jesus of Nazareth, 20, 28–35,
37–38, 68–69, 75–78,
109–10
John the Baptist, 67, 149
John, gospel of: abrogating anti-
Judaism, in, 148–49; christology of, 135–37, 140–48,
173–74; dualism in, 135–
37, 171; evaluative claims
in, 140–41; Jewish symbols
in, 145–47; and "Jews,"
148–49, 152–72; law in,
141–44; Pharisees in, 138–
39, 155; rejection in, 150–
53; sabbath in, 145–46;
subordinating polemic in,
145–47; and the synoptics,
137–38; and "the world,"
150–52; mentioned, 35
Johnson, Luke T., 14, 16, 64
Judaism, 3–5, 14, 16, 18–20,
67–68
Judas, 150
Judas the Galilean, 67
Juel, Donald, 35–36, 42, 50,
105, 110

Kahler, Martin, 32
Koran, 5
Kysar, 146

Leibig, J. E., 173
Leviticus, 76
Lowe, Malcolm, 101, 163, 164–
65, 168
Luke, gospel of: and abrogating

Clemens Thoma and Michael Wyschogrod, editors, *Parable and Story in Judaism and Christianity* (A Stimulus Book, 1989).

Eugene J. Fisher and Leon Klenicki, editors, *In Our Time: The Flowering of Jewish-Catholic Dialogue* (A Stimulus Book, 1990).

Leon Klenicki, editor, *Toward a Theological Encounter* (A Stimulus Book, 1991).

David Burrell and Yehezkel Landau, editors, *Voices from Jerusalem* (A Stimulus Book, 1991).

John Rousmaniere, *A Bridge to Dialogue: The Story of Jewish-Christian Relations*; edited by James A. Carpenter and Leon Klenicki (A Stimulus Book, 1991).

Michael E. Lodahl, *Shekhinah/Spirit* (A Stimulus Book, 1992).

STIMULUS BOOKS are developed by Stimulus Foundation, a not-for-profit organization, and are published by Paulist Press. The Foundation wishes to further the publication of scholarly books on Jewish and Christian topics that are of importance to Judaism and Christianity.

Stimulus Foundation was established by an erstwhile refugee from Nazi Germany who intends to contribute with these publications to the improvement of communication between Jews and Christians.

Books for publication in this Series will be selected by a committee of the Foundation, and offers of manuscripts and works in progress should be addressed to:

Stimulus Foundation
785 West End Ave.
New York, N.Y. 10025